The Videogame Industry Does Not Exist

T0323369

The Videogame Industry Does Not Exist

Why We Should Think Beyond Commercial Game Production

Brendan Keogh

The MIT Press
Cambridge, Massachusetts
London, England

The MIT Press would like to thank the anonymous peer reviewers who provided comments on drafts of this book. The generous work of academic experts is essential for establishing the authority and quality of our publications. We acknowledge with gratitude the contributions of these otherwise uncredited readers.

This book was set in Stone Serif and Stone Sans by Westchester Publishing Services. Printed and bound in the United States of America.

Library of Congress Cataloging-in-Publication Data

Names: Keogh, Brendan, author.
Title: The videogame industry does not exist : why we should think beyond commercial game production / Brendan Keogh.
Description: Cambridge, Massachusetts : The MIT Press, [2023] | Includes bibliographical references and index.
Identifiers: LCCN 2022030010 (print) | LCCN 2022030011 (ebook) | ISBN 9780262545402 (paperback) | ISBN 9780262374149 (epub) | ISBN 9780262374132 (pdf)
Subjects: LCSH: Video games industry. | Video game designers—Interviews.
Classification: LCC HD9993.E452 K46 2023 (print) | LCC HD9993.E452 (ebook) | DDC 338.4/77948—dc23/eng/20230120
LC record available at https://lccn.loc.gov/2022030010
LC ebook record available at https://lccn.loc.gov/2022030011

10 9 8 7 6 5 4 3

For April Tyack, who made the Australian videogame field a better place.

Contents

Acknowledgments

Fieldwork for this book was conducted on the unceded lands of numerous indigenous people and nations. In Australia, this included but was not limited to the lands of the Turrbal People, the Yuggera People, the Eora Nation, the Kulin Nation, the palawa people, the Kaurna People, the Barunggum People, the Ngunnawal People, and the Noongar People. I pay my respect to all Elders past and present of these peoples and nations. In North America, fieldwork sites included but were not limited to the unceded lands of the Kanien'kehá:ka Nation, and the Duwamish Tribe.

This book would not exist without the insights, articulations, honesty, and time of my participants. I'm deeply humbled by the trust shown in me by those who agreed to an interview and those who completed my survey. Numerous gamemakers let me into their offices, their coworking spaces, their conferences, and their homes. Not all my participants are quoted in the following pages, but all my participants nonetheless contributed to how I came to understand videogame production. This book would not exist without their insights, but any errors or misrepresentations herein are entirely my own.

The time and resources required to undertake such an extensive period of fieldwork was made possible by a Discovery Early Career Research Award fellowship (DE180100973), funded by the Australian Research Council. My thanks to the council, as well as my application reviewers for having the confidence in me to undertake this project.

Parts of this book draw on and extend on arguments I have made in articles and chapters published throughout this fellowship. An early version of the theoretical foundations of chapter 1 is found in "The Cultural Field of Video Game Production in Australia," *Games and Culture* 16 (1): 116–135. My conceptualization of the phases of the videogame field's history extends on my article "From Aggressively Formalised to Intensely In/

formalised: Accounting for a Wider Range of Videogame Development Practices," *Creative Industries Journal* 12 (1): 14–33. Parts of chapter 6 draw from my previous work on videogames and scenes in my chapter "The Melbourne Indie Game Scenes: Value Regimes in Localized Game Development," in *Independent Videogames*, edited by Paolo Ruffino, 209–222 (New York: Routledge, 2021). The discussion of gameworker collective action in chapter 7 builds on my article coauthored with Benjamin Abraham, "Challenges and Opportunities for Collective Action and Unionization in Local Videogame Industries," *Organization* (DOI: 10.1177/13505084221082269). My thanks to all the reviewers, editors, copyeditors, and collaborators of these previous publications, as well as of this current book, for constantly challenging and strengthening my work.

My ability to obtain the fellowship and to successfully undertake the subsequent years of fieldwork, research, and writing that led to this book is deeply indebted to the mentorship I have received as a member of the Digital Media Research Centre (DMRC) at Queensland University of Technology. I have been privileged to work alongside and learn from generous mentors, including Jean Burgess, Michael Dezuanni, Terry Flew, Patrik Wikström, Amanda Lotz, Kevin Sanson, and John Banks. In particular, I want to single out Stuart Cunningham, who has provided me with a humbling level of guidance, insight, suggestions, patience, and friendship. It is not modest to say that without Stuart, this project simply would not have happened.

I have also greatly benefited from the broader DMRC community. My thinking has been enriched greatly by the insights, questions, comradery, and reflections of my colleagues, including postgraduate students, within the DMRC's Transforming Media Industries program, led by Amanda Lotz. In particular, I'm tremendously grateful to my game studies colleagues, Benjamin Nicoll, Ben Egliston, Dan Padua, and Erin Maclean for the countless conversations and draft feedback sessions.

Two research assistants made significant contributions to this work. Dr. Taylor Hardwick located, collected, compiled, and analyzed the details of Australian videogame development tertiary programs used in chapter 4. Dr. D. Bondy Valdovinos Kaye transcribed and coded a significant number of my interviews after my fellowship ended and I returned to teaching duties. Both provided valuable insights and feedback throughout the project, and I'm deeply grateful to both Taylor and Bondy for all their work.

My professional life and personal life have both been enriched throughout this research project through the close friendship of Benjamin Abraham, Terry Burdak, and Dan Golding. Their support, insights, friendship, memes, garden photos, and typos have made a trying few years much easier to bear.

Finally, my eternal gratitude to my partner and love, Helen Berents, who is always there to listen to my bad ideas, to stop me overworking, to provide me with baked goods, to always ask "So what?" and to ensure, to the best of her ability, that none of my sentences are longer than a hundred words.

Introduction

"I just want to get better and make cool stuff."

This was the 60th interview I had conducted with an Australian game-maker. My participant was Nicole Williams, a 23-year-old artist who had, three weeks prior, become the fourth employee at an independent game studio in Melbourne. We were sitting on brightly colored beanbags in the common area of The Arcade, a coworking space in Melbourne's inner south, housing many of the city's growing number of videogame companies. Williams and I had already discussed their background and education, and what they found challenging and enjoyable about being involved in videogame production. Then I asked the dreaded question: "Where do you see yourself in five years?" Previous responses had, regardless of the discipline or seniority of the gamemaker being interviewed, typically included nervous laughter, blown raspberries, semi-joking accusations that it was a cruel question, reinterpretations of the question to be about "dream jobs," and, on two occasions, tears. Williams spent some time in silence, thinking about their answer, before shrugging and waving off the careerist pretentions of the question: "I just want to get better and make cool stuff."

This response stayed with me in the subsequent years of the research project that has led to this book. In lieu of any access to long-term job security or predictable career trajectories, more young workers are joining the ranks of what Silvio Lorusso (2019) has labeled the *entreprecariat*, focusing on investing in their own skills and networks—"getting better"—and on the intrinsic reward of creative fulfillment—"making cool stuff." Williams's vague but intrinsic ambitions highlight the increasingly individualized focus of young workers in the cultural industries who, confronted with increased precarity and decreased long-term employment prospects, are conscious that they need to build portfolio careers by "becoming [their] own enterprise" (McRobbie 2016, 20).

But Williams's response stuck with me for contrasting reasons too. It captured an aspect of making videogames that was ubiquitous across my interviews but which academic, popular, and industrial discourses rarely consider in detail: that those who create videogames—those I am calling "gamemakers"[1]—often have working lives and subjectivities that are structured less like tech workers and more like cultural workers—that is, artists, musicians, actors, writers, and so on. They are driven by cultural and creative desires to express themselves and improve their craft, and they often accept situations of extreme job precarity and low (or no) pay in order to achieve this. At the same time, they are often conscious and articulate of the notorious work conditions within videogame companies such as excessive and unpaid overtime, misogyny and harassment, and aggressive individualization (Dyer-Witheford and de Peuter 2009; Legault and Weststar 2017). Many gamemakers I interviewed expressed, on the one hand, a deep political consciousness of how the rhetoric of passion and creativity have long been used to exploit and underpay professional gamemakers and, on the other hand, a strongly articulated desire to nonetheless prioritize improving their craft and making good art over obtaining financial security.

It's become common practice, to the point of cliché, to begin any piece of writing about videogame production by proclaiming that "the videogame industry" generates over a hundred billion dollars every year—perhaps more than any other entertainment sector, depending on what revenue sources you include or omit (Kerr 2006, 51; Hesmondhalgh 2018, 316). This total generated revenue has become a reactionary shorthand in journalism articles, policy documents, academic research, and trade association reports for the economic and cultural significance of videogames. Once relegated to the sidelines of cultural relevancy at best, actively excluded at worst, champions of the videogame medium now hold up the revenue generated by the top videogame firms as proof that videogames do, in fact, matter.

But this financial measurement of videogames' worth is far removed from the individual ambitions and work conditions of a 23-year-old Melbourne artist working in a four-person team who wants to "get better and make cool stuff." Indeed, this is true literally in a geographic sense: the top 25 global companies in terms of revenue generated from videogames all have ownership concentrated in North America, western Europe, or East Asia (*NewZoo* 2020). But it is also true in terms of what we imagine "the videogame industry" to be, how we imagine it to operate, and who we think belongs to it. While videogame production is most commonly imagined as happening in large, multinational corporations with campus-sized studios producing Hollywood-quality blockbusters for home consoles, today there are just as many gamemakers working in teams smaller than five people as there are working in teams larger than 250 (Game Developers Conference 2021, 22). The majority of gamemakers now use preexisting technological frameworks and software tools, such as the Unity and Unreal game engines, and produce much smaller videogames for digital platforms, such as Apple's App Store or Valve's Steam marketplace. Instead of relying on resources supplied by a publisher in exchange for copyright ownership, more and more gamemakers fund their work with their own savings (albeit sometimes subsidized by government grants, private investment, or a partner's income), hoping against hope that the investment will pay off—even though it rarely ever does. Just like most musicians, most actors, most writers, and most painters, most gamemakers won't make much money from their gamemaking activity, if they make anything at all. But most gamemakers know this. They nonetheless want to get better and make cool stuff.

The central claim of this book is that a disconnect exists between the diverse range of lived experiences, identities, ambitions, work conditions, communities, and skills of videogame makers, and the ways in which videogame production is typically understood and depicted by researchers, journalists, policymakers, education institutions, and gamemakers themselves as narrowly happening within the domain of a lucrative and centralized videogame industry. "The videogame industry" as a concept, as a defined and distinctive area of commercial activity, only accounts for a small, particularly lucrative, and geographically concentrated aspect of gamemaking activity while failing to account for a much broader and complex range of gamemaking identities, cultures, and sites. This did not happen by accident. After the first videogames were created by hobbyists, students, and tinkerers in the late 1960s, commercial firms and entrepreneurs emerged through the 1970s to "privatize the cultures of games and play" (Boluk and LeMieux 2017, 8; see also Dyer-Witheford and de Peuter 2009, 10). What we call the videogame industry has "convinced its employees"—and to this we could add legions of aspirational students, as well as researchers and policymakers—"that [the industry is] the only gateway to videogame creation" (Anthropy 2012, 18). In this book, I want to undermine this conviction by paying close attention to other sites of videogame production and to other ways of being a videogame maker.

In doing so I'm indebted to the growing, nebulous, interdisciplinary body of research elucidating the realities of videogame production—a subfield of game studies that Olli Sotamaa and Jan Švelch (2021) have fruitfully called "game production studies." Political economic approaches to understanding the flows of capital and extractions of surplus-value across transnational value chains have provided insights into how global videogame markets are unequally shaped (Kerr 2017; Dyer-Witheford and de Peuter 2009; Nieborg, Young, and Joseph 2020; Jiang and Fung 2019). Similarly, researchers of the governance logics of dominant digital platforms have not only revealed how videogame production and consumption have been restructured in the networked age but also provided insights into the expanding reach of what Nick Srnicek (2017) has called platform capitalism (Nieborg and Poell 2018; Jin 2015; Chia et al. 2020; Boluk and LeMieux 2017; Joseph 2021). Most extensively, and most relevant to this book, ethnographic and qualitative approaches to studying the cultures and labor practices of studios and creators in specific local contexts have increased greatly over the past decade, from the still-rare ethnographies of larger studios (Banks 2013; O'Donnell 2014; Bulut 2020), to a number of empirical studies of independent and smaller-scale studios and communities (Whitson 2018; Parker and Jenson 2017; Jørgensen, Sandqvist, and Sotamaa 2017; Banks and Cunningham 2016; Ruberg 2019; Young 2018; Ruffino and Woodcock 2020), to the invaluable historical analyses of local gamemaking cultures of previous decades that directly challenge the "global" videogame industry's hegemonic origin myths (Swalwell and Davidson 2016; Švelch 2018; Fiadotau 2019; Nicoll 2019; Nooney 2020; Swalwell 2021; Garda and Grabarczyk 2021).

I wish to bring this emerging subfield of game production studies and the work of videogame history into closer conversation with the rich body of critical work on the cultural industries. Cultural industries as a research focus refers to "those [industries] involved in the production of 'aesthetic' or 'symbolic' goods and services; that is, commodities whose core value is derived from their function as carriers of *meaning* in the form of images,

symbols, signs and sounds" (Banks 2007, 2; original emphasis). As a theoretical allegiance, cultural industries signals "a lineage from the Frankfurt
School and Adorno in particular through to the Birmingham [Centre for Contemporary Cultural Studies]" and a "Marxist legacy" that risks being defanged
by "more pragmatic ideas of creative industries" (McRobbie 2016, 10).[2] As for
Kate Oakley and Justin O'Connor (2015, 10), I find that the component words
culture and *industry* provide a "productive juxtaposition not just of culture
and economy but more particularly the traditional artistic-centred mode of
cultural production with that of mass-industrialised production." Yet, while
David Hesmondhalgh (2018, 316), in the fourth edition of *The Cultural
Industries*, calls videogames "without doubt the most important new cultural
industry . . . to emerge since 1980," videogame production and videogame
makers are only visible in limited ways in cultural industries research to date.
The sheer economic value of videogame companies, their early adaption of
platform-based and digital distribution models, and the perpetually unrealized
promise of videogame technologies to usurp all other modes of storytelling
are mentioned frequently throughout this literature. The lived experiences of
videogame makers—themselves cultural producers with relationships to creativity and commodification no less ambivalent and complicated than those
cultural workers in any other discipline—remain underexamined.

Put simply, while the ways in which videogame production is industrialized have been well articulated, the ways in which videogame production
is *cultural* production, remains underexamined. Casey O'Donnell (2012, 21)
made a similar point when he argued against videogame production being
understood—as it still pervasively is—as a software industry, arguing instead
that "video game production viewed as an art world, rather than 'industry'
constructs a much more critical and nuanced perspective" of videogame
production. Thus, while cultural industries research has fruitfully articulated
juxtapositions and tensions as they have emerged in other cultural fields in
their industrialized state (the music industry, the film industry), that videogame production has only ever been understood as an industry makes the
term prematurely limiting for understanding the broader experiences and
contexts of videogame makers.

This isn't just true for the semantics of scholarly debate but is felt acutely
by gamemakers themselves. For instance, 26-year-old Georgia Symons
works primarily as a playwright but also contracts as a writer for the small

Melbourne game studio Ghost Pattern. When I asked Symons if she would consider herself part of the videogame industry, she reflected:

> We talk about "the theater industry" all the time and people are aware that industry isn't quite right, but we don't really know what is the right word so people just say the theater industry and get on with it. . . . But when people say "the video-game industry" I think of more like triple-A games and big companies that repeatedly churn stuff out. . . . It feels weird to say you're a part of the industry when in the videogame sector specifically those things seem to be kept quite consciously apart: the industrial production of games and then the local, independent games that might still be sold and might still turn a profit but seem to really resist some of the ethos of the industrial companies.

For Symons, despite accepting the use of "industry" when discussing theater work, she feels that when one invokes "the videogame industry" they are not referring to her own independent and locally situated practice.

This was a common perception among videogame makers marginal to the most dominant and commodified sites of videogame production, even though such videogame makers account for the majority of videogame production activity. The limited sites of videogame production that are often conceptualized *as* the videogame industry, I argue throughout this book, are a misrepresentative synecdoche for a much larger space of cultural and economic activity that includes hobbyists, artists, gamemakers with day jobs, gamemakers working in non-entertainment sectors, modders, and students. As will become clear over the coming chapters, these alternative and marginalized sites of videogame production do not simply *also* exist alongside the videogame industry. They instead form the foundations of skills, cultures, genres, communities, technologies, and aesthetics that are a necessary precursor for any industrialized videogame production to occur. For videogame production, as with all forms of cultural production, "industry produces culture" but also "culture produces industry" (Negus 1999, 14).

With this book, I want to comprehend a broader range of sites and subjectivities that in turn allow us to understand videogame production as a cultural, social, *and* economic phenomenon. I draw on Pierre Bourdieu's work on fields of cultural production to theorize, holistically but not homogeneously, *the field of videogame production*—or more simply, *the videogame field*. I am far from the first researcher to apply Bourdieu's concept of the field to the cultures of videogame play and production (e.g., Consalvo 2007; Kirkpatrick 2015; Parker 2013). Nonetheless, as chapter 1 will detail, articulating videogame production as occurring within and as a field of cultural production expands our conceptual frame to consider cultural and social forms of capital (prestige, awards, acclaim, scenes, etc.) and a broader range of positions occupied by competing agents. The videogame field—as a space in which cultural, social, *and* economic values flow between differently positioned producers—remains largely unarticulated in conceptualizations of videogame production, yet it is this much broader space of activity from which videogame industries emerge in specific local contexts. Just as one could not hope to understand the global music industry without first situating it within the broader music field—accounting for Taylor Swift, the countless anonymous Sunday pub cover bands, punk subcultures, and everything in between—here I want to seriously investigate the ramifications of truly considering videogames as a field of cultural production constituted by a vast range of competing positions, just like any other cultural field.

In fact, researchers in other cultural fields have similarly denounced the "industry" framing as conceptually limiting. In a 2014 article, Jonathan Sterne (2014, 50) critiques popular music scholarship for considering the music industry as too narrowly "the monetization of recordings." For Sterne, to speak of a music industry "crystallizes a particular historical formation of music production, circulation, and consumption as ideal-typical" (51). Ultimately, he argues, "There is no 'music industry.' There are many industries with many relationships to music" (53). Likewise, I find the notion that a singular videogame industry is the sole site of all forms of videogame production activity to be both reductive and obfuscating. As such, underpinning this book is a similar provocation: a singular videogame industry, as it is typically and narrowly imagined, does not exist. The videogame industry is a selective and limited framing that excludes all but the most commodifiable gamemaking activities. There is no videogame industry; there are many industries, many communities, many creators, and many audiences with different relationships to videogame production. With this provocation I want to clear a conceptual space that allows us to more adequately account for the broader, more varied field of videogame production from which any commercial videogame production necessarily emerges. I want to shift the focus away from the traditional geographical centers of the videogame industry of a select few North American, western European, and East Asian cities to instead understand how commodified videogame production *emerges from* a vast range of local, political, cultural, educational, and economic contexts. Effectively, this book is an attempt to more holistically and less selectively articulate videogame production as *cultural* production.

I strive to do this through firsthand accounts of videogame makers themselves: from those employed in massive blockbuster (or "triple-A") studios and indie start-ups, but also those videogame makers we less frequently hear from: artists, hobbyists, students, part-timers, educators. I have found ethnographic methods of semistructured interviews, surveys, and observations to be—as Sarah Thornton (1995, 166) notes—"best suited to emphasizing the diverse and the particular," and to allow me to challenge the often too-simple, top-down, triumphalist trade association and press reports that obscure at least as much as they reveal in their reduction of a vast range of gamemaking experiences to "full-time equivalent" employee numbers. Between 2018 and 2020 I conducted 205 interviews with videogame makers, educators, students, curators, and relevant government officials. Interviews were conducted primarily in Australia's capital cities (162 across Brisbane, Sydney, Melbourne, Hobart, Adelaide, Canberra, and Perth) but also in regional Australia (5), Seattle (6), Montreal (12), Berlin (3), the Netherlands (15 across Amsterdam, Utrecht, and Rotterdam), Jakarta (1), and Singapore (1).[3] Further, in 2018 I ran a survey for "people who are involved in the making of videogames in Australia" that received 288 responses. I also attended a range of videogame production events such as A MAZE Festival (Berlin), Freeplay Independent Games Festival (Melbourne), Melbourne International Games Week, and the Game Developers Conference (San Francisco). Of the interviewees, 72 percent were cisgender men, and 78 percent of survey respondents identified their gender as male. While this imbalance is unfortunate and inevitably influences the analysis that follows, it also aligns with trade association reports that consistently put the gender (im)balance of videogame production at around 70 to 80 percent male (e.g., Game Developers Conference 2021; Interactive Games and Entertainment Association 2019). Fieldwork was conducted solely in English, and this of course further limits the representativeness of the collected data. For the most part, and where consent was provided, I have attributed quotes to my participants. Occasionally, quotes are anonymized where requested by my participants or where I have determined topics to be of a particularly sensitive nature.

Gamemakers from all my fieldwork sites make appearances on the following pages, but it is Australian gamemakers who are my primary focus. As chapter 2 will describe in more detail, Australia provides a case study that is at once exceptional and exemplary for making sense of the videogame field. In the early 2010s, Australian videogame production was radically altered as events surrounding the global financial crisis (GFC) saw extensive studio closures and wiped out two-thirds of gamemaking jobs across the country. Through the decimation of Australian videogame companies and their subsequent regrowth in a radically different form, we can see the field of videogame production that is typically hidden from view. Australian videogame production is exceptional in its unique history of a work-for-hire industry collapsing to be replaced with a dispersed community focused on small-scale independent production. But it is also exemplary in that small-scale independent production is the dominant mode of videogame production in most local contexts today. Australian videogame makers are physically removed from the field's dominant sites but remain subservient to the North American, western European, and East Asian publishers, platforms, and investors through which the field's economic capital is overwhelmingly concentrated. Just like all gamemakers outside of the field's dominant sites, Australian gamemakers have little hope of obtaining employment at a large, well-known, lucrative company like Ubisoft, Nintendo, BioWare, or Activision, any of which would require moving one's life halfway around the world. Instead—again, like most of the world's gamemakers—most rely on small, entrepreneurial, start-up approaches much closer to home, with the hope that digital distribution platforms will allow them to reach global markets. Australia's liminal circumstances between center and periphery provide an opportunity to start seeing more clearly what else exists but remains largely invisible in the field of videogame production around the world.

However, importantly, this is not to imply that the experience of Australian videogame producers is identical to those of videogame producers globally. Australian gamemakers still possess many privileges not available to gamemakers in much of the world. Indeed, as we will see especially in chapter 6, even within Australia each city I visited had its own distinct communities shaped by geographic, infrastructural, and political landscapes. Videogame production requires approaches and conceptualizations that are pluralist and scalable, that can focus on not just "the field" but on local fields, national fields, regional fields, global fields, and translocal fields. Each exists as a subset or superset of the others. This requires us to not just pan our focus across the field, as one might do with a paper map, but to zoom in and out as necessary, as one might do with a smartphone map application, to bring in and out of focus different struggles and positions and relationships. By focusing on the diverse experiences of Australian gamemakers, supplemented by those gamemakers from my other fieldwork sites, I don't intend to suggest there is a globally uniform experience of making videogames. Rather, I wish to argue quite the opposite: that a broad, pluralistic, sometimes contradictory range of gamemaking experiences and identities exists, mediated by both local and global economic and cultural conditions. Through my Australian case study, I am confident the non-Australian reader will find insights, dynamics, and questions just as applicable to gamemaking in their own local context, even as the exact layout of the terrain will surely differ.

Book Outline

The goal of this book is to articulate the broader videogame field that exists before, beyond, and beneath those dominant positions of the videogame field that have historically been perceived as the sole site of legitimate videogame production. Chapter 1 begins by shifting the conceptual frame of reference from a singular videogame industry to a videogame field working at a plurality of scales and sites, driven by a variety of markers of success. It introduces in more detail Bourdieu's key concept of fields of cultural production and demonstrates its relevancy to the contemporary state of videogame production. Central to Bourdieu's theory is that a cultural field is, cyclically, the collective struggle to define the cultural field such that one's own position is legitimately within it and others' positions are not. In this sense, "the videogame industry" itself can be understood as one particularly dominant and narrow conceptualization of the field that has ensured all nondominant positions are delegitimized. This chapter demonstrates how such processes of legitimation and disavowal are playing out in contemporary videogame production within the context of platformization and creative entrepreneurism, where professional and amateur gamemaking identities are increasingly blurred. In chapter 1's final section, we will hear how videogame makers themselves, like Symons above, articulate their position within this videogame field in terms of whether or not they consider themselves to be "videogame developers" working within "a videogame industry." Many, despite making videogames, do not.

Chapter 2 then introduces Australia's videogame field as the main case study for the chapters that follow. It traces the transitions undertaken by Australian gamemakers and companies through the seismic restructure brought about by the GFC in the late 2000s. If the titular claim of this book is meant primarily as a provocation to jolt us into thinking about the limitations of our current frames of reference for videogame production, it has a much more literal meaning in Australia where, following widespread studio closures brought about during the GFC, many videogame companies literally ceased to exist. The decimation of Australian videogame companies revealed a much more complex and far-reaching field of videogame production that includes independents, artists, students, and activists.

If the field of videogame production in Australia looks radically different from the ways in which the videogame industry is traditionally conceptualized, then chapter 3 asks what this means for how we understand the politics of making videogames as cultural work—or "gamework" as it is increasingly being called by the field's burgeoning unionization movements. The gig workers of the "creative precariat" (Arvidsson, Malossi, and Naro. 2010, 296) are often seen to be role models of late capitalism and neoliberalism (de Peuter 2014), showing managers in other sectors of the economy how to structure their own workers' lives around individualized goals and piecemeal careers while lowering expectations of job security, explicit work hours, or other entitlements hard-won by workers of previous generations. Videogame makers are no different, and the exploitation of an intrinsic passion or desire to be creative are pervasive throughout the videogame field—leading to what Ergin Bulut (2020, 166) has called videogame production's "governmental logic of precarization." In the context of contemporary videogame production in locations such as Australia where, as one participant explained to me, "everyone is indie," there are particular instantiations of precarity and self-exploitation that look less like those of start-up tech companies and more like the vocations of musicians and writers. This, then, raises other challenges for articulating gamework. Few would consider four young friends trying to start a band in their garage on the weekend as "self-exploiting," but what of the same four young friends trying to produce their first videogame under similar circumstances? Ultimately, this chapter strives to paint a picture of videogame-making work that is far removed from popular stereotypes of a lucrative and growing industry and instead more aligned with what we would typically expect to see in other cultural fields: precarious, unpredictable, and driven by symbolic aspirations at least as often as by economic ones.

If the realities of working within the videogame field are drastically different from how the field is typically imagined by those outside it, this has ramifications for how newcomers enter the field—and which newcomers are most able to enter. Chapter 4 thus examines the role of formal education in both sustaining and potentially challenging the dominant configuration of the field. Only a handful of researchers have looked directly at the cultures and structures of game development education (e.g., Harvey 2019; Zagal and Bruckman 2008; Ashton 2009), even as many game researchers themselves teach such courses, and as videogame producers endlessly debate the efficacy and relevancy of formal education. In Australia alone, by one trade association's estimation, there are thousands of students studying in game development programs even as only one thousand people actually possess jobs in videogame production companies nationally (*Game On* 2016, 3). For many, this is a sign of a clear oversupply of students for an industry that doesn't need them. But one rarely discusses an oversupply of music students, creative writing students, or acting students—or, rather, graduate oversupply in such fields is seen less as a problem to solve and more a simple reality of studying a cultural practice. Through an examination of what students, educators, and gamemakers have to say about game development education, and an analysis of the advertising and student-facing material of courses available from Australian institutions, chapter 4 shows that more than a straightforward "pipeline" priming junior workers to be pumped into videogame companies, different institutions are differently focused on enrolling junior videogame makers into the field varyingly as artists, entrepreneurs, or potential employees.

Crucially—and again, just like practitioners in every cultural field—many videogame development graduates find pathways to employment other than through the autonomous creation of new intellectual property, instead finding other ways to deploy their skillsets for a financial return. Indeed, some researchers argue that cultural industries' perspectives overstate the precarious nature of creative work, as they often ignore those creative workers embedded in noncreative sectors of the economy (Hearn et al. 2014): filmmakers employed to produce television ads; artists who become graphic designers; poets who become PR agents. Those with creative skillsets might not find full-time employment pursuing their vocation, but they take these skillsets into other sectors of the economy. Chapter 5 explores a common yet unromantic strategy of small-scale independent videogame production teams seeking financial sustainability: undertaking contract work for clients in other economic sectors. The past decade has seen increased enthusiasm for the educational and advertorial potential of videogames from a range of sectors, and some independent teams hire out their services to meet these needs. These gamemakers are a type of embedded creatives (Cunningham 2011): creative workers deploying their skills beyond the cultural industries traditionally defined to instead provide creative services. For gameworkers in this space, client work poses an alternative to self-funded passion projects but often fails to meet the creative ambitions of the gamemakers involved. Instead, for many, it provides a carrot-on-a-stick hope that, one day, they will have done enough client work to have accumulated enough funds to undertake their desired passion project—a goal that is rarely realized. Together, chapters 4 and 5 beg the question: Just what are the skills that constitute videogame production? What do these independent game studios offer their clients that an IT professional or a graphic designer does not? Embedded gamemakers regularly felt that their clients misunderstood their skills as being primarily technical in nature, when they saw themselves as offering more creative and design-oriented approaches to a problem. Chapter 5 concludes with a consideration of what it means to consider videogame production as being constituted of skills that can be transferred out of the field.

Embedded gamemakers hold a peripheral position in the videogame field, often not knowing exactly where they fit as videogame makers. Some have offices in videogame coworking spaces, and some attend local gamemaker meetups and community events. Others, however, feel detached from their local videogame production communities due to the fact they don't work on original intellectual property. When looking at videogame production in specific local contexts, we must be careful not to homogenize those local contexts that are themselves experienced in a variety of ways. Chapter 6 considers the local and translocal contexts in which the gamemaking field is constituted through personal relationships, socioeconomic and politic contexts, collaborations and competition, coworking spaces, parties, festivals and conferences, public infrastructure, and private property. Far from homogenous, every city where I interviewed gamemakers—both in Australia and elsewhere—had overlapping and competing gamemaking cultures, each of which was influenced by employment opportunities, government funding programs (or lack thereof), student cohorts and curriculums, coworking spaces, and broader cultures and politics. While several cities are discussed throughout chapter 6, the chapter directly compares the gamemaking cultures of the two southern Australian state capitals of Melbourne and Adelaide, looking at how funding opportunities, public infrastructure, studio sizes, and informal communities shape each city's field. Chapter 6 draws from popular music theorists such as Will Straw (2004), Holly Kruse (2010), and Sarah Thornton (1995) to consider how a "game scene"—or perhaps even multiple competing game scenes—takes root in particular locales. Game scenes and communities aren't just local, however; they are also intricately *translocal*, with social media and software platforms not simply globalizing the videogame field but intimately connecting disparate geographic contexts of videogame production.

By chapter 7, the book will have disassembled conventional understandings of videogame production by exposing the broader field of videogame production cultures, identities, and contexts that "the videogame industry" fails to represent. Crucially, however, this broader field of videogame production does not simply exist parallel to the companies and games we are more familiar with. Rather, it provides the skills, communities, and activities that form the foundations of and are exploited by the field's dominant videogame companies. Building off Karl Marx's theory of surplus-value and Maurizio Lazzarato's theory of how the immaterial labor of consumers builds brand value, here I propose the notion of *surplus cultural value* to understand how the videogame field's dominant players have come to rely on the precarious, informal work of those at the field's margins to build their own cultural and economic value. On the flip side of this, as the dominant players of the videogame field increasingly rely on the cultural labor of a broader field of gamemakers while, at the same time, refusing to directly employ them, the potential exists for the videogame field's current power hierarchies to be disrupted. What we see in Australia, and indeed around the world, is extensive precarity and exploitation but also an opportunity to reimagine videogame production as communal and collaborative, rather than competitive and secretive. Unionization is becoming an increasingly hot topic among videogame workers since the birth of the grassroots Game Workers Unite (GWU) in 2018. As more and more GWU chapters around the world formalize into actual gameworker unions, it bears remembering that the GWU movement began with outsiders on the field's margins. Among the creative precariat at the periphery of the videogame field, there is a political consciousness emerging that, if organized, could shift the balance of power in the field.

Finally, the conclusion turns to the future of videogame production. By considering the full field of videogame production in all its complexity and plurality, and not just the dominant subset known as the videogame industry, we are able to reimagine just how formal, informal, and embedded sites of videogame production interact and coconstitute the field. If local and national videogame fields beyond the dominant global sites of production are to build more sustainable businesses and careers, the conclusion argues, it will occur not solely by attracting the field's dominant triple-A companies to parachute large studios into cities but by fostering robust, grassroots local ecologies. The videogame industry does not exist before the skills, identities, tastes, communities, and resources fostered by the broader videogame field. By shifting our conceptual frame, from a top-down global videogame industry toward a bottom-up videogame field emerging within local and global contexts, videogame makers have an opportunity to imagine a different, more collaborative and collective politics of videogame making that might eventually allow them to "get better" and produce "cool stuff" in more sustainable and less precarious circumstances.

1 From Videogame Industry to Videogame Fields

In Sydney, on Australia's east coast, four young friends in their early twenties started a games studio called Chaos Theory Games. Their dream since childhood, as for many young people who wish to make a career in videogame production, was to create sprawling role-playing games for home consoles—videogames just like the ones they had grown up playing themselves. However, they quickly came to realize that for such a small team with a shoestring budget, their first game would have to be much smaller and would be unlikely to generate the revenue required to produce large-scale entertainment products. Instead, after releasing a small mobile game, Chaos Theory pivoted toward making videogames for clients in other sectors: advertising games, educational games, training simulations, or sometimes other digital products that aren't videogames at all but that use similar skillsets, such as websites. Now, as told to me by Nico King, the studio's 24-year-old creative director, the focus is on sustaining the company, not expanding it. Instead of sprawling console games, the team is "starting to realize it would just be better to create small, more impactful experiences." Now, instead of a studio of hundreds making massive games like the ones he grew up with, King explains how he wouldn't want Chaos Theory to grow any larger than 20 employees because "I would very much like to be involved in the creative direction of our projects and know everybody on our team." Eventually, Chaos Theory wants to move away from client work and focus on their own games. This would be more financially risky but also more creatively fulfilling. It sounds like a poor business strategy, but as managing director James Lockrey, also 24, noted, "If we were more in it for doing work for money, we would probably not have picked games as an industry in the first place."

I left Chaos Theory's two-room office and took a train to the suburb of Chatswood, where I met with 39-year-old Meghann O'Neill. O'Neill is a music teacher and freelance journalist, and has worked on a range of game projects both in Australia and overseas (remotely) as both a writer and a composer. "With the game development stuff" O'Neill has been "contributing to projects for the last four or five years." Like most of the gamemakers I interviewed in notoriously expensive Sydney, O'Neill doesn't have a studio or office external to her home, and so we met in a food court above Chatswood train station. O'Neill works primarily from her laptop, finding brief moments between her responsibilities as a parent: "I've taught myself to work when [the kids] are at gymnastics, for example. They do a three-hour block of gymnastics several times a week, so I just tune out the noise and work." O'Neill doesn't describe herself as having a job in gamemaking so much as having a range of gamemaking activities she undertakes, some of which are paid and many of which are not. "I've done a lot of music for free, and a lot on a kind of informal amateur kind of basis [but also] a mix of profit share and upfront payments." Such work can be unpredictable and unreliable, and O'Neill muses that "I don't know how a person without a partner with a full-time job would be able to do this at all."

Several months later, in the southern city of Adelaide, the state capital of South Australia, I met with 25-year-old Samantha Schaffer in a local theater collective's workspace—effectively an old shop space above a shopping arcade. A software developer by training, Schaffer was unemployed at the time we spoke, living on their savings from a previous software job while they focused on their creative practice of photography, poetry, and making videogames. Schaffer enjoys working from the theater collective's space because "They're very non-techy. . . . You meet lots of cool people who aren't in the tech or games space, which I really like." Schaffer has been producing small narrative games with the free software tool Bitsy and uploading them to their profile on itch.io (an unregulated distribution site for independent and amateur games) where they can be played for free. While Schaffer isn't currently getting paid for their gamemaking work, they are not too fussed about this. Rather, they appreciate "the low level of investment in [making small, free games] because the industry can be quite hostile towards femme people and queer people. I didn't want to go all in on an industry that might get mad at me." Schaffer's ideal goal for the near future is to be working part-time in software "to fund the stuff I do on my off time, because I find that software can pay well enough that if you just work part-time you make a modest living that's plenty to make art." For

Schaffer, this isn't a defeatist acceptance that a full-time job making videogames is too hard to obtain. It's a conscious decision to live within their means and avoid what they perceive as the poor labor conditions and toxic culture of formal videogame employment, while continuing to produce videogames and be part of a creative community nonetheless.

The diverse range of creative and commercial experiences and ambitions of Chaos Theory, O'Neill, and Schaffer are not exceptional. For videogame makers in Australia, and indeed in most of the world, there are no campus-sized studios owned by multinational corporations looking to regularly hire dozens or hundreds of juniors into full-time jobs. In a stark contrast to popular imaginings of the lucrative videogame industry, most of the gamemakers I spoke to were barely getting by on their gamemaking activity. Like O'Neill, reliance on a partner's more stable income was a constant refrain. Some rented studio spaces for their small teams, others took advantage of local coworking spaces, but many either worked from home or public spaces such as cafés or libraries. Their employment status was rarely stable or ongoing; instead they stitched together piecemeal and fixed-term contracts without benefits such as paid holiday or maternity leave. Many ostensibly worked in formally registered "companies," but often for purely legal or practical reasons such as opening a bank account, accessing a government funding program, or filling out necessary fields when submitting builds to distribution platforms. Few could straightforwardly answer the question "What is your job title?" For most videogame makers, making videogames is not simply a job one is employed to do but a liminal and precarious cultural activity that is sometimes commodified but often undertaken as unpaid hobby or artistic craft.

This is not how gamemaking is typically imagined, but it aligns with how we understand cultural production activity to occur in the cultural industries more broadly. While the work of gamemakers is now regularly described by both researchers and policymakers as occurring within a cultural or creative industry[1]—and while gamemakers, players, and critics regularly insist on the cultural and creative significance of the videogame medium—the actual experiences, identities, and conditions of gamemakers have not received sustained and nuanced attention *as* cultural producers, especially in the ways in which gamemakers take on high levels of personal risk as they strive to balance both creative and commercial ambitions. Musicians, artists, actors, writers, and painters are well understood to hustle from project to project, cobbling together a precarious existence through personal networks and unpaid (but fulfilling) work—remember that the broader phenomenon of the "gig economy" is effectively named after the gigs that a musician depends on in lieu of steady employment. If one looks closely enough, the experiences of videogame makers are no less diverse, and no less precarious.

This first chapter develops the concept of the videogame field, drawing from Pierre Bourdieu's work on fields of cultural production, to account for these gamemaking experiences more holistically. Field theory provides a framework that takes seriously both the economic necessities of contemporary cultural work as well as the underpinning noneconomic drivers such as creative fulfillment, self-expression, and peer recognition. Indeed, through Bourdieu, we can examine how the commercial and noncommercial ambitions articulated by gamemakers are deeply intertwined and symbiotic. The first section introduces the key terms and concepts of Bourdieu's theory of cultural fields that will be deployed throughout the rest of the book. The second section turns to the contemporary state of videogame production that, over the last decade, has undergone radical changes with the rise of more accessible production and distribution tools. Videogame production, I show here, was once *aggressively formalized*, making it difficult to conceive of videogame production occurring beyond formal companies, but is now *intensely in/formalized*, where just who is or isn't producing videogames in a formal or professional manner is now difficult to distinguish. It's this in/formalization, this ambiguity of who is "in" and who is "out," that makes Bourdieu's field theory particularly valuable for understanding contemporary videogame production since a cultural field is, ultimately, "the site of struggles in which what is at stake is the power to impose the dominant definition of [cultural producer] and therefore to delimit the population of those entitled to take part in the struggle to define the [cultural producer]" (Bourdieu 1993, 42). Finally, to show how this intense in/formalization and the formative tensions of the field are playing out for videogame makers themselves, the final section of this chapter turns to my participants and their complex responses to two seemingly straightforward questions: "Are you a professional videogame developer?" and "Are you part of a videogame industry?" Answers to these questions were multifaceted and provide initial insights into the sites of struggle, and the stakes at play, in the contemporary field of videogame production.

The Field of Videogame Production

Bourdieu's theory of the field of cultural production is developed over a series of essays written between 1968 and 1987 (compiled together in *The Field of Cultural Production* [1993], which I reference throughout this book), and forms a foundational component of his broader investigations into the production and perpetuation of class distinction through taste, culture, and education. Underpinning Bourdieu's work is the notion that a wide range of capitals are unevenly distributed among societal classes and, through them, social mobility is more or less feasible. Where *economic capital* is well understood through Marxist economic theory to be money that is turned into more money through the buying and selling of commodities (including, and most importantly, the labor-power of workers), Bourdieu (1986, 242) sees economic exchange as but "a particular case of exchange in all its forms." To economic capital, Bourdieu adds the concepts of *cultural capital* and *social capital*—which he sometimes collectively refers to as *symbolic capitals*—as qualitative, nonmonetary forms of value that can be, in the long run, converted into economic capital. Perhaps the most significant contribution of Bourdieu's body of work is a more sociologically robust articulation of how the dominant classes reproduce their own dominance not simply through the concentration of economic wealth but through the ability to define broader social and cultural practices and tastes in such a way that they also grow their own concentration of cultural and social wealth, while suppressing such wealth in the dominated classes.

For cultural production theorists, Bourdieu's theory allows us to go beyond, without ignoring, economic markers of value when working to articulate the contexts and drivers of cultural activities and labor. This has seen Bourdieu's idea of cultural capital adopted and adapted across a wide range of fields and case studies. Yet the concept remains nebulous and vague across Bourdieu's work—perhaps an inevitability when describing something that is itself intrinsic and often intangible. In one passage of his essay "The Forms of Capital" (1986, 243; original emphasis), Bourdieu does provide a general explanation of the three main forms of capital:

> Capital can present itself in three fundamental guises: as *economic capital*, which is immediately and directly convertible into money and may be institutionalized in the form of property rights; as *cultural capital*, which is convertible, in certain conditions, into economic capital and may be institutionalized in the form

of educational qualifications; and as *social capital*, made up of social obligations ("connections"), which is convertible, in certain conditions, into economic capital and may be institutionalized in the form of a title of nobility.

As a simple example, we can think of the hypothetical situation of two different students attending an elite, exclusive university: one from an upper-class family that has attended equally exclusive private schools for generations, and one from a working-class background, who attended public schools, and who was awarded a scholarship to attend the university. While both students have the same access to the university's material resources of teachers, social clubs, and alumni networks despite their varied economic capital, the student from the upper-class background would likely possess numerous advantages to get the most out of these resources: stronger previous education through which to approach new subjects, familial experiences and general knowledge of the "hidden curriculum" (Margolis 2001) of university life, experience with particular cultural events and traditions, and existing social networks throughout the university community. These constitute the unequal social and cultural capitals that make it easier for the upper-class student to extract even more value from such an education than for the working-class student and, ultimately, even more economic capital in the future.

The unequal distribution of economic and symbolic capitals, and the power to impose laws and norms most favorable to the reproduction of these capitals among those already most rich in them, forms the foundations of Bourdieu's theory of *fields*. A field is the structured space of social relationships where differently positioned agents compete for access to the accruement of the different forms of capital (or, simply, for power). Just as in its everyday usage, to speak of a field in the Bourdieusian sense is to denote an ambiguous, contested, yet shared arena of common principles and agreed-upon markers of success. For Bourdieu, the most all-encompassing field is *the field of class relations* in which all members of a society are constituents. Within the field of class relations are countless subfields: the education field, the biology field, the literary field, the political field, the stamp collecting field, the videogame field. Cyclically, a field becomes more or less recognizable *as* a field as those that strive to be part of the field come to agree on the forms of cultural and social capital (such as awards, publishers, exhibitions, endorsements) that determine success within the field. That is, a field becomes a field as it develops a limited *autonomy* from the broader field of class relations, where success and capital within that field may be measured by different metrics than that of economic value or political power. Fields are thus *homologous* to the field of class relations in that they inherit a similar structure between dominant and dominated positions, and a similar logic based on the exchange of symbolic values, but the specific structures and recognized forms of capital themselves differ. For instance, we can consider how in academia a relatively younger area of study (such as that of videogames) transitions over time from being considered solely as a topic within existing fields (such as media studies, narratology, or computer science) to instead being autonomous *as* an academic field (such as game studies) with its own recognized journals, conferences, pioneers, awards, publishers, concepts, and debates.

A *field of cultural production*, then, is a semiautonomous space of relationships between creators that compete to accrue the forms of cultural capital recognized within the field as legitimate. A cultural field becomes autonomous as a field as it more successfully "consecrates" (Bourdieu 1993, 38) its own markers of legitimacy and value (such as awards, review scores, recognition by other producers in the field) separate from those external markers of economic and political profit (such as sale figures, popularity, sponsorship deals). But then, just which markers of legitimacy the field consecrates is constantly contested within the field as different cultural producers strive to have their own positions legitimized. Each producer within a cultural field strives for their own work to be considered more legitimate, and, consequentially, for others' work to be considered less legitimate. Here we can think of common, perpetual struggles in various cultural fields over authenticity, such as the debates of the early 2010s, with the rise of new communities and tools, as to just what constitutes a "real" videogame (Harvey 2014; Consalvo and Paul 2019), or debates in popular music scenes as to who is an authentic member of a particular subculture and who is a sellout (Thornton 1995). Importantly, a field of cultural production is not a predetermined or static space with uniform or pregiven markers of quality or success but a continuous struggle to define the field—a struggle played out between those already recognized as existing within the field (who have a stake in ensuring the current shape of the field persists) and those striving to be recognized as existing within the field (who have a stake in upending the current shape of the field). Thus, we could say the videogame field is the site in which creators take positions and compete to determine whose positions are the most authentic videogame maker positions (i.e., generative of the most symbolic capital recognized within the field, and most able to be exchanged for economic capital in the future) and, perhaps as importantly, whose positions are the least authentic (generative of the least symbolic capital).

Here, Bourdieu's concepts of *position*, *disposition*, and *position-taking* are crucial. Firstly, *positions* are, most simply, where within a field a cultural producer sits in relation to the positions of all other cultural producers within the field. Positions are relative and "every position, even the dominant one, depends for its very existence, and for the determinations it imposes on its occupants, on the other positions constituting the field" (Bourdieu 1993, 30). When a cultural producer takes a position in a field, they do so in relation to all the existing positions. This could include alliances of closely related positions with similar interests and values that set themselves apart from other positions in the field. Positions that define themselves as "alternative" or "indie" or "post-" are explicit examples of such relative positions. When mapping a field, a position can be at either the dominant or the dominated pole along axes of different forms of capital. One could thus be in a position that is highly generative of economic capital but weak in generating the forms of cultural capital recognized within the field, such as a commercial blockbuster film that makes millions of dollars but has no chance of winning an Oscar or being shown at Cannes. Alternatively, a position in a cultural field could be weak in generating economic capital but highly generative of cultural capital, such as a critically acclaimed poet who might win awards and prestige but is unlikely to sell many copies.

Not all positions in the field have equal power, and not all positions are equally available to everyone. Rather, the field presents itself to potential constituents as "a *space of possibles* which is defined in the relationship between the structure of average chances of access to the different positions" (Bourdieu 1993, 64; original emphasis). Each constituent forms "a subjective basis of the perception and appreciation" of these objective chances through their ability or inability to access different forms of capital, and this subjective basis is the constituent's *disposition*. One's disposition entails a vast range of social, economic, and culture pretexts—such as access to education and resources, the diversity or lack thereof of the field—that all inform the actor's consideration of which positions in the field it is possible to hold and which positions it is not possible to hold. Here we can think of how videogame production is often presented by schools and job ads as a technological, rather than artistic, endeavor, which requires a lifetime passion of playing videogames. This perpetuates the gender disparity in most videogame production companies by making the positions within seem less possible to those who haven't played blockbuster videogames their entire life. Alternatively, we can consider a hypothetical Indian film actor who is much more likely (but in no way certain) to end up, within the cinema field, positioned in Bollywood rather than Hollywood, due to the opportunities more directly available to them in terms of proximity, resources, language, and racial bias.

But one's disposition does not determine one's position straightforwardly. Women still can—and of course do—come to be employed in large videogame production companies despite the heterosexist and masculinist legacies that ensure such spaces remain dominated by male gamemakers. The Indian actor, despite the objective chances of success, can still accrue the savings, language proficiency, and visa to move to California and strive to make it in Hollywood. One ultimately takes a position in the field through an act of *position-taking* (*prises de position* in Bourdieu's original French) that is itself a "taking a stance" in relation to the space of possibles available to one's disposition. One's position-taking receives its value "from its negative relationship with the coexistent position-takings to which it is objectively related and which determine it by delimiting it" (Bourdieu 1993, 30). That is, by choosing to take a position, the cultural producer chooses to not take all the other available positions, and in so doing changes the "universe of options" that exist in the field and, ultimately, the meaning of all other position-takings. Thus, an agent's position-taking can change over time even as their position stays the same, due to its changing relationship to other positions. Here we can think of the daring, new, avant-garde artist who, decades later, has become the incumbent, established classic that newcomers to the field position themselves in contrast to. Or we could think of the scholar who was forward-thinking and field-defining for their time but now gets critiqued as conservative and outdated as a rite of passage by each new postgraduate student in the field.

Dispositions and position-takings matter because cultural fields always exist within the broader field of class relations. Regardless of how autonomous a cultural field becomes, one's ability to take a position in the field is always determined, in part, by factors external to the field, such as access to funding, access to education, access to the right social networks, and so on. Thus, a field of cultural production never fully achieves the autonomy it perpetually strives for. Here, we come to the fundamental contradiction at the heart of all cultural production: the tension every cultural producer faces between creating "art for art's sake" that is recognized as such only by a small circle of peers, and "selling out" to focus on what is recognizable as art by a much broader audience and so more likely to be exchangeable for economic return. As Bourdieu (1993, 39) puts it, "Whatever its degree of independence, [a field of cultural production] continues to be affected by the laws of the field which encompasses it, those of economic and political profit." And so any field of cultural production is driven by parallel but contradictory principles of hierarchization: the autonomous principle and the heteronomous principle. The *autonomous principle of hierarchization* is the "degree of recognition accorded by those who recognize no other criterion of legitimacy than recognition by those whom they recognize" (Bourdieu 1993, 38). That is, for a cultural producer to achieve success through the autonomous principle they would have to be recognized by their peers within the field as a legitimate cultural producer. Whereas the *heteronomous principle of hierarchization* "is *success* as measured by indices such as book sales, number of theatrical performances, etc. or honours, appointments, etc." (Bourdieu 1993, 38; original emphasis). That is, for a cultural producer to achieve success through the heteronomous principle they would have to be recognized by those external to the field such as general audiences, marketers, and investors. If the autonomous principle reigned unchallenged, "the field of production [would] achieve total autonomy with respect to the laws of the market" (Bourdieu 1993, 38). If the heteronomous principle reigned unchallenged, "losing all autonomy, the . . . field [would] disappear as such (so that writers and artists became subject to the ordinary laws prevailing in the field of power, and more generally to the economic field)" (Bourdieu 1993, 38). All cultural producers find themselves negotiating the two principles through their position-taking: even the most autonomous poet still needs to obtain food and pay rent, and even the most commercial musician needs to adhere somewhat to the autonomous principles recognized by the music field if they are to be recognized as a musician at all. Thus, a field of cultural production "is at all times the site of a struggle between the two principles of hierarchizations" (Bourdieu 1993, 40). How videogame producers navigate the constant push-and-pull of autonomous and heteronomous principles of hierarchization will be a recurring theme in the following chapters.

Most importantly, and worth repeating, is that the structure of a cultural field is never static. With each new position-taking of a newcomer to the field, the meaning of every other position-taking changes, as too does the distribution of the available capital—both economic and symbolic. And so what is at stake in the constant struggle that is the field of cultural production is the boundary of the field itself—that is, the shared understanding as to just which positions are, at any given time, legitimately within or without the field. Bourdieu stresses that, due to this dynamism of the field, it is not the researcher's task to draw a hard and fast dividing line between those who are and those who aren't in the field. To do so would simply impose the researcher's own biases through their own position. Instead, the researcher of a field should aspire to "describe a *state* (long-lasting or temporary) of these struggles and therefore of the frontier delimiting the territory held by the competing agents" (Bourdieu 1993, 43; original emphasis). If a researcher chooses to only focus on those cultural producer positions perceived as already the most legitimate within the field, they are "blindly arbitrating on debates which are inscribed in reality itself . . . as to who is legitimately entitled to designate legitimate [cultural producers]" (Bourdieu 1993, 41). Instead, by examining how producers strive for autonomy (internal success) and how they strive for heteronomy (external success), we make the struggle between the two principles itself—the struggle that *is* the cultural field—the focus of our inquiry. This is why the chapters that follow do not simply define or outline the videogame field in terms of which positions are within it and which are without it. Rather, following Bourdieu's warning, I seek to examine the videogame field's *frontiers* at the time of writing— the sites that are most contested and perceived by some to be within the field and by others to be without it.

By focusing on the contested boundaries of the field of videogame production we can expose a wider range of differently positioned gamemakers with varying degrees of power within the field that are deploying economic and symbolic capital—or feel hindered by their lack thereof—in either pursuit or disavowal of more capital. Considering the field as the full holistic site of videogame production, rather than just those activities and identities that are formalized industrially in a narrow sense, allows us to better identify, appreciate, and examine the noneconomic values that influence and shape videogame production while, at the same time, neither romanticizing nor downplaying the equally important influence of the uneven distribution of economic capital both within the videogame field and in the broader field of class relations. In other words, looking at videogame production as occurring within a cultural field striving for autonomy, but always still constrained by heteronomy, allows us to consider how "necessity [becomes] internalized and converted into a disposition that generates meaningful practices and meaning-given perceptions" (Bourdieu 1984, 17). Put simply, it allows us to consider more holistically who makes videogames, with what resources, and toward what ends.

The In/formalization of Videogame Production

To adapt Bourdieu's words (1993, 42), the field of videogame production is a site of struggle where what is at stake is the power to impose the dominant definition of videogame maker and therefore to delimit the population of those entitled to take part in the struggle to define the legitimate videogame maker. The videogame field is today in a paradoxical position where the cultural relevancy of its texts is now more or less given, but where conceptualizations of the production of these texts as itself a cultural practice remains limited. If one were to draw the field of videogame production on a piece of paper as a network of positions related through their competition over different forms of capital and thus through their struggle for legitimation, what is traditionally referred to as "the videogame industry" would itself form a much smaller subset of this broader network. This dominant subset, to achieve its dominance, obscures and delegitimizes the rest of the field that it is fundamentally and continuously shaped by. While a legitimate "musician" or "writer" is not necessarily someone who works full time in the music industry or the writing industry, it remains difficult to image a "videogame developer" who exists external to the "videogame industry" due to the success of the field's dominant positions in limiting what products and practices are understood as legitimate within the field.

Such a limited understanding of who legitimately makes videogames is increasingly unsustainable. Chaos Theory's cofounders, while determined to build a commercial company, began making their own games in high school and now primarily work for private clients, making websites or other forms of software just as often as they make games. Schaffer has little interest in ever making videogames as a full-time job, yet they have undertaken short-term work with commercial game studios in Adelaide and regularly attend and organize meetup events that are themselves vital for local studios and gamemakers to network and collaborate. O'Neill is sometimes a hobbyist, sometimes a journalist, sometimes a paid contract worker, but always primarily a musician and music teacher. Each of these gamemakers are sort of part of a videogame industry and sort of not. How might we then articulate the videogame field's current dynamics where more and more legitimate gamemaking positions are visible beyond the dominant positions of commercial videogame companies?

Where once a clear distinction could arguably be made between the professional studios that employed hundreds of people and the bedroom amateur tinkering in their spare time, the 2010s saw a drastic reconfiguration of the videogame field that has disrupted and blurred categories and practices. *Minecraft*, one of the most successful videogames of all time, began life as a side-project of a single programmer working around a day job. *Untitled Goose Game*, one of the biggest releases of 2019, was produced by four friends who gradually, over a number of years, transitioned from a hobbyist group to a formal development studio. In a time of indie start-ups, viral hobbyist successes, and artistic interventions, just which gamemakers are "professional" and which are not is harder to define than ever before.

I find the concepts of *formal* and *informal* cultural activity valuable to articulate this broader gamemaking field and the increasingly fuzzy lack of distinction between professional and amateur modes of videogame production. I take these concepts from Ramon Lobato and Julian Thomas's *The Informal Media Economy* (2015, 7), which conceptualizes informal media economies broadly as "a range of activities and processes occurring outside the official, authorized space of the economy." Crucially, informal media is not detached from the regulated practices of formal media and software organizations. Rather, the activities of different individuals and organizations, the affordances of different technologies and policies, and cultivated tastes and behaviors of audiences of different cultural moments continuously *formalize* and *informalize* media economies and, more important for this book, cultural industries.

Lobato and Thomas demonstrate this with the example of the recorded music distribution industry that, at the turn of the twenty-first century, was dramatically reshaped by the rise of software that made it easy to rip CDs into digital MP3 files that could then be shared directly between networked computers. Services like Napster and LimeWire dramatically informalized music distribution, allowing peer-to-peer distribution of music without the formal mediations of record stores and publishing labels. Companies like Apple in turn reformalized these informalizing practices, regulating the management, distribution, and use of MP3 files through iTunes and the iPod once the concept of keeping a digital library of song files had become normalized. The music industry did not simply suppress these informal practices but formalized them, subsuming them into its regulated economic practices to reinsert dominant commercial positions back into the flow of capital. The story of media economies—and indeed cultural production—is a Möbius strip of informal practices circumventing or emerging beyond the regulations of the formal economy, and the formal media economies adapting to, co-opting, and incorporating informal practices in turn.

The pendulum of formality and informality has swung particularly far in each direction during the history of videogame production. As numerous historical accounts have shown (Swalwell 2021; Nooney 2020; Nicoll 2019; Švelch 2018; Jørgensen, Sandqvist, and Sotamaa 2017; Rocca 2013), videogame production was born from the informal activity of hobbyists, hackers, artists, and students, and it was only later formalized through the capture and commodification of this informal activity through companies such as Atari, Taito, Activision, Nintendo, and Sega. Technologies and business models such as the coin-operated arcade machine and the home television game console formalized and commodified videogame production. But through the 1970s and 1980s, videogames also continued to be created and distributed through informal capacities. With the growing availability of the microcomputer, users were able (and often required) to write their own game programs, leading to the formation of ecosystems that would create, share, duplicate, remix, and reshare a number of "homebrew" games (Swalwell 2021).

This balance of formal and informal videogame production in the field shifted dramatically through the 1980s. Much like the music industry several decades later, videogame companies struggled to adapt to the ease with which digital media could be duplicated and redistributed. That is, the formal industry at the time struggled to find means through which to adequately regulate prolific informal practices such as homebrew development and copyright infringement. This eventually led to the infamous

North American videogame industry crash of the early 1980s. From 1981 to 1984, the coin-operated videogame industry almost halved from just under US \$5 million to US \$2.5 million thanks to the rise in popularity of home console machines (Donovan 2010, 98). At the same time, the sheer number of low-quality videogames available for home consoles such as the Atari VCS saw consumer trust plummet, retailers lowering prices to clear unsold stock, companies going under, and liquidators flooding the market with drastically underpriced titles (Donovan 2010, 99). Importantly, a wide range of factors contributed to this crash such as a nationwide recession in the United States and an increased public anxiety about the effects of videogames on children. Further, the financial impact of this crash beyond North America is often overstated in popular retellings. Nonetheless, a flood of unregulated, cheap, low-quality titles and subsequent plummeting consumer trust would be perceived by videogame companies and players as the leading reasons for the crash.

When Nintendo entered the post-crash American market with the Nintendo Entertainment System (NES; Famicom in Japan) in 1985, they established a business strategy that defined the videogame field for the following decades. As O'Donnell's (2014) analysis of the NES details, Nintendo worked to reassure American consumers (both children and parents) as to the quality and appropriateness of their products through technological, legal, and discursive strategies. To make games for the NES at all, gamemakers required a software development kit (SDK) that Nintendo would only provide if one abided strict editorial guidelines. Any attempt to circumvent the need for an SDK was suppressed by Nintendo through patent law. Public facing, the Nintendo "Seal of Approval" that stamped first-party Nintendo games was an explicit reassurance to customers that these professionally made videogames were more trustworthy than the amateur offerings that bloated the Atari VCS shelves. Meanwhile, the Nintendo-run magazine-slash-marketing-brochure *Nintendo Power* provided a discursive basis—echoed throughout the nascent videogame press—that fostered a transition of videogame playing culture from family-oriented computer use to an edgier, juvenile, technophilic, male-dominated consumer culture (Kirkpatrick 2015; Arsenault 2017; Nicoll 2019; Shaw 2014). A hegemonic force took form to constitute what Graeme Kirkpatrick (2015), also drawing from Bourdieu, calls the gaming field, where the markers of internal legitimacy that first consecrated videogame play as an autonomous field (as opposed to just one aspect of computing) emerged side by side with the industrialization and professionalization of videogame production, and the deliberate and gendered stabilizing of videogame target audiences. Nintendo, followed by the likes of Sega, Sony, and Microsoft, successfully framed the formal videogame industry as *the* place where legitimate videogames were made, to the exclusion of a range of alternative, noncommercial potential videogame-making positions.

As console manufacturers competed to convince consumers to commit to their platform over the competition, increases in computational power and graphical fidelity became a significant selling point of the "console wars"—most significantly in the transitions from 2D to 3D environments in the mid-1990s. Every few years, a new "generation" of home consoles would emerge with supposedly greater technological affordances—the Super NES replacing the NES, the PlayStation 3 replacing the PlayStation 2—and, consequentially, the resources required to produce videogames for each new platform constantly rose to meet these heightened expectations. Budgets and development team sizes grew exponentially, as did the financial burden of accessing console manufacturers' SDKs. Meanwhile, through marketing and critical discourses, players were taught to evaluate a videogame's quality through technologically determinate markers of "technobabble" (Arsenault 2017, 77). Discussions of aesthetics or style became subservient to considerations of polygon counts, framerate, and hardware memory capacities. PC developers were spared the need to access SDKs or appease console manufacturers but were still confronted with the need to increase the scale of their products to meet the technological expectations of consumers increasingly interested in the field's dominant values of gameplay, content, and graphics if they were to take a position recognized as legitimately existing within the videogame field at all (Kirkpatrick 2015; Arsenault 2017).

This period from the mid-1980s until the late 2000s can be understood as the time in which the field of videogame production was *aggressively formalized*. The dominant commercial positions within the field in this time successfully narrowed the range of positions considered legitimate to their own. Commercial videogame production became increasingly dependent on contracts with large publishers and console manufacturers that could provide the financial resources, technological infrastructure, and global distribution networks required to produce and distribute commercially feasible (that is, legitimate) videogames. The rise of the studio-publisher model effectively priced out smaller independent teams and hobbyist creators from the dominant development and distribution platforms. Without the visibility of alternative forms of videogame production, this period of aggressive formalization normalized a cultural imagination of the videogame as consumer software driven by innovations in processing power and graphical fidelity, an ever-increasing amount of content and scale, and limited to a finite number of action-centric genres. While it remained possible to create and distribute smaller videogames on personal computers through software such as *ZZT* (see Anthropy 2014) or Flash (see Salter and Murray 2014), videogames made with such software could not compete with the commercial offerings of the large development studios financially backed by console manufacturers and third-party publishers in terms of technological spectacle and, hence, legitimacy. Ultimately, the dominant positions within the videogame field successfully determined how videogames would be evaluated in such a way that only the dominant positions would have the resources and ability to develop and distribute videogames that would be evaluated as being of commercial quality.[2]

The aggressively formalized videogame field greatly narrowed the ability of researchers, the public, policymakers, and gamemakers themselves to imagine a broader field of videogame production beyond its most commodified and commercial positions. In the mid-2000s, however, the structure of the videogame field again began to shift drastically in ways that have directly challenged these established understandings of where videogame production occurs and who undertakes it. High-speed Internet and the rise of digital distribution platforms weakened the distribution bottlenecks imposed by the large console manufacturers between videogame developers and potential players. The rise and eventual ubiquity of smartphone devices, such as the Apple iPhone, opened up new audiences and demographics, and created new opportunities and business models for videogame producers (Leaver and Willson 2016; Nieborg 2020). The emergence and ubiquity of financially and technologically accessible software such as the Game-Maker, Unity, and Unreal game engines converged the skillset and resources of professional and amateur gamemakers alike (Foxman 2019; Nicoll and Keogh 2019). On the margins of formal videogame production, new subcultures and communities of creators beyond the dominant demographics of young, white, cisgender, heterosexual, university-trained men began making *different* kinds of videogames for different audiences with different tools. Tools such as Twine and later Bitsy were picked up by marginal gamemakers and truly revolutionized understandings of what videogames are allowed to be (Harvey 2014; kopas 2015; Ruberg 2020b; Reed 2020). As Anna Anthropy noted in 2012, "We have one foot in an era when creative people will no longer need publishers to distribute their games" (2012, 19). While the years since have not necessarily produced the utopia of democratized game creation Anthropy alludes to (see chapter 3), she was correct in her sense that the field was transforming.

Writing particularly of the queer, transgender, and otherwise marginal creators of the Twine scene, Alison Harvey (2014, 104) notes that as these marginal gamemakers become increasingly visible within the videogame field, researchers "need to address what constitutes our dominant construction of game designer and challenge those rubrics in order to understand the subversive and radical contributions of those who do not align with the normative constitution." Just as "the established definition of the writer may be radically transformed by an enlargement of the set of people who have a legitimate voice in literary matters" (Bourdieu 1993, 42), the explosion of more accessible tools for videogame production and unregulated platforms for videogame distribution has given rise to "videogame zinesters" (Anthropy 2012) and "everyday gamemakers" (Young 2018) that point toward new lines of tension in the struggles for legitimization within the field. As in any field of cultural production, the arrival of what Bourdieu would call "newcomers" to the videogame field challenges dominant understandings of just what practices constitute the field at all and shifts the values associated with existing position-takings.

These tensions have played out explicitly in videogame discourse over the past decade with extensive debates across blogs, reviews, message boards, social media, conference talks, and academic publications as to just what might even be considered a "real" videogame in the first place, and just who might be considered a "real" videogame maker (Consalvo and Paul 2019). While indie games had already claimed to split from the mainstream industry in the mid-2000s (a claim critiqued in chapters 2 and 3), the diverse range of independent gamemakers that emerged in the early 2010s, particularly in queer and transgender gamemaking subcultures

> consciously and deliberately rejects indie's failed split from the mainstream and its poorly-concealed capitalist underpinnings, and instead upholds personal expression

as the highest ideal, the only goal that matters. And in order to do that successfully, they must break off completely [from the videogame industry], not at a branch
somewhere on the tree but at the very root of the established order. (Burns 2013)

Here, we have a classic case of newcomers to a field of cultural production
making a claim of legitimacy through the principles of autonomous hierarchization and a complete disavowal of heteronomous hierarchization. Yet,
it is worth stressing that these "newcomers" to the videogame field in the
early 2010s (women, queer folk, transgender folk, poor folk, artists, etc.) of
course always existed at the peripheries of the videogame field. They were
newcomers to the field only insofar as the positions they held have become
newly legitimized within the field as videogame production and distribution, and so their activities have come more in focus under the lens of
videogame production researchers, including myself.

The accepted borders of the videogame field are shifting so that a vast
range of informal hobbyist, amateur, and enthusiast creator positions are
now legibly within the field. As the following chapters will detail, the traditionally understood formal videogame industry and the informal activities of the broader field are now deeply codependent. The evidence of this
is in the shifting discourses around the developer and consumer cultures
that have taken place in recent years as a wider range of creator demographics find their labor increasingly validated and visible around what has
historically been a stubbornly hegemonic industry. As Christopher Young
highlights: "[As everyday gamemakers] increasingly contribute to the economic development of the video game industry, the industry has simultaneously enabled these gamemakers to contribute to the cultural discourse
surrounding working conditions, information practices, and definitions of
games" (2018, 12). A wider range of gamemakers with different values and
ambitions (that is, gamemakers who are taking a wider range of positions in
the field) now have a louder voice in the videogame field and an increased
say in the autonomous principles that underpin and motivate it. They are
interviewed and reviewed by game journalism outlets, winning awards at
legitimized (and legitimizing) festivals and conferences, followed by players and other gamemakers on social media, and selling their videogames on
legitimized (and legitimizing) platforms such as Steam and the App Store.
Consequentially, new sites of tension are emerging where these new positions clash with those values and ambitions established by the dominant
positions that aggressively formalized the field in previous decades.

The videogame field is thus no longer aggressively formalized as a small handful of console manufactures no longer have the sole power to determine who is a legitimate videogame maker. But neither has the field returned to a period of informalization, such as existed in the 1960s and 1970s. The legacy of aggressive formalization persists, and the largest companies continue to hold the most power even as a wider range of positions are legitimized and challenging the state of the field. Whereas informalization would suggest a weakening of the dominant formal positions in the field, as Lobato and Thomas trace in the music industry, the videogame field has now entered a period of what I call *intense in/formalization*, defined by a blurring of relationships and positions that gamemakers now occupy between the formal and informal—between the need to strive for autonomous (cultural) and heteronomous (economic) modes of success. Today, once clear distinctions between triple-A and indie, professional and amateur, player and developer have broken down. Previously stable dominant positions in the field have lost their ability to present themselves as the entire field, while marginal positions in the field have successfully gained legitimacy. Crucially, the legacy of aggressive formalization and the values it instilled in videogame production and consumption discourses persists. Intense in/formalization thus points to the specific, transitionary historical moment of the videogame field in the late 2010s and early 2020s where access to (but not necessarily ownership over) the means of production and distribution of videogame works has greatly outpaced public, industrial, government, and academic conceptualizations of what is understood as legitimate and successful videogame production.

In its intensely in/formal phase, the videogame field now operates more explicitly like every other cultural field that has achieved some degree of autonomy: a lot of people make videogames in a lot of different contexts, and some of those people make money doing so. Yet, the legacy of aggressive formalization persists and still strongly influences perceptions of just what videogame creation is among researchers, policymakers, students, and videogame makers themselves. Empirically researching the lived experiences of those who make videogames in different geographic contexts helps to address this. While the videogame industry still risks being imagined as globally homogenous, Aphra Kerr's unparalleled political economic analysis of global videogame production makes clear that the videogame field is defined by its variability rather than its uniformity, and thus "the industry and culture of digital games" must be placed "firmly within local and regional economies and societies" (2017, 30). To decenter the most formalized and dominant positions of the videogame field, the global videogame industry needs to be reconceptualized as emerging from the multitude of local videogame making cultures that exist—have always existed—in specific regions, countries, cities, towns, and suburbs.

This makes the specific cultural, social, and economic contexts in which videogames are produced particularly important if we are to adequately understand the in/formalized videogame field. Gamemakers I spoke to consistently referred to issues of space and place that mediated their gamemaking activities: the cost of local rent (both commercial and domestic); the value (or lack thereof) of coworking spaces; the vibrancy (or lack thereof) of the local scene; the difficulties and flexibilities of remote work (even before the COVID-19 pandemic); the presence or absence of local government funding programs; the presence or absence of large videogame companies or university programs; the cost and length of flights to North American or Asian conferences and exhibitions; the crunch-inducing external deadlines of consumer expos and industry conventions; the quality of local Internet infrastructure; the presence or absence of social safety nets such as health care and social welfare income. *Where* videogames are made underlines *what* videogames are made, *who* makes them, and *how* they go about making them.

It is historical accounts of videogame production's formalization in specific local contexts that have best exposed the ways in which aggressive formalization narrowed how we imagine the field by showing how videogame production has always been "a multiplicity that has no monolithic center, no representative feature, especially not once we formulate on planetwide scales" (Nooney 2020, 142). Examples include Jaroslav Švelch's (2018) account of how Czech hobbyist gamemakers built a grassroots local industry in the 1980s; Melanie Swalwell and Michael Davidson's (2016) account of New Zealand videogame production between local identity and global imitation through the case study of *Malzak*; Laine Nooney's (2020) examination of the professional women involved in the operation and success of Sierra Online; and Benjamin Nicoll's (2019) account of the early days of South Korea's videogame field (today one of the largest and most lucrative national game industries in the world) as that of deliberate, opportunistic, and patriotic poaching and reappropriating of Japanese technology and intellectual property. These various case studies, as Kristine Jørgensen, Ulf

Sandqvist, and Olli Sotamaa (2017, 458) note in their own history of Nordic videogame production, demonstrate that "the major industries [of the United States and Japan] supported by large home markets provide a very particular and somewhat limited perspectives on the origins of the global game industry."

To Jørgensen, Sandqvist, and Sotamaa's claim I would add, however, that it is not just perspectives on the "origins" of the global game industry that are sorely limited, but our ongoing understanding of how videogame production is still continually formed and contested by those who are neither necessarily absorbed into nor replaced by the formalizing and industrializing of the videogame field. Local videogame production communities do not simply exist beyond a videogame industry but are the broader field of informal, creative, affective, and social activity through which formal videogame production sometimes emerges to be understood *as* a videogame industry. Examining the cultural field of videogame production in this transitionary moment of intense in/formalization provides an opportunity to take seriously the diverse, often contradictory positions that have *always* been taken by gamemakers in the struggle between autonomy and heteronomy, between different markers of success and legitimation, between different forms and distributions of capital. The current moment allows us to move beyond the reductively economic markers of success that persist from the period of aggressive formalization to instead better account for the full range of contexts in which videogames are produced—have always been produced—and the full range of people who produce them.

Who Is a Videogame Developer in the Videogame Industry?

In 2019, I received an email inviting me to participate in the Game Developers Conference's (GDC) annual "State of the Industry" survey. At this point, I had been making my own videogames in what I feel most comfortable calling a hobbyist capacity for four years.[3] I was directly invited to participate in the survey as a previous attendee and speaker at GDC, and thus I was clearly someone whose experience the survey designers hoped to capture. However, the questions of the survey immediately made me doubt just how appropriate it would be for me to submit my answers. Questions asked about my game development salary ($100 over the previous year, solely from voluntary donations), the number of videogames I've worked on (over 50, but few took more than a week to create), my workplace (on the couch in front of the television), and attitudes toward my employer (myself). I did not feel explicitly unwelcomed by the survey, but I worried that by truthfully contributing my own experiences I would poison the well of the survey data, preventing it from adequately representing "real" videogame makers who "actually" work in the industry.

This personal experience of doubting the legitimacy of my own position within the field of videogame production echoes the curiosity that inspired this research project: just which positions within the intensely in/formal videogame field are captured and presented *as* the videogame field, at the exclusion of which other positions? Yet again, Bourdieu (1993, 42) preempts this concern when he warns that "every survey aimed at establishing the hierarchy of [cultural producers] predetermines the hierarchy by determining the population deemed worthy of helping to establish it." This curiosity led me to end both my interviews and survey with two questions directly influenced by Adrienne Shaw's (2012) research on which videogame players do or don't identify as gamers: (1) Are you a professional videogame developer? (2) Are you part of the videogame industry? Having so far in this chapter outlined how a field of cultural production is the struggle to determine the legitimate positions within the field, and how this is particularly complicated in the contemporary videogame field, here I want to explore the responses to these two questions specifically to consider how this foundational tension of the videogame field plays out through the perceptions, embodiments, and understandings of those that strive to take positions within it.

Are You a Professional Videogame Developer?

When I initially designed this project, I suspected it would be "professional" game developers who were more likely to fill out trade association surveys, while "amateur" game developers would not. And so I thought it made sense to determine which gamemakers consider themselves to be professionals. However, when I began asking gamemakers "Are you a professional videogame developer?" I was surprised that all three words in the label were contested by different gamemakers. *Professional* raised questions about *how* the participant went about their work, with what kind of commitment, and toward what kind of success. *Game* raised questions as to what sort of work or products participants spent their time producing. And *developer* raised questions as to their personal position within the videogame production process, at times differentiated from roles such as designer or artist or producer.

One student survey respondent succinctly exposed the problem with my simplistic categorization of professional videogame developer as meaning "those who are paid to make videogames" when they answered, "Well, I've made $2 from [my games], so I guess? But also, I've made $2 from [my games], so I guess no." Even if professionalism could be reduced to being paid, the question of just how much one needs to be paid before they become a professional demonstrates that it remains a nonetheless subjective label deeply informed by the field's dominant formations. An ambiguous relationship with professionalism is a common quandary for cultural producers since many who see their primary occupation as cultural production support this work through "a secondary occupation which provides their main income" (Bourdieu 1993, 43). For some gamemakers, professionalism had less to do with how much money they were making and more to do with how they approached their gamemaking practice. John Kane, a 33-year-old gamemaker in Sydney, made his income primarily from a day job in web development. This meant he did not feel that he was part of the videogame industry, but nonetheless he did consider himself a professional videogame developer because "[gamemaking] is something I do on a regular basis and take seriously." In contrast, an anonymous gamemaker from South Australia felt they could not consider themselves to be a "pro dev" until "I am earning a solid, stable salary from just developing videogames" but nonetheless insisted that they "have a professional work ethic and treat development in a professional manner."

Many did consider professionalism narrowly as tied to a financial income, as I first had. Scott Purcival, a 32-year-old programmer who worked remotely into a small team from his home in a small town in regional Queensland, mused that he would "class myself as a professional when I have something that I start showing to people and say 'give me money to make more of this.'" Curiously, perceiving professionalism as tied to income was also a reason why some gamemakers felt ambivalent about professionalism. Riad Djemili, 39, in Berlin, was cofounder of the videogame collective Saftladen. The collective takes its name from their first coworking space, which was situated in an old juice factory, a *saftpresserei* in German. *Saftladen* (meaning juice shop) softens *saftpresserei*, according to Djemili, to connote a "particularly nonprofessional business": "So I consider myself a professional but I really also like the idea of being an amateur artist and being able to combine this commercial need to sustain myself with this naïve thing of just doing things I like and saying stuff about the world." Here, for Djemili, professionalism's affiliation with financial income puts it at odds with his desires as an autonomy-driven artist.

Game developer was more overwhelmingly agreed upon as an identity that participants shared, professional or otherwise. However, despite the sheer ubiquity of the term in all forms of discourse around videogame production, ownership of the title was still far from unanimous among gamemakers. Casey O'Donnell (2012) highlights how the title of game developer emerges from, and is often equated with, that of the software developer. While this might have made sense in the early days of videogame production, today "*game developer* is often assumed to be synonymous with 'game programmer,' with many designers, artists and audio producers responding to such carelessness with 'we live here too, you know'" (O'Donnell 2012, 21; original emphasis). Indeed, those involved in videogame production in nontechnical roles, such as community managers, producers, and writers, expressed a sense of uncertainty as to whether or not they were a developer. Lee May was a 34-year-old narrative designer at a studio in Brisbane, having recently shifted into the role after previously being the studio's community manager. For May, this shift in role changed his relationship to the claim of game developer:

> [When I was a community manager] I felt like there should be a distinction between what I was doing and what the people who were legitimately working on the game were doing. And I struggled, particularly when I was at shows and conventions, showing the game off and people were like "Oh are you one of the devs?" and I was like "Uhhhh." But then once I actually started getting into the editor and writing for the game, that's when that went away because clearly I am developing the game now.

Similarly, Georgia Symons in Melbourne, a writer on *Wayward Strand* who primarily works as a theater playwright, took issue with the title of developer due to which aspects of the production process she was involved with:

> I think the only word that sticks for me is "developer" because I think I associate that with the people who write the code or whatever. . . . But I would say I am a "videogame professional" because I'm getting paid to make a videogame, which is

kind of like the textbook definition of that term. . . . If someone was like "you're a professional videogame maker" I'd be like, yep, I guess that's factually accurate. . . . I have not looked at the game in Unity [the game engine] once. I have no idea what that looks like! I just write the script and I also direct the voiceover, and then they take it from there.

For both May and Symons, *game developer* is articulated as having connotations of being aligned with specific aspects of the videogame production process most directly involved in the manipulation of code and assets, and not with other aspects of the process such as scriptwriting, quality assurance, or community management—a finding echoed in Nooney's (2020) research on the uncredited women working for game studio Sierra in the 1980s in typically unrecognized business and administrative roles.

Those in part-time contract positions, such as freelance artists working simultaneously on multiple projects across different media formats, also felt less of an identity as a game developer as videogames was only one of the many formats they work in. Tania Walker, 31, is a contract illustrator in Hobart who has worked on a range of projects, including videogames, board games, and websites. She reflected:

> I put so much concentration into building my business as an illustrator, and often solo my own comic projects, that games almost become like a "nice to have" venue. So I don't consider myself a professional videogame developer in that clear-cut way of "I am always working on and producing assets for commercially viable games."

For Walker, the lack of resonance with game developer was less about her particular skillset as an illustrator and more the infrequency with which she directed these skills toward the production of videogames as opposed to other products. This is not a rare position to be in, as the examples of both Chaos Theory and O'Neill in this chapter's introduction demonstrate. For my own part, as a full-time academic who makes videogames in my spare time, I feel highly uncomfortable calling myself a game developer and instead call myself a gamemaker.

Are You Part of the Videogame Industry?

Participants had, broadly, two diametrically opposed perspectives on the term *videogame industry*. The first was that the videogame industry referred to a global or local *community* of videogame makers. The second was that the videogame industry referred to a distinct and hegemonic subset of a broader game development community that the participant either could not or did not wish to participate in. The former speaks to how the dominant positions of the field are imagined as the full extent of the legitimate positions that can be held in the field (and so the community and the industry become synonymous); the latter speaks to how those beyond these dominant positions feel very much marginalized by such an imagining.

For those working in commercial game studios or with ambitions for eventual commercial sustainability from their videogame work, when asked if they were a part of the videogame industry, both yes and no answers conceptualized the industry as something more than a simple sector of employment, instead seeing it more like a professional community in which involvement also required socializing, information sharing, and networking:

> I mean yes and no. Like, yes, I do [consider myself part of the videogame industry], because I'm working at a company. But at the same time, no, because I don't actively engage that much with the community and I feel that's an important part of it. (Anthony Massingham, 33, Brisbane)

> [No, I'm not part of the videogame industry because] we're a two man team that's released a relatively successful Android title that was developed apart from the local community. (Anonymous survey respondent, Western Australia)

In these framings, employment at a videogame company is not sufficient in itself to be "part of the industry."

Others, though, saw the videogame industry similarly to how I conceptualize it in this book as a particularly dominant subset of videogame production. This played out in a number of ways. First, commercial gamemakers working in small teams or by themselves felt that when the videogame industry was invoked, it was not independent developers that people had in mind but the larger industrial mode of production more commonly associated with triple-A. Henry Smith, a 39-year-old solo developer in Montreal, mused that

> usually when we talk about the industry we're talking about non-indie companies. At least when I'm talking with friends and colleagues I talk about the industry as big companies like EA and Bioware and Ubisoft and Warner Brothers. There are a lot of big companies just in Montreal, and indie is a counterpoint to that. When I talk about my history I say "I spent ten years in the industry" and so I guess I don't consider myself as part of the industry anymore. It's not particularly industrial what I'm doing. It's more grassroots, and it's not really business like. It's on that verge of hobby game development because I'm doing it mostly because

> I have a drive to build games and I've found ways to support myself, and they're often non-traditional means. But because of that it's not a normal business and so I see myself on the fringes of the industry, I guess. I'm doing what they do, selling games to people, but I like to think of myself as outside the industry as well to distinguish myself from the machine.

In Utrecht, 21-year-old game designer Ruben Naus works in the four-person collective Sokpop and likewise did not consider himself part of the video-game industry. Naus had an "aversion to the word industry" as, for him, "it's more like an art scene. . . . Like, I don't know a lot of people that work at studios. I only know people who either have perhaps like a really small collective or like a team of two or three people or who make games on their own." In Melbourne, 28-year-old Jake Strasser works as part of the four-person team House House. Strasser said the team "think of ourselves as being part of a videogames community rather than an industry. It feels like a big network of people supporting one another rather than some kind of industrial machine." At the time of our interview, House House was working on *Untitled Goose Game*, which would go on to become one of the best-selling games globally of 2019. This is an important reminder that who is and is not in the videogame industry cannot be reduced to simply who is and is not creating commercially viable videogames.

The videogame industry as the defining site of gamemakers' activity was also rejected by gamemakers making videogames in informal communities centered around local scenes or particular tools. Such gamemakers had a strong sense they were not part of the videogame industry specifically because of either *how* they were making games:

> No, I don't think [I am part of the game industry]. But I couldn't say whether that's because I don't like the games industry as a being or whether it is because I don't consider my products to be—well I don't like the word products for a start—for my works to be associated with the kinds of things that are made by the capital-G games industry or whether it's because I don't really adhere to that business model. I suspect it is a combination of these things. (Zachariah Chandler, 21, Melbourne)

Or *who* they were, as someone not perceived as welcome within the video-game industry:

> [No, I am not part of the videogame industry] because I don't make videogames in a commercial capacity. I also don't feel represented by the "industry," at least groups like IGDA [International Game Developers Association] whose interests in the medium seem to have little to no overlap with mine. Also, I hear too many

horror stories from people—mostly marginalized folk—who *are* in the industry (or were before they were chased out by shitheads). (Anonymous survey respondent, New South Wales)

[No, I am not part of the videogame industry because] my local games chapter is bad for minorities. The heads seem very complacent or like they can't do much for issues surrounding minorities in the community. The local meetup is set up in a location every time with a mural of a lady pulling a sexy pout speaking in a speech bubble "Eat, Sleep, Game . . . Repeat" (this is placed in a games co-working space) which is problematic in both the overworking practices facing the industry and the more general trends of sexism within the games industry. . . . I have also been treated different from my male colleagues by clients in obvious ways (I am a person of color and haven't told anyone I'm nonbinary and am seen as female). I am treated differently by peers in the community due to the same reasons. It's great to see the diversity in the national game developers community but I rarely see women or nonbinary people of darker skin being invited to speak or be recognized or thrive here so colorism is an issue that hasn't been addressed. Mostly it's sexism and racism. (Anonymous survey respondent, Canberra)

Importantly, these participants express not only feeling unwelcome in or unable to take positions in the part of the field known as the videogame industry, but also not necessarily *wanting* to take such positions due to the industry's notorious poor working conditions and rampant discrimination. This goes beyond a simple desire to not sell out to instead, politically and personally, not wanting to be associated with those toxic and impersonal sites of videogame production responsible for poor and unequitable working conditions that workers and researchers alike have been identifying for decades (Kline, Dyer-Witheford, and de Peuter 2003; Dyer-Witheford and de Peuter 2009; Legault and Weststar 2017; Cote and Harris 2020).

As the videogame field has become intensely in/formalized, with distinctions between professionals and amateurs blurring and overlapping on digital platforms and in local communities, simple questions of how gamemakers identify themselves and their position—as professional or not, as videogame developers or not, as in the videogame industry or not—highlight all sorts of struggles and ambivalences between commercial workplaces and creative communities, between artistic practice and employed profession. These struggles exist and have long existed in all fields of cultural production. Musicians and writers similarly muse as to when they become professional and whether they are part of a music or writing industry. Until recently, however, the fact that these struggles *are* struggles has been largely hidden from view in the videogame field due to the aggressive formalization of the dominant positions obscuring the rest of the field. The intense in/formalization brought about by the rise of digital platforms but no concurrent rise in stable employment opportunities exposes the struggles that continuously define and redefine the field of videogame production. We need to expand how we consider the videogame field, who we consider to be a part of it, which works and markers of success we measure it by, and, consequentially, what this means for our attempts to conceptualize the experiences of videogame makers in terms of labor, culture, politics, identity, and practice.

In my interviews, 85 percent of gamemakers said they would consider themselves to be videogame developers, but only 66 percent considered themselves to be *professional* game developers. Further, only 78 percent considered themselves to be part of the videogame industry.[4] Of the survey respondents who were asked to categorize what sort of gamemaker they are, we see a clear distinction between gamemakers formally employed at a company and others in terms of how they relate to the label of professional videogame developer, despite all respondents having explicitly opted into the survey as someone involved in the making of videogames (see Table 1.1).

Ultimately, while *videogame developer* is used broadly in popular, industry, and scholarly discourses to refer to videogame makers, the ambivalent responses of my participants suggest a need for us to reflect on how such a title might connote and perpetuate selective understandings of which skillsets and roles of videogame production are, as May put it above, considered to be legitimately working on the game. Such a reflection would not be dissimilar

Table 1.1

Percentage of gamemaker participants who responded affirmatively to "Are you a videogame developer?" and "Are you part of the videogame industry?"

	Identify as a professional videogame developer	Identify as part of the videogame industry
Survey respondents (282)		
Employed at or run a company (81)	85%	94%
Self-employed gamemaker (49)	44%	54%
Hobbyist, amateur, enthusiast, or student (112)	7%	63%
Contract/Freelance worker (40)	26%	41%
Interviewees (160)	66%	78%

to how recent years have seen a reconsideration as to just who is included or excluded when researchers use the "gamer" label to refer to videogame players (Shaw 2012). It's for this reason that throughout this book I use the terms *videogame maker* or *gamemaker* to refer to those involved in the production (not just development) of videogames.[5]

Conclusion

The videogame industry as it is typically imagined by researchers, players, and policymakers as a collection of formal videogame companies employing videogame developers fails to account for the full field of videogame production. A diverse range of people make videogames in different contexts for different reasons with different skillsets. The videogame industry is no longer, indeed if it ever was, an adequate conceptual frame to define the space they work in. Nor is the common moniker of videogame developer, with its technological connotations, always an adequate label through which to capture the type of work this diverse range of people undertake. Many are taking alternative positions in the videogame field.

The ways in which the videogame field was aggressively formalized through the 1990s and 2000s has led to a popular imagining of videogame production as first and foremost a commercial enterprise, and only abstractly as a creative and cultural practice. While videogames are now broadly understood to be a cultural form—to be art by certain broad definitions—we are yet to adequately consider what it means to account for videogame producers as themselves cultural producers—as artists by certain broad definitions—working within a cultural field.

It's the goal of the following chapters to rectify this, to show the much broader, more complex, and often contradictory ambitions, identities, and cultures that underpin videogame production. In this initial chapter, I've introduced the concept of the field of videogame production as an alternative concept through which videogame production can be understood in its multiplicity, in the contradicting struggles of differently positioned gamemakers striving to accrue different forms of both economic and symbolic capital. These struggles are formative of the videogame field, and the field is ultimately nothing but the struggle of videogame makers striving to have their own position legitimized as existing within the field. I've detailed how the context of these struggles in videogame production has shifted drastically since the early 2010s, with the rise of digital distribution and more accessible development tools underpinning the field's intense in/formalization giving a much wider range of creators and audiences a say in how the videogame field should be structured: what approaches should be valued, what achievements count as success, and which skills count as gamemaking skills.

This period of intense in/formalization, mirroring broader shifts in a range of digital and creative sectors toward precarity and a blurring of personal and professional identities, all but demands a Bourdieusian analysis of videogame production, of videogame production as happening within and as a field of cultural production. Bourdieu warns that the social scientist's job is not to delimit which positions are or are not within a cultural field but to describe how the cultural producers at the frontier of the field are struggling to be included or excluded. As such, the rest of the book turns to those videogame makers most on the periphery of videogame production that least fit within traditional understandings of the videogame industry: independent videogame makers, hobbyists, students, contract workers, and communities. Doing so will, I hope, both broaden and demystify the contexts and drivers of videogame production as no more or less complex than the contexts and drivers that underpin all fields of cultural production: the desire, as Nicole Williams put it, to get better and make cool stuff.

2   Videogame Production in Australia

Melbourne, the capital of the southern state of Victoria, is one of Australia's largest cities and is home to many of the country's most vibrant scenes in music, theater, comedy, art, screen, and videogames. Late every year since 2015, Melbourne hosts Melbourne International Games Week (MIGW). Organized and subsidized by the Victorian government agency Creative Victoria, MIGW operates as an umbrella over a cluster of small and large, public and private, producer- and consumer-oriented events connected in one way or another to the cultural field of videogame production. At the start of the week is Games Connect Asia Pacific (GCAP), a producer-facing conference where gamemakers share practical insights, network, and present awards to their peers. In the middle of the week, the long-running Freeplay Independent Games Festival presents Parallels, a one-night showcase of alternative and experimental videogames made by Australian (and a handful of Asian Pacific and New Zealand) students, artists, hobbyists, and independent commercial creators. At the end of the week is the Australian Penny Arcade Expo (PAX Australia), the self-claimed largest consumer-facing pop culture expo in the Southern Hemisphere, where local gamemakers and international publishers present upcoming games to the public. PAX is the lynchpin of MIGW, drawing the national and international consumers, creators, publishers, and investors to Melbourne that the other events held during the week then take advantage of.

Later in the week, typically once PAX Australia is over and all the meetings with potential investors and publishers are wrapped up, various social events are held for the local, national, and international gamemakers in town. The biggest of these is the Megadev party, a massive, semipublic event with corporate sponsors and organized by the International Game Developers Association's Melbourne chapter (IGDAM). This party functions as a networking event for Australian commercial gamemakers, many of whom only get to see each other in person this one week in the year, and as an opportunity for a professional community to let off steam after not only a massively taxing week but also after months of frantic work ensuring demos are ready, talks are prepared, pitch decks are designed, and investor meetings are scheduled. A very different party I attended during 2018's MIGW was the "arty after party," which took place in an empty, graffiti-covered warehouse in the inner-east suburb of Richmond. This party was public and free but only advertised through personal social networks of those affiliated with local, in-the-know gamemaking fringe communities. LCD projectors sat precariously atop milk crate pillars to project bespoke art-games onto the walls of the gutted shop (see Figure 2.1). Cash was traded for beer on an old counter. Some attendees were employees, contractors, or founders of local game companies, but just as common were attendees who were primarily artists or hobbyist creators, or creators from other disciplines entirely.

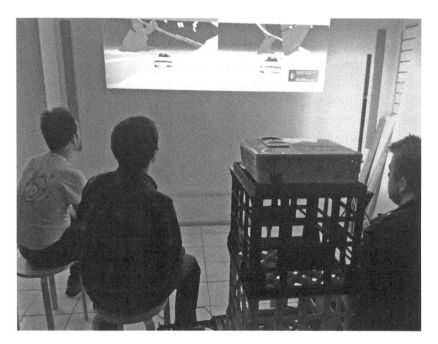

Figure 2.1
Partygoers of the 2018 arty after party play *Need 4e + 9 Speed* by Kalonica Quigley and Jason Bakker, projected onto the wall of a warehouse from a pillar of milk crates. Photo by author.

Others had simply heard about the party through a mate and had no professional interest in videogames at all; they were just attending a cool party. One of the party's organizers later told me that the 2018 arty after party was the first that continued to its scheduled end time, rather than being shut down early by the police for their lack of liquor license.

Large events such as MIGW or the annual Game Developers Conference (GDC) in San Francisco have traditionally been where researchers and observers can most clearly trace the full range of positions that constitute the videogame field. Within a few city blocks one can find suited investors, government representatives, hardware manufacturers, cosplaying fans, ambitious and entrepreneurial indie developers, esports teams, venture capitalists, celebrity triple-A auteur creative directors, PR firms, queer communities, livestreamers and influencers, and fringe arty types who otherwise have little to do with each other. Visible during MIGW is the truth of videogame production globally: videogames are made at a range of scales, in a variety of contexts, across different networks of people whose relationship with others in the field may be positive, antagonistic, or indirect.

Historically, this full range of positions in the field has been obscured by the dominance of the largest, most secretive companies and publishers. But in Australia, the complexity of the field exemplified during MIGW now remains traceable throughout the year as such secretive companies are almost entirely absent. At the time of writing, there are three, perhaps four, studios in all of Australia that employ more than 100 gamemakers. Instead, the vast majority of gamemakers across the country are working in smaller teams (on average in teams of nine but in the majority of cases in teams of five or fewer), sometimes in formal companies but just as often not. In most Australian cities, established development studios, entrepreneurial coworking spaces, artist collectives, student cohorts, bedroom coders, countercultural scenes, government funding bodies, pubs and bars, and slick consumer expos all interact within and as the local videogame field. Indeed, many of these are no longer discrete positions at all, as a gamemaker at a commercial studio may also work on a side-project with a local art collective, and a small team of friends may, as Melbourne four-person team House House did in 2019 with *Untitled Goose Game*, produce a cultural and commercial phenomenon. In Australia, without the veneer of stability provided by massive blockbuster studios, the intense in/formalization of videogame production is explicit and felt keenly by the everyday experiences of local gamemakers.

This chapter maps the transition that videogame production in Australia undertook through the 2000s and 2010s from an aggressively formalized network of commercial videogame firms largely detached from a fringe of new media artists and hobbyists, to a diverse and dispersed in/formalized field in which just who is or isn't a "professional game developer" is no longer clear. As a case study of a site of videogame production, Australia is both exceptional and exemplary. It is exceptional in its specific history, as will be detailed in this chapter, that saw established companies and their workforce crumble in a few short years following the global financial crisis (GFC). As studios closed, employment opportunities dried up, and a deep cynicism toward the commercial publishers that abandoned local gamemakers during the GFC took root; scenes and collectives and alternative ways of being a videogame maker emerged and restructured the field and its flows of both symbolic and economic capital. But despite these unique conditions, Australia's videogame field is also exemplary of contemporary videogame production globally in the way that, like most sites of videogame production, it is physically removed from the field's dominant sites (North America, western Europe, East Asia), yet still subservient to and dependent on the publishers, platforms, and investors located therein. Australian gamemakers have little hope of obtaining employment at a large studio. Instead, the majority of Australian gamemakers, just like gamemakers residing in most parts of the world, now rely on entrepreneurial start-up approaches in lieu of external support, with the hope that digital distribution will allow them to reach global markets. Ultimately, the historical dominance and more recent absence of larger studios make Australia a valuable case study through which to expose more clearly the frontiers of the videogame field more generally as it transitions from aggressively formalized to intensely in/formalized modes of production. From this chapter's history of Australia's field, the sorts of overlapping spaces and networks of videogame production that constitute the positions and dispositions of the videogame field globally will be made apparent.

First, the chapter provides a brief history of videogame production in Australia, with a particular focus on the seismic restructuring that occurred in the late 2000s as midsized work-for-hire companies shut their doors and their workforce dispersed, in part, into a wide range of small indie teams producing original intellectual property (IP). The second section turns to these indie firms as they are shaped by specific sociopolitical, economic, infrastructural, and geographic conditions to consider the changing nature of professional videogame creation in local contexts, where teams are much more likely to consist of fewer than five employees (by the broadest definition of "employee") than more than 100. What will become apparent here, and which underpins the next chapter's analysis of videogame production labor, is that these conditions have shaped the ways Australian gamemakers understand the structure of the local field, their own craft, their identities, and ultimately their position-taking in ways that significantly jar with how commercial videogame production is traditionally imagined. Next, the chapter sticks a spanner into this too-neat depiction of a videogame field of large firms fragmenting into a videogame field of small firms by considering the other forms of gamemaking that have been occurring at the margins of the Australian field since at least the mid-1990s, more aligned with new media art and cultural institutions than with commercial videogame companies. Looking particularly at cultural clashes around the Freeplay Independent Game Festival in 2013, this section shows how the Australian "videogame industry" has not simply rebuilt itself, but how the Australian videogame field has been reshaped—and intensely in/formalized—by global shifts in capital and power brought about by the struggles between dominantly and marginally positioned gamemakers.

The Other Game Industry Crash

Videogames have been made in Australia since at least 1980, with parallel histories of commercial, hobbyist, and artistic gamemaking having been well documented by local researchers through these times (see, for instance, Wilson 2005; Stuckey 2005; Swalwell 2007; Banks 2013; McCrea 2013a; Apperley and Golding 2015; Swalwell 2021). Narratives of this history begin, most commonly, with Melbourne House. Founded in 1977 by Naomi Bensen and Alfred Milgrom as a book publisher and distributor, they expanded into videogame production with the founding of Beam Software in 1980, releasing successful microcomputer games including *The Hobbit* (adapted from the novel) in 1982 and *Way of the Exploding Fist* (an early entry in the one-on-one fighting game genre) in 1985. Documented most exhaustively by the Play It Again[1] project run by Melanie Swalwell, Helen Stuckey, and Angela Ndalianis, and Swalwell's *Homebrew Gaming and the Beginnings of Vernacular Digitality* (2021), through the 1980s Australia was home to an eclectic range of independent game "companies" (sometimes simply the name under which an individual or a group of friends chose to release a game, more like a band than a company) such as Strategic Studies Group (SSG), HoneySoft, Micro Forté, and Armchair Entertainment. Through the 1980s, Australian teams were primarily producing games for microcomputers such as the Sega SC3000, the ZX Spectrum, the Commodore 64, and Amstrad CPC.

However, throughout the 1990s, the aggressive formalization of the videogame field took hold, and the necessary resources, team size, and funds required to undertake commercially feasible videogame production increased dramatically. To stay in the game through this period of drastically increasing costs and consolidated audiences, Australian videogame production through the 1990s and 2000s coalesced into larger and larger studios, typically either owned by or reliant on the investment from a small number of foreign, risk-averse publishers such as EA, Activision, Sega, and Ubisoft. While studios in some nations were able to build more collaborative relationships with North American, Japanese, and European firms in large part thanks to proximity, Australia's geographic and temporal displacement from North America and Europe, and its cultural displacement from Japan, hindered these relationships. Australia still produced several successful new intellectual properties during these decades with foreign publisher assistance, such as racing game *Powerslide*, created by Adelaide studio Ratbag Games in 1998 and published by GT Interactive, and real-time strategy game *Dark Reign*, created by Gold Coast studio Auran (later N3V) in 1997 and published by Activision. However, increasingly crucial to the survival of Australian videogame firms through the period of aggressive formalization was less the original creative ideas of Australian gamemakers and more the relative low price of Australian gamemaking labor for North American, European, and Japanese publishers, making Australian studios an attractive site for outsourcing.

Outsourcing has a long but rarely visible history in videogame production, with large multinational publishers such as EA, Ubisoft, and Rockstar regularly subcontracting lower-level aspects of videogame production—such as porting existing titles to new platforms, the more tedious programming work, or producing lower priority art assets (Dyer-Witherford and de Peuter 2009, 50; Chia 2022). Australia, geographically located in proximity to Southeast Asia while primarily culturally identifying with North America and Europe through its colonial history, for a time provided videogame publishers an ideal site of cheap, highly skilled, and English-speaking labor. Locally owned studios such as Krome (Brisbane, Adelaide, and Melbourne), Torus

Games (Melbourne), and Big Ant Studios (Melbourne) occasionally produced original IP, but primarily worked with a variety of existing videogame, film, or sport franchise licenses to fill the catalogues of foreign publishers. Other foreign-owned companies such as Pandemic (Brisbane), THQ Australia (Brisbane, Melbourne), Sega Studios Australia (Brisbane, formerly Creative Assembly Australia), and 2K Australia (Canberra, formerly Irrational Games Australia) contributed extensively to blockbuster games such as *Bioshock: Infinite* and *Borderlands: The Pre-Sequel*. Team Bondi (Sydney) meanwhile, produced detective title *LA Noire* for publisher Rockstar Games under an exclusivity deal with Sony. In many of these examples, Australian gamemakers were responsible for a wider range of high-level design decisions than we would typically associate with "outsourcing," and Australian gamemakers themselves more typically refer to this relationship as one of "work-for-hire." Nonetheless, the term remains apt as the work was conducted for and controlled by overseas companies that chose Australian companies to conduct the work, mainly, because of the affordability of Australian gamemaking labor.

The Australian videogame field through the 1990s and 2000s was driven disproportionately by the principle of heteronomous hierarchization, at the expense of the principle of autonomous hierarchization. Or, in plainer language, Australian gamemakers at the time were necessarily driven by the economic requirements of success in the broader field of class relations rather than by the symbolic requirements of success internal to the field such as crafting novel or experimental experiences. Consequentially, as the studios that populated the Australian field in the 1990s and 2000s were increasingly funded to work on preexisting franchises rather than to conceptualize new intellectual property, over time they became richer in technical skills and knowledge but poorer in design skills and knowledge. This is reinforced by John Banks's (2013, 40) sustained ethnography with Queensland studio Auran, which heavily invested in not just videogame production but in "[becoming] a technology provider" through its bespoke game engine software.

The more heteronomous a cultural field (that is, the less autonomous), the more tied to and dependent it becomes to external economic and political conditions. Thus, the GFC of 2008 had a particularly crippling impact on Australian videogame studios. While Australia was spared the worst of the GFC's economic fallout due to a mining boom sustaining a strong trade partnership with China, alongside extensive stimulus packages from the Labor federal government, Australia's economic resilience and America's economic collapse saw the usually disparate exchange rate between the two countries' currencies hit parity. In late 2010, for the first time since the Australian dollar was floated in 1983, it cost more than one American dollar to buy one Australian dollar, and this significantly impacted Australia's export-oriented manufacturing sectors, and likewise Australia's outsourcing-focused videogame studios. Abruptly, Australian game studios were no longer a cheap source of labor for American publishers—publishers that were themselves undergoing financial hardships during the GFC, as Nick Dyer-Witheford and Greig de Peuter (2009, xviii) have detailed. The business model of most Australian game studios rapidly became untenable.

As Christian McCrea (2013a, 204) summarizes, Australian studios' learned dependency on foreign publishers that viewed them as cheap and disposable outsourcing labor rather than vital creative partners sparked an "inexorable vicious cycle" that devastated the national field once the cost of this labor rose:

> The lack of Australian games publishers isolated the production system from the decision-making process, especially in the United States and United Kingdom. As other Western centers of production bolstered their industries with tax incentives, and others were able to undercut on labor costs, Australia became part of a crowded global game production system, beset by the tyranny of distance. With the increasing desperation of the work-for-hire system, the lack of original intellectual property meant that experienced developers—especially artists and designers—were moving overseas to further their careers, leaving local production bereft of talent or creative assets.

By 2011, "nearly all the companies that were focusing on work-for-hire console games were bought, shrunk, merged, or closed—often all four in that order" (McCrea 2013a, 204). The studio closures hit the Australian videogame field hard and fast. Pandemic shut in 2009; Krome in 2010; THQ Australia's Brisbane and Melbourne studios, EA's Visceral Games, and Team Bondi in 2011. Sega Studios Australia closed in 2013; 2K Australia held on until 2015. Between 2007 and 2012, according to the Australian Bureau of Statistics, the official number of Australians employed by digital game developers shrunk by 60 percent, from 1,431 to 581. As something of a punctuation mark on this dark period, in 2014 the newly elected Liberal-National Coalition government, led by conservative prime minister Tony Abbott, introduced a brutal austerity budget that included the dismantling of a fledgling federal funding scheme for Australian-owned videogame companies, immediately removing $10 million of previously earmarked funding that local studios were at the time finalizing their applications for (Hopewell 2014).

The impact of this crash on the collective psyche of contemporary Australian videogame makers cannot be overstated. Some Australian gamemakers I interviewed who had been around since the 2000s (now considered "veterans" of the community less than 20 years later) told stories of surviving consecutive redundancy rounds, continuing to work under conditions of extreme uncertainty, finally losing their job in the next round, being hired by another studio, and having the same process happen all over again several months later. The emotional trauma wrought on the workers at the time remains vivid when they speak of it more than a decade later. One anonymous Australian expat gamemaker who now works in a triple-A studio overseas explains what happened after their employer in Brisbane shut down:

> My first move was to Sydney because there wasn't much work in Brisbane. . . . But there was always this feeling of just like treading water. You're always on a four-month contract, maybe six months if you're lucky, and then nothing. That's quite a stressful way to live. . . . After [Sydney studio] shut down I got contacted by a recruiter for [European studio]. . . . We were pretty tired of the situation [in Australia] so we decided let's go work on real triple-A games at a reasonable steady country.

This same gamemaker remembers their time working in Australia bitterly as "one of backstabbing and hissing and jealousy" in stark contrast to their later work in North American and European studios, which were "nothing but experiences . . . of people trying to help me succeed and propping me up." Like this gamemaker, many Australian gamemakers left Australia in the late 2000s and early 2010s to seek employment overseas, where many still remain. Many others left videogame production for good, finding work in adjacent fields such as software development, engineering, VFX, web design, or retraining into entirely different fields.

The crash is fundamental to the ways in which contemporary Australian videogame makers talk about their careers, craft, and community. At the time of my interviews, the GFC provided the contemporary Australian videogame field a foundational myth and identity of having "done it tough" and "come through the war together." For instance, Leena van Deventer, a 33-year-old writer, educator, and community organizer in Melbourne, explained that "after the decimation of the industry that happened after the GFC . . . I think there's an attitude of collaboration and helping each other out that you only get out of adversity and everyone kind of panicking about survival." For trade association lobbyists, game journalists, students, and aspiring gamemakers, this foundational myth of economic crisis and government abandonment often sees the pre-GFC era of Australian videogame production framed as the time when Australia had a triple-A industry that no longer exists but, with the right tax incentives, could perhaps return. Here, the larger studios that collapsed during the GFC paradoxically symbolize a more prestigious, legitimate, and secure mode of videogame production than the smaller scale independent teams (detailed below) that are now the field's bread and butter. This story is told formally by the Australian videogame trade association, the Interactive Games and Entertainment Association (IGEA),[2] which has long advocated for tax breaks for its member companies, and regularly holds up Montreal, home to 10,000 gamemaking jobs, as an exemplar of what Australia could and should imitate (Walker 2018). In early 2021, the IGEA made the dubious but emotionally charged claim that "Every other developed nation in the world has government incentive packages in place for game developers. Everywhere except Australia" (Biggs 2021). It's unclear what is counted as a "developed nation" here, but the strategic point for the IGEA is to connect the collapse of Australia's large videogame companies with the lack of financial support provided by the federal government.[3]

I, too, understood the history of Australian videogame production as the collapse of triple-A before speaking to several disillusioned gamemakers who had lived and worked through the crash—such as the above anonymous gamemaker who left Australia to work on "real triple-A." In Melbourne, one of my first interviews was with Trent Kusters, the 31-year-old director and cofounder of independent studio League of Geeks. Before helping to found League of Geeks in 2011, Kusters worked as a designer at Torus Games, a larger studio specializing in work-for-hire production. When I casually referred to the collapse of Australia's triple-A studios, Kusters interrupted me to note:

> Australia never had triple-A development. Apart from 2K [Australia], maybe, and they were developing American triple-A games for Irrational in Boston. But we had that traditional publisher-studio model and I think . . . triple-A has kind of become a catch-all for before when everything was just the traditional studio-publisher model.

For those developers who were there at the time, the fact that Australia functioned under a studio-publisher model did not necessarily mean everyone was working on the most prestigious and legitimized triple-A titles. Instead, this revised version of history retroactively broadens the concept of triple-A in a way that exemplifies aggressive formalization's gutting of the middle ground of videogame production—if it wasn't triple-A, it's difficult to imagine what other form of legitimate videogame production it could possibly have been. In Australia specifically, the retroactive application of the triple-A label romanticizes what was largely thankless outsourcing or contract work. Gamemakers from this time derisively refer to the games they and their peers produced as either "shelf-fillers" or "shovelware" (labels that imply a title only has commercial value and no intrinsic creative value). Further, they express how foreign managers rarely acknowledged the gamemakers of Australian studios as themselves creative contributors to the games they produced. When Australian studios *were* working on high-budget triple-A titles such as *Bioshock Infinite*, gamemakers saw this primarily as unrecognized technical—as opposed to creative—labor. Indeed, very few people globally would consider *Bioshock Infinite* an Australian-made videogame, despite the significant amount of labor gamemakers at 2K Australia contributed to the game. Generally, commercial Australian gamemakers in the 1990s and 2000s were producing not prestigious, original titles but cookie-cutter genre games for specific franchise licenses. The work of these studios was not particularly high in cultural capital, and their economic capital was on loan from offshore publishers who themselves would leave once it became too expensive to stay.

Thus, the foundational narrative of the GFC destroying Australian videogame companies only tells part of the story, and by itself obfuscates the shape and nature of videogame production that was occurring in Australia at the time. Issues among Australian studios prior to the GFC—poor working conditions, fraternal and secretive cultures, excessive crunch, and managerial incompetence and corruption—have been well documented by local journalists and researchers. As McCrea (2013a, 204–205) summarizes the pre-GFC period of Australian videogame production:

> some companies were overcommitting to projects of little potential value, had entirely rotten work cultures, or were run in semicorrupt conditions. Interzone, a medium-sized games company in Perth, was withholding pay and benefits from staff for 18 months when it suddenly closed doors one morning, locking out staff. Melbourne-based Transmission Games was suddenly closed with some staff reorganized under Trickstar Games, leaving some employee entitlements

unpaid. Working conditions across the game industry internationally are notorious, but Australia's precarious position left it more open to the consequences of poor management.

To this list we could add the extensive issues that plagued Team Bondi during *LA Noire*'s production, including hundreds of contributors to the game going uncredited—a major hinderance to finding future employment (McMillen 2011); the extended development hell of 2K Australia's *The Bureau: X-Com Declassified* (Plante 2013); the collapse of Australian distributor Red Ant alongside questionable loans from the company to its own managing director (Lien 2010); or the surreal mismanagement that led to the planning, production, and eventual cancellation of an *Avengers* game at THQ Australia that would have coincided with Marvel's 2012 eponymous film (Serrels 2020). My interviewees recollected consistent tales of extensive crunch, unpaid overtime, sexual harassment, bullying, and mismanagement across Australian studios in this time.

The narrative, still popular with younger Australian gamemakers and players, that the GFC destroyed the Australian videogame industry actively frustrated veteran developers, who saw it as allowing incompetent managers off the hook for poor business decisions. In Seattle, I interviewed Dan Teasdale, 38, who left Australia in 2005 after working at a number of larger studios. As Teasdale saw it, "The GFC was just an excuse to buck everything off . . . in terms of like studio leadership and emphasis. . . . There was no management sense at the top of how to maintain a studio through that time." Jon Cartwright, 47, in Brisbane, also spoke of jumping rather than waiting to be pushed at the large company he worked for due to concerns around mismanagement:

> I left a bit before the studio shut down. The writing was on the wall. [Management] were wanting to spend more money on the projects than I knew we could make back. . . . The amount of money they paid for the license for [animated film franchise] was just insane. And then when we were doing [blockbuster film franchise], we were like "How much did [management] pay for this?" None of it added up from a profit point of view. It was not going to go well.

For Morgan Jaffit, 41, also in Brisbane, the state of Australian videogame production before the GFC was a squandered "golden age" that could have been better used to grow a resilient, self-sustaining local field instead of the learned dependency on easy foreign contracts that ultimately fell apart when the economic situation changed:

> I think we squandered it. We were Western, English-speaking, technologically literate. Australia's uptake of the Internet and programming were very, very high

compared to the rest of the world, and we had a cheap dollar. If you were going to outsource, Australia actually was great through the late '90s up to the GFC mark. And then we blew it.

It's undeniable that the GFC was a formative, destructive event for the Australian videogame field and that its effects were amplified by the subsequent stripping back of government support. But it's important that this narrative doesn't erase the shortsighted managerial decisions that prioritized profit over worker well-being or long-term sustainability that ultimately ensured the GFC was such a formative, destructive event for Australian videogame makers in the first place.

Economic factors, management factors, skills factors, government factors, geographic factors all converged to prove, abruptly and traumatically, that the pre-GFC model of Australian videogame companies providing cheap labor for foreign publishers through the studio-publisher model was not sustainable. It was Australian videogame workers who suffered the brunt of this as jobs were lost, wages and entitlements went unpaid, contributions to games went uncredited, senior talent moved either overseas or to other sectors, and skills and institutional memory were lost. Australian commercial gamemakers suffered financially, mentally, and physically at the hands of Australian and foreign management alike. Even as some Australian gamemakers today lament the absence of triple-A from Australian shores—and its perceived prestige and employment opportunities—many others hold a deep-seated cynicism and skepticism of the studio-publisher model and its reliance on foreign companies and relationships that they feel were responsible for the destruction of the local field in the late 2000s.

Forced Autonomy

As Australian videogame companies were decimated at the start of the 2010s, over a thousand newly unemployed Australian videogame makers—along with an indeterminate number of now unemployable graduates from the nation's many game development tertiary programs—were faced with one of three options: leave Australia to find gamemaking work overseas, leave commercial gamemaking entirely, or find alternative means of commodifying their gamemaking skills other than employment within the studio-publisher model. As we saw in the previous chapter, they were not alone in this predicament as, at the same time, the organization of the videogame field globally was undergoing major, deeply interconnected changes.

The parallel platformization of both videogame distribution and development shattered the distribution bottlenecks that the dominant firms used to perpetuate their dominance in the period of aggressive formalization. Valve's Steam and Apple's App Store and, later, Microsoft, Sony, Google, and Nintendo's own digital storefronts shifted the console business model of editorial regulation and forced scarcity to a platform business model of maximum royalty capture. Whereas the Nintendo Seal of Approval was all about building consumer trust that a game released on a Nintendo console had been through particular editorial oversight and thus deserved its premium purchase price (O'Donnell 2014, 198), digital platforms instead promised audiences maximum access to a maximum quantity of content. ("There's an app for that," as Apple's marketing promised.) Platform owners take a cut from every purchase of a product while under no obligation to invest in the product's development or marketing costs or the employment of its producers (Nieborg, Young, and Joseph 2020; Srnicek 2017; Whitson 2019). The subsequent normalization of high-powered 3D game engines available at no upfront cost through Unity and Unreal would further open up videogame production to the broader field. A broader range of gamemakers no longer had to rely on personal programming skills, amateur tools, or modding preexisting corporate games. Instead, they now had access to comparably sophisticated development tools as the larger firms and distributed their products on the same platforms (Nicoll and Keogh 2019).

In public discourses, these shifts are discussed most directly as the rise of "indie" videogame development, beginning in the mid-2000s, as an entrepreneurial and romanticized alternative to working in the larger, risk-adverse videogame firms. Early publicized successes such as *World of Goo*, *Braid*, and *Cave Adventure* inspired videogame makers to go it alone. At the same time, toward the end of the 2000s, the "casual revolution" (Juul 2010) started on social media platforms and Nintendo's Wii console but came into its own with the ubiquity of high-powered, Internet-connected smartphone devices. If independent developers were already primed to make smaller videogames for digital distribution, targeting demographics typically ignored by the triple-A publishers, then the burgeoning casual market, looking for cheap, small games for their smartphones, fitted these developers perfectly. This is the essence of the field's shift from aggressive formalization to intense in/formalization: a blurring of formal and informal means of production and distribution, an opportunity for a wider range of producers to make claims to a legitimate presence within the field.

While many unemployed Australian gamemakers and unemployable graduates left the field entirely or sought employment overseas, many others thus "went indie," forming independent small businesses producing smaller games, with fewer resources, for digital distribution on social media platforms or smartphone devices (and then, in later years, console and PC). In the same 2007 to 2012 period in which the Australian videogame workforce shrunk by 60 percent, from 1,431 to 581, the number of registered videogame *businesses* nearly doubled, from 45 to 84. Put another way, in 2007 Australia was home to 45 videogame companies that employed, on average, 32 workers; in 2012 Australia was home to 84 videogame companies that employed, on average, 7 workers. This signifies the Australian videogame field's almost exhaustive transition to indie modes of production.

A number of these studios were highly successful in their readjustment to the new realities of Australian videogame production. Halfbrick, in Brisbane, had been producing licensed titles for foreign publishers since 2001, but then in 2010 saw huge commercial success on the iPhone with their own game *Fruit Ninja*, and again in 2011 with *Jetpack Joyride*. Firemint, in Melbourne, had been producing games independently since 1999, and had been one of the few Australian studios focused on producing mobile games for Nokia mobile phones before the advent of smartphones. Their early iPhone success with *Flight Control* saw them bought by EA and merged with fellow Melbourne studio Iron Monkeys to form EA Firemonkeys, which is now one of Australia's largest studios at approximately 150 employees. Back in Brisbane, Defiant Development, formed by Brisbane industry veterans from Krome and Pandemic in 2010, had a breakout hit in 2012 when they published *Ski Safari* for iPhone, originally a hobbyist project of one of their contractors, allowing the studio to grow dramatically and bankroll the much larger *Hand of Fate* project for PC and consoles (Serrels 2012). Today, with both PC and console platforms embracing digital distribution and relying on indie gamemakers to fill out their digital catalogues, a large number of small teams have moved beyond the now-crowded and devalued casual mobile space to produce larger-scale, narrative- or systems-driven titles for console and PC with titles such as *Necrobarista* (Route 59), *Assault Android Cactus* (Witch Beam), *Hollow Knight* (Team Cherry), *Golf Story* (Sidebar), *Hand of Fate*, *Satellite Reign* (5 Lives), *Webbed* (Sbug), *Unpacking* (Witch Beam), and *Untitled Goose Game* (House House).

While the number of gamemakers formally employed in Australia is still smaller than it was before the GFC, it is steadily growing; IGEA surveys estimated 1,300 full-time equivalent positions in 2021. Studios remain small, at an average of nine people per company, with this number still blown out by a small handful of 50 to 150 person studios, such as EA's Firemonkeys in Melbourne, Wargaming in Sydney (born after Belarusian company Wargaming Group acquired Australian middleware firm Big World Technology in 2012, itself having grown out of early Australian studio Micro Forté), and Mighty Kingdom in Adelaide (founded in 2010 by former employees of Midway Australia and Krome Adelaide). While data on the median Australian studio size is unavailable, I would suspect it to be much closer to five. Most Australian studios now primarily work on original intellectual property, as opposed to outsourced work-for-hire, but as chapter 5 details, some find more economic stability in contract work for the professional sector, producing serious games, advergames, or training simulations. Meanwhile, the attendance numbers of national industry events such as GCAP (over 1,000 in 2019), and the registered number of people in the various local game development Facebook groups (6,200 members of the IGDA Melbourne group alone), point to a much greater and unmeasured local field of gamemaking activity beyond that captured by formal employment statistics.

John Banks and Stuart Cunningham (2016, 130) detail this national transition to indie development as one of "creative destruction" that indicates "a major restructuring of the core of Australia's videogames development industry." As Thomas Apperley and Dan Golding (2015, 61) observe in their own overview of the Australian videogame field, the entrepreneurial startups and small companies that "would have once been labeled 'indie' or at least as outside the mainstream for the Australian industry . . . now form the backbone of Australian game development." The politics of indie game development and how it fits within broader shifts in the cultural industries will be unpacked in the following chapter. For this current chapter's consideration of the structure of the Australian videogame field, it suffices to say that in the same period that many Australian gamemakers and graduates found themselves confronted by a videogame field providing no employment opportunities, they also found available for the first time feasible alternative ways of making and distributing commercial videogames beyond the traditional employment contract with a larger studio dependent on the resources of a foreign publisher or console manufacturer. Here, going indie is less a romantic, countercultural alternative to "working for the man" and more the only viable option remaining after "the man" has packed up and left. Australian videogame makers were thrust into a disposition through which the only available positions in the field required them to prioritize and reevaluate the field's autonomous principles of hierarchization as the heteronomous principles became increasingly unobtainable with the withdrawal of foreign investment and contracts.

In Australia, and indeed in much of the world, "indie" does not define a single mode of videogame production so much as it defines a range of videogame production contexts that are *not* American and *not* triple-A. As will be investigated in much more detail in the following chapter, this reshaped field is defined by small teams, high personal risk, small budgets, intense volatility, heightened self-exploitation, greater creative freedom, strengthened interteam community and solidarity, and boom-or-bust economics. Echoing a broader rhetoric of entrepreneurism that has become "a commonsense way of navigating the inevitable, irreproachable, and apparently unchangeable reality of global capitalism" (Szeman 2015, 473), Australian gamemakers I interviewed regularly offered the satisfaction of being their own bosses as a positive spin on the country's mass studio closures and the loss of steady employment opportunities—especially in the context of the poor and often impersonal management of those studios. As Bourdieu says of how one's dispositions inform one's position-taking within cultural fields more generally, Australian indie developers made a virtue out of necessity.

We must thus be careful not to frame the transition of Australian videogame production to indie as too simply a redemptive narrative of the creative and entrepreneurial phoenix rising from the corporate ashes. Of the above examples of early Australian indie success stories in Australia, Halfbrick has undergone a series of restructures after failing to replicate their successes of the early 2010s, EA Firemonkeys fired approximately 50 staff in early 2019, and Defiant Development ceased development and effectively let go all of its staff in mid-2019. According to an IGEA survey, in 2019 55 percent of Australian studios were less than five years old, and 23 percent of Australian studios were still working on their first title (International Games and Entertainment Association 2019). On the one hand, this potentially suggests the field is growing rapidly; on the other hand, the fact that the number of new studios does not align with a significant increase in the number of workers in the sector suggests that few independent ventures in the field successfully gain financial sustainability. The transition to indie has not reduced the volatility of making a career of videogame production—if anything, as the following chapter will show, it has only intensified the precarity felt by Australian gamemakers.

Further, while the entrepreneurial nature of indie development might seem to break down systemic barriers of entry into the videogame field, the high risk, necessary personal investment, unclear career trajectories, and persistent misogynistic cultures perpetuate entrenched inequalities. Gender diversity remains poor, with approximately 20 percent of the nation's gamemakers identifying as other than male in both industry surveys and my own survey; however, this is nonetheless a significant improvement from 2012, when this number was only 8.7 percent (Serrels 2013). The field remains even more homogenous when it comes to race, with over 90 percent of respondents to a GDAA survey in 2017 identifying as Caucasian—a shocking statistic given both Australia's geographic position near Southeast Asia and 2016 national census data showing that a quarter of Australia's population have Indigenous or non-European backgrounds . Age, too, is a major area of concern. Of the respondents to my own survey, 61 percent were under 30 years old, and only 11 percent were over 40. This replicates well-trodden patterns across the cultural industries that suggest the precarity and unpredictability of independent cultural work can only be tolerated for so long before workers leave for more reliable and less risky work elsewhere.

So far, this chapter has outlined the historic shifts in formal Australian videogame production from primarily large companies dependent on foreign publishers to smaller companies focused on producing original IP for digital platforms. However, this narrative is currently too straightforward and economically deterministic. Long before Australian gamemakers were forced to go indie in lieu of any other employment options, a rich parallel history of independent videogame production existed in Australia, and the following section turns to this.

How to Destroy Everything

In 1992, VNS Matrix, a feminist artist collective based out of Adelaide, launched *All New Gen*, a new media artwork using the language and aesthetic of videogames to "disrupt the machismo world of video games with a female non binary centric computer game" where "an omnipresent supershero collaborates with her band of DNA Sluts to bring down Big Daddy Mainframe" (VNS Matrix 1992). This project formed part of VNS Matrix's broader cyberfeminist efforts to "hijack the toys from technocowboys and remap cyberculture with a feminist bent." Very few contemporary Australian gamemakers have any knowledge of VNS Matrix or *All New Gen*—the majority of them were not even born in 1992. I am only aware of VNS Matrix due to a passing reference in Dyer-Witheford and de Peuter's *Games of Empire* (2009, 18).

Peripheral and parallel to the dominant historical narrative of Australian game companies growing through the 1990s, being obliterated in the late 2000s, and restructuring through the 2010s, other modes of videogame production were happening across the Australian field. While the aggressive formalization of the 1990s and 2000s did indeed make it harder for small independent teams to release and distribute videogames without the support of a large publisher and the blessing of console manufacturers, this does not mean that large-scale videogame production is the only kind that happened during this time. A rich underbelly of homebrew and artist-gamemaking scenes persisted in Australia through the 1990s and early 2000s. Much of this history remains, sadly, unrecorded or unacknowledged (see Wilson 2005 for one exception).[4] These alternative modes of videogame production relied on close collaborations and connection with (and ambiguous borders between) informal gamemakers and the field of new media art. While Australia's videogame companies in this time largely focused on shelf-filler commercial titles most able to sustain an ongoing company, cultural institutions, particularly in Melbourne, such as the Australian Centre of the Moving Image (ACMI), Film Victoria, and the Freeplay Independent Games Festival helped to instill early and radically political approaches to crafting and comprehending videogames as culture.

Under Helen Stuckey's role as games curator, ACMI became home to the Games Lab from 2003 to 2008, providing an early institutional home to artistic videogame production, including the development of the "virtual public space" of AcmiPark, created by artist collective SelectParks (Stuckey 2005). Elsewhere, artist and SelectParks member Julian Oliver and game developer Katharine Neil (working anonymously at the time) produced the acclaimed and notorious *Escape from Woomera* with funding from the Australia Council for the Arts, now widely viewed as one of the first political or "serious" games. The *Escape from Woomera* team worked with refugees detained in the Woomera detention center to provide a virtualized firsthand account of Australia's refugee imprisonment regime after journalists were banned from entering the center (Swalwell 2007; Golding 2013). A deeper investigation of these pre-GFC movements are, sadly, beyond the scope of this book. Nonetheless, the fact that independent videogame production at artistic, hobbyist, personal, and otherwise noncommercial scales persisted in Australia peripheral to the rise and fall of formal outsourcing-dependent companies—and also peripheral to indie videogame development—reminds us that the videogame field's period of aggressive formalization was not a period in which *only* commercial videogames existed but a period in which other positions struggled for legitimacy at the field's border.

Independent videogame production existed long before the increased visibility and necessity of indie development—both in Australia and elsewhere. Indie developers, in taking alternative commercial positions within the field, built upon established cultures, skills, aesthetics, and movements of independent videogame production that persisted in the shadows of the aggressively formalized field. At the same time that the label of indie games "valorize[s] only certain kinds of precarious labor practices—the ones that paid off" (Boluk and LeMieux 2017, 33), it also relies on and obscures all the other forms of independent videogame production in the field that are unable to speak directly to the most dominant commercial positions. Thus, as indie development became more common, and as the autonomous principles of hierarchization became more valued in the Australian videogame field (with original IP becoming prioritized over work-for-hire contracts), the once peripheral informal and artistic gamemakers suddenly found their practices and positions newly legitimized by and in conversation with a field that instilled them with new amounts of cultural (if not economic) capital.

The tensions between Australia's long history of independent videogame production and the formal field's transition to indie modes of production are most vivid in the long-running Freeplay Independent Games Festival, an explicitly political and fringe countercultural festival for independent videogame producers. Freeplay was founded by Katharine Neil and Marcus Westbury in 2004 as a satellite event of the Next Wave arts festival. Instead of a typical games conference with talks about monetization strategies and opportunities to network with publishers and investors, Freeplay was a coming together of interdisciplinary creators to discuss craft and politics around videogame production. In its first year, held at the World Wing Chun Kung Fu Association's dojo on Flinders Street in central Melbourne, the festival banner included the dramatically crossed-out words "Innovation in the Field of Excellence," which Neil notes was "a dig at the bullshit corporate themes

Figure 2.2
Festival banner for the inaugural Freeplay Independent Games Festival (2004). Photo by Katharine Neil (used with permission).

that the Australian Game Developers' Conference used to go with" (Neil 2020). As Mark Gibson (2018, 6) notes in his own detailed account of Freeplay as part of Australia's contemporary fringe culture, "[Freeplay's] founding aspiration was to stake out a different kind of space, a space in which conversations could be developed not about games as a business, but about their aesthetic, political, and social dimensions—their status as cultural forms" (see also Hardwick 2023).

Freeplay persists to this day as a beacon for countercultural videogame producers in Australia, and I have personally been attending its events since 2010. It provides a particularly visible site in which to articulate the struggles of differently positioned gamemakers at the field's frontiers. Here, I want to focus on a presentation given at the 2013 festival by two gamemakers, Marigold Bartlett and Sam Crisp (using the pseudonym Stephen Swift for the talk), who at the time were game design students at a local university. Bartlett and Crisp's talk "How To Destroy Everything, Or, Why Video Games Do Not Exist (And How This Is Great For Everyone)" connected the Australian context with major shifts taking place in the early 2010s within independent game discourses in North America, centered on figures such as Anna Anthropy, Liz Ryerson, Porpentine, merrit kopas, and Mattie

Brice. As part of the process of intense in/formalization outlined in the previous chapter, these marginal game creators had begun to draw attention to the ways in which popular constructions of indie games, far from being countercultural or politically radical, centered on the same limited and hegemonic understandings and values of videogame production as did triple-A. Through a number of manifesto-like publications and explicitly queer and subversive games, such gamemakers worked toward a reclaiming of the countercultural nature of independent videogame production that indie was swiftly gentrifying (Anthropy 2012; kopas 2013). In a lecture theater at the State Library of Victoria, to an audience of Australian indie videogame makers, Bartlett and Crisp brought these debates home to the Australian field with a far-reaching, globally connected, incendiary inditement on the contemporary culture of indie gamemaking. To illustrate, it is worth quoting several segments of Bartlett and Crisp's talk at length:

> What is considered "good aesthetics" in indie game circles carries discriminatory undertones of class, race, and gender. When indie culture is Western-centric, when major events take place in only certain cities, when festival award ceremonies or online marketplaces require arbitrary entrance fees of up to $100:[5] All these barriers inform what we perceive as a body of work. It paints an image of video games in our mind that is dictated by the privileged. And this happens, most of the time, without us realizing it. . . .
>
> As young, impressionable game students, we're sold these narratives of success stories in the indie games scene. *Indie Game: The Movie* encourages us to lock ourselves into a room for months and months on our own and express ourselves through the language of the games we played in our childhood. Or there's the idea that maybe one day we, too, can run a successful Kickstarter or get our games on [Steam] Greenlight. . . . But what we see as the state of games today didn't arrive simply from a series of successes, even though those are the stories we are most exposed to.
>
> By celebrating failure, we can shift our perception, and instead of looking at games which don't sell or don't get critical acclaim as games which must be doing something wrong, we can realize that these games are the only ones which can truly offer us emancipation. From a certain perspective, they're the only games doing something right. Voices that are queer, feminist, or trans, who are implicitly seen as failures by society's notion of success, are on the forefront of transgressive game design and criticism. . . .
>
> "Games are art" means listening to voices of dissent. It means engaging in these discussions about what our culture and our games say. That collection of words, as a predicate, is not a belief. It is a practice. It's something you do, not

something you say. Seemingly innocuous opinions on what constitutes a video game, or how polished a game should be, or what aesthetic fits in to your taste: All these things are politically charged, whether you think they are or not. They're all informed by a culture where certain parties control the means of production, who control the conversation. (Bartlett and Crisp 2013)

Many in the audience, including myself, found the talk to be an energizing, invigorating call to arms for a new generation of Australian gamemakers to take new positions and redefine the field and its possible values and modes of expression. Others, especially those newly indie gamemakers of the nation's many burgeoning start-ups, found it alienating and patronizing—heretical, Bourdieu might say. Here were two young undergraduate students—Bourdieu's classic "newcomers to the field"—lecturing a room of professional videogame developers, proud of their resilient pivot to indie following industrial collapse, about political discourses in videogame creation. In one of my interviews, an older gamemaker employed at a larger Melbourne studio noted to me that it was political talks such as Bartlett and Crisp's that saw them stop attending Freeplay. The festival's countercultural politics felt disconnected to their own interest and identity as an indie gamemaker trying to make a living in the field.

Yet, at the same time, it is the artistic and countercultural peripheries of videogame production that Bartlett and Crisp's talk alludes to that assisted the transition of the formal sector through its period of "creative destruction" (Banks and Cunningham 2016). While entrepreneurial videogame businesses took advantage of new digital platforms and broader consumer markets to go indie, they also relied on the cultural capital of institutions such as Freeplay, ACMI, and Film Victoria, and the creative and artistic skills of the new media arts movements that found their way into local gamemaking communities and classrooms. Bartlett and Crisp's talk specifically, and the Freeplay festival in the early 2010s more generally, signifies a moment when a field exclusively populated by gamemakers that identified as independent or indie had to come to terms with the fact that those terms did not mean the same thing to all of them, and that there were conflicting markers of legitimacy circulating the now intensely in/formal, and increasingly autonomous, field of videogame production in Australia. What this situation most explicitly exposed in the restructured Australian videogame field is the perpetual "struggle between the established figures and the [socially] young challengers" (Bourdieu 1993, 60) that is core to any field of cultural production but which has long been difficult to trace in videogame fields due to the exhaustive dominance of the established figures.

This is the current shape of the Australian videogame field: a nebulous range of creators and companies with varying values and goals, many of whom self-identify as indie or independent, very few of whom are working with the resources or scale traditionally considered to be available to video-game companies, even fewer of whom are making a living wage from their gamemaking work. For those readers more familiar with cultural industries literature, none of this should seem particularly exceptional. However, as videogame production has historically been understood first and foremost as occurring within a formalized videogame industry—as an economic and technologic field and not an autonomous cultural field—this field's dif-fuse agents and their diverse activities remain difficult to account for. Thus, the creative destruction that Banks and Cunningham recognized among Australian videogame firms following the GFC, inflected by the calls from the countercultural fringes of the local field to "destroy everything" and "dethrone the technocowboys," doesn't point to a new monolithic position emerging out of the ashes of the old. Rather, through the disappearance of those companies and actors that enforced the field's aggressive formalization, alongside the emergence of new avenues and identities and business models that encouraged the field's intense in/formalization, the Australian video-game field was drastically reshaped so that a much wider range of videogame-creating positions became legible, legitimate, and able to contest just which autonomous and heteronomous markers of success the field would abide.

Conclusion

The dramatic restructuring of the Australian videogame field exemplifies how intense in/formalization blurred any clear distinction between profes-sional videogame developers and amateur hobbyist, but similar transitions were occurring across the field globally. In the Nordic countries, a range of grassroots hobbyist activities and government funding programs have given rise to a range of homegrown videogame production cultures primar-ily constituted by small teams surrounding a few larger companies such as Supercell and Rovio (Jørgensen, Sandqvist, and Sotamaa 2017; Sotamaa, Jørgensen, and Sandqvist 2019). In the Netherlands, a small number of triple-A studios exist, including Guerilla and Nixxes, alongside the entrepreneurial coworking space of the Dutch Game Garden and vibrant independent communities such as the Sokpop Game Collective working out of Utrecht. In Southeast Asia, countries including the Philippines, Indonesia, Hong Kong, and Malaysia are each in different ways working to transition videogame fields, not unlike Australia's, from a focus on outsourcing for Northern Hemisphere companies to entrepreneurial start-ups focused on original IP for digital distribution (Chung 2016; Fung 2018). In Iran, teams of gamemakers work in semiformal environments—sometimes privately, sometimes with government support—to produce a range of videogames that counter dominant Western narratives about the region, but struggle to access professional-standard US-owned software such as Unity or Unreal (Šisler 2013; Daiiani and Keogh 2022). Even in North America, home to some of the largest studios and most powerful publishers in the videogame field globally, informal scenes and collectives abound, such as the Twine scene, which emerged in 2012, primarily driven by trans women gamemakers working out of Oakland (Harvey 2014), or the vibrant independent scenes of numerous Canadian cities such as Toronto and Montreal (Joseph 2013; Young 2018; Parker and Jenson 2017; Rocca 2013).

What the highly particular tale of construction, destruction, and fragmented reconstruction of the Australian videogame field allows us to see more broadly is the wider range of videogame-making positions struggling, with increased success, to have their position-taking recognized as legitimately within and as the field of videogame production. As employment opportunities disappeared and were replaced with the tools, cultures, and rhetoric of entrepreneurial and independent development, Australia transitioned across and after the GFC from a homogenous videogame field of commercially focused companies and excluded artists to a diffuse and contested field of differently positioned gamemakers struggling to define the field through different markers of success, quality, and legitimacy. The particulars are unique to Australia, but they nonetheless give us insights into what the videogame field now looks like globally. While each local and national videogame field of course has its own political, economic, social, and cultural conditions, the vast majority do not have a major presence of large triple-A studios and publishers. We can go so far as to say that large-scale triple-A development is something of an anomaly in videogame production, both currently and historically. It's time we account for everything else.

By outlining Australia's rocky journey from an aggressively formalized cluster of videogame companies to a contested and dynamic, intensely in/formalized videogame field, this chapter has also highlighted the need for a similar conceptual shift in how we understand the sites, identities, and ambitions of videogame makers. The shift to intense in/formalization through digital platforms and the obliteration of job opportunities, especially in a context such as Australia with a large existent skill base, exposes the struggles that continuously define and redefine the field of videogame production. They demonstrate a clear need to expand how we consider the videogame field, who we consider to be a part of it, which works and markers of success we consider to drive it and, consequentially, what this means for our attempts to understand the experiences of videogame makers in terms of labor, education, creativity, community, and value generation. The remaining chapters of this book look to each of these issues in turn.

3 Getting by in the Videogame Gig Economy

In 2018, I spent several days interviewing employees at Brisbane studio Defiant Development. Defiant was one of Australia's post-GFC success stories. A start-up founded by former employees of defunct local studios Pandemic and Krome, following the success of *Ski Safari* in 2012 they were able to grow into one of Australia's largest independent studios, approximately 25 people, producing complex and highly polished 3D titles for PC and console, including *Hand of Fate* in 2015 and its sequel in 2017. A senior designer I spoke to was grateful that following the upheaval of the GFC described in the previous chapter he had landed at a (relatively) larger studio like Defiant as his personal interest was in 3D game design, and most of the smaller studios in Brisbane were focused on 2D genres for mobile platforms. When asked about his plans for the future, the senior designer was conscious that there were no other studio in Brisbane of comparable size or output to Defiant: "I couldn't tell you another studio I would want to be working at. That's not a good thing for [job] security." For this senior designer, this led to a much more ubiquitous sense of anxiety than before the GFC. Then, if you lost your job there was always one or two other studios of comparable size in town that might take you on. But today, most other teams in Brisbane are small groups of two to five friends, neither looking for nor able to afford more staff: "The *Assault Android Cactus* team [Witch Beam] can't hire anyone. The *Yonda* team [Prideful Sloth] can't hire anyone. Literally you are standing on your own two feet and if it goes belly up, I don't know what you can do." Eighteen months after our interview, and to the shock of the Australian gamemaking community, Defiant Development abruptly announced it would be letting go all of its development team and going into hibernation after failing to obtain external funding for a new project (Prescott 2019).

No question that I posed to gamemakers caused as much reflection, insight, or existential angst as "Where do you see yourself in five years?" This is unsurprising considering that in the 2019 International Game Developers Association (IGDA) Developer Satisfaction Survey, nearly two-thirds of respondents had worked in videogame development for less than ten years, and half of respondents for less than six (Weststar and Kumar 2020). No wonder gamemakers don't know where they see themselves in five years when there's a 50–50 chance they won't even be making games anymore by then. What Ergin Bulut (2020, 166) calls a "governmental logic of precarization" haunts videogame production of all scales. Many videogame makers struggle to imagine or predict a future making videogames beyond their immediate circumstances. For those working in small teams or on subsequent short-term contracts or balancing personal projects alongside day jobs, the future is entirely contingent on the eventual unpredictable reception of the project they're currently working on. Larger companies, at first glance, offer more security with clear promotion pathways such as junior designer, designer, senior designer, creative director on which to plan a career trajectory, but even gamemakers employed at such companies, such as the senior designer above, are conscious that no amount of critical or commercial success is sufficient to assuage the feeling that any studio could fold, or any developer could be made redundant, at any time.

As a passion- and lifestyle-driven vocation dependent on individualized skills and convictions, and taken up primarily and historically by young, middle-class men in the Global North, previous research has suggested that workers in formal videogame companies typically consider "game production as a neutral, meritocracy-based creative profession rather than concrete work defined by politics" (Bulut 2020, 167; see also O'Donnell 2014; de Peuter and Dyer-Witheford 2005). The insecurity and volatility become normalized as part of the adventure. Academic, journalistic, and gamemaker discourses have long documented the structurally poor working conditions that have scaffolded videogame production for decades, such as crunch, burnout, discrimination, unpaid overtime, individualization, uncredited labor, harassment and bullying, the possibility of being laid off even after releasing a successful title, and pervasive regimes of surveillances (Dyer-Witheford and de Peuter 2009; O'Donnell 2014; Peticca-Harris, Weststar, and McKenna 2015; Legault and Weststar 2017; Bulut 2020; Cote and Harris 2020). Foundational myths of creativity, entrepreneurism, and libertarianism have long worked to normalize and naturalize videogame production's poor working conditions while, at the same time, make traditional collective responses to such conditions by workers seem unfeasible.

The volatility of pursuing a career in videogame production is felt acutely by those working at smaller, independent scales. As the previous chapters have already shown, most videogames are today produced by small independent teams or individuals in more autonomous yet even more precarious situations than their large studio counterparts. In many such cases, gamemakers aren't employees in the traditional sense at all. Despite popular claims of "going indie" as an escape from the worst corporate excesses of the studio-publisher model (Lipkin 2013), this broader, dispersed field of independent gamework is just as, if not more, susceptible to the range of issues plaguing the large studios (Whitson 2019). Yet it should hardly be a radical or shocking observation that the overwhelming majority of videogame production labor occurs locally, precariously, anonymously, at a small scale, and for a financial loss at least as often as for a profit; this reflects the very common and well-documented experiences of most cultural workers in most cultural fields. If I were to note that most musicians or painters or actors do not make enough money to live from their creative work, no reader would blink twice. Yet, in the cultural field of videogame production, the decades of aggressive formalization mean that the largest corporations and most successful (and lucky) indie millionaires cast long shadows that obscure the broader field of cultural activity where economic capital circulates in much smaller and unreliable quantities. The notion of "successfully" making videogames without it being your full-time job is a difficult thing to imagine.

In a 2017 blog post titled "lol we're all poor," independent gamemaker Robert Yang responded to the particular anxieties of independent videogame makers finding themselves increasingly unable to compete in crowded digital marketplaces—a phenomenon a number of indie developers and commentators labeled an "indiepocalypse." Whereas the videogame field, through the legacy of aggressive formalization, still holds economic success as the ultimately goal of videogame production, Yang argues that "most of us will always fall short of [astronomical blockbuster commercial success] in ways that often feel out of our control." Yang proposed a somewhat more radical approach to making videogame production less volatile and more sustainable, asking, "Why is it so important for us to make our living from selling our games? Why can't we make our living from doing something else?"

Here, Yang is proposing that perhaps the videogame field's dominant and economic-centric signifiers of success are better abandoned than pursued by most gamemakers. For Yang, sardonically, we can now tell videogames are definitely art since "there are so many of us [gamemakers] and we are all stressed-out and poor, and the world oppressively devalues our labor, just like all the other artists in other fields." Perhaps the most sustainable way to produce videogames isn't to pursue more stable employment but to reject turning it into a job at all—to become even more disinterested in economic interests.

These tensions in how gamemakers navigate the conditions and politics of gamework have not emerged in a vacuum; rather, the videogame field has found itself impacted by wider trends of middle-class precarization brought about by post-Fordism, neoliberalism, platform capitalism, and the gig economy. Game production researchers are increasingly identifying a fruitful overlap in game studies approaches to gamework labor issues and the literature and debates around the politics of cultural work in the so-called creative economy through authors such as Angela McRobbie, Susan Luckman, Mark Banks, David Hesmondhalgh, Kate Oakley, and Stuart Cunningham. As Greig de Peuter (2011, 421) notes of media and cultural workers more broadly, independent gamemakers as they have emerged since the late 2000s have been among the protagonists of "a laboratory of labor politics [that has led to the] de-standardization of employment, de-unionization of labor, dis-aggregation of production, [and] de-industrialization of economies [to undermine] workers' earlier sources of organizational power and economic security." For those striving to find ways to "be creative" (McRobbie 2016) through career aspirations that are more personally fulfilling than they are financially stable, just which activities are and are not *work* becomes increasingly blurred as creative work becomes defined less by occupation and more by a collection of personal skills, social networks, and dispositions that converge into a "portfolio career" across projects and side hustles. The growth of smaller-scale, independent, precarious creative production— including that within the videogame field—is effectively "labor reform by stealth, since the objective is to re-route young people into spheres that are unprotected in advance" (McRobbie 2016, 58). In this context, chapter 2's narrative of Australia's videogame makers adapting entrepreneurially to sector-wide collapse could be reframed as the local videogame field being reconfigured so that the major firms of the field can still capture and commodify the aspirational labor of independent videogame creators (through platformization) while no longer needing to provide formal employment arrangements, offsetting production costs onto gamemakers themselves.

This chapter explores how gamemakers navigate the precarious and strenuous conditions of gamework within intensely in/formalized modes of videogame production. How are we to consider issues of crunch, burnout, discrimination, and unpaid work in a seemingly "democratized" field of self-driven independent creators? Are we to consider the unpaid work of a gamemaker who explicitly considers making games on the weekend around a full-time job to be a rejection of capitalist commodification or a self-exploiting "passionate play slave" (de Peuter and Dyer-Witheford 2005)? The answer, inevitably, is not straightforward. The first section begins by introducing cultural studies critiques of how individualization and precarization under neoliberal post-Fordism are restructuring the nature of cultural work. Perhaps the most striking parallel between cultural studies critiques of the creative economy and the self-articulations of Australian gamemakers is the ways in which narratives of adventure and autonomy paint an attractive veneer over situations of extreme and externally enforced insecurity. The second section turns to the particular identity and brand of indie game development as it is deployed by Australian gamemakers to add a sense of countercultural edge to a precarious situation where *not* being independent is simply not an option. Here, parallels are traced with the use of "entrepreneurism" in creative economy discourses more broadly. Finally, the chapter turns its attention to those gamemakers who, like Yang, for one reason or another, explicitly claim to *not* want to be paid for their gamework. A tension exists here between, on the one hand, seriously and critically considering the external forces that exploit creators while also convincing them to work for free and, on the other hand, trusting and respecting gamemakers' own articulations of how they wish to remove themselves from exploitative and alienating processes of capitalist commodification. This provides a significant and urgent challenge for game production researchers specifically and cultural industries researchers more generally: if the commercial companies of these fields are so exploitative of their workers, then is there an emancipatory potential in finding ways to opt out of economic ambitions either partially or entirely?

The Politics of Cultural Gamework

Economic capital has an ambivalent relationship with cultural work, and its accumulation is often a secondary consideration for cultural workers after the accumulation of the cultural and social capital recognized within the field. For many cultural workers, accruing economic capital is prioritized only insofar as it makes the accrual of other forms of capital more feasible—artists still have to eat and pay the rent! For Bourdieu, the strong influence of non-commercial markers of success within the field of cultural production leads him to call it "the economic world reversed" (1993, 29). The more autonomous a cultural field, the more the field adheres to its own "disinterested [symbolic] values which constitute the specific law of the field" and the more its "economy of practices" is based on "a systematic inversion of the fundamental principles of all ordinary economies" (Bourdieu 1993, 39). The tensions between making "art for art's sake" (for intrinsic reasons determined by the field's internal markers of success) and "selling out" (to make a living more reliably from commodified artistic practice in the economic world) is an everyday struggle for cultural practitioners striving to take legitimate or authentic positions, and one that has been extensively interrogated in other cultural fields (Thornton 1995; Banks 2007; McRobbie 2016).

In sharp contrast to perceptions of the videogame industry as a lucrative space of campus-sized studios and savvy entrepreneurs, gamemakers I spoke to were commonly frank about how monetary reward was a secondary ambition in their work and how this created difficulties in regard to still needing to sustain themselves. More often than not, it was a desire to express an idea or to be creative that they articulated as their main driver for making videogames. For instance, Jason Bakker, 31, left his relatively stable employment at a larger mobile studio in Melbourne to cofound his own small team, Ghost Pattern, to work on what he describes as his "dream game." With piecemeal government grants and the savings accrued by himself and his cofounder through contract work at other studios, Bakker insists he is able to ensure his contractors get paid for the work they do. But at the time we spoke, Bakker and his cofounder had themselves spent almost two years on the project, unpaid. For Bakker, this was justifiable since:

> I have limited time on earth, and I should try to do this thing so I can feel like I've done it. I've taken this thing that I've been thinking about for years and years and

actually, you know, given it a shot as opposed to thinking in ten or twenty years like, "Oh, what if I'd done that?" or whatever.

In addition to willingly going unpaid during the production process, many gamemakers had little hope of their products being economically successful even upon completion. Jake Strasser, 28, worked in the four-person team House House with several friends in Melbourne. Strasser explicitly attributed the financial unreliability of videogame production to its creative nature:

> There's no delusion in any other creative field, I don't think. In every other field, making money is the amazing thing you aspire to eventually after making things for a long time. . . . If you're doing any other creative field the baseline is that the thing you make won't make you money. It's built into the work.

Yet, the fact that financial gain wasn't their main driver often jarred with how those external to the field understood the work of these gamemakers. Georgia Symons, 26, a writer hired on a contract basis on Bakker's team, explained how:

> When we talk to people about *Wayward Strand* [the game] . . . always the first question is "oh like who is the market for that, though?" These bizarrely market-driven questions. It's actually quite degrading, really, the extent to which everyone in your whole life, from art professionals through to your own parents, the first thing they want to ask you about an artistic product has to do with the profit motive and the marketability. . . . People at the moment are quite limited in their thinking [of videogames as an art form], or at least mainstream games seem to be that way. More and more games are challenging that, and we want to contribute to that as well.

For Bakker, Strasser, and Symons, creative and cultural values motivate their work and their expectations, often in direct tension with external perceptions of the field as driven primarily by commercial imperatives.

Deprioritizing economic imperatives to prioritize cultural or creative ones is complicated when cultural practice *is work*—both a source of financial income for the individual and a means of accruing capital for the employer (or publisher or platform) through the surplus-value generated by the worker's labor. For Mark Banks (2007, 12), cultural work—"the act of labor within the industrialized process of cultural production"—is "the very axis point of political struggle between the forces of art and commerce," and the cultural worker is the embodiment of the art-commerce relation, "who must most evidently balance the desire to indulge in disinterested, creative self-expression against the necessity of accumulation" (2007, 8). If we are to think of the site of videogame production as an industrialized cultural field, then this complicates how we are to understand and discuss the politics of undertaking and being compensated for gamework as itself cultural work. If videogame production is a cultural field, we must consider not only the distribution and imbalances of economic capital but also its disavowal and deferral alongside the striving for and accruing of cultural and social capital.

Such a task becomes more complicated still if we wish to balance a trust that interviewees are the best subjects for representing their own lifeworld with a more critical understanding of how a desire for disinterested, creative, and autonomous cultural work has been co-opted by a widening range of professional sectors to justify longer hours, lower pay, and individualized performance metrics. Angela McRobbie (2016, 15) has provided a searing assessment of how creativity is deployed under neoliberalism to mask worsening work conditions and a lack of opportunities, especially to younger workers, with "an invitation to discover one's own capabilities, to embark on a voyage of self-discovery," turning the insecurity of necessary self-employment into a seemingly self-chosen adventure. Here, the cultural producer's ability to "turn necessity into a virtue" (Bourdieu 1993, 50) is exploited to particularly malicious ends by employers who are all too happy for workers to be motivated by other than economic means. While pursuing cultural autonomy can "progressively challenge or moderate the pursuit of market values," the cultural worker's desire for such autonomy is prone to exploitation by commercial concerns "safe in the knowledge that [cultural workers] will feel sufficiently 'aesthetically motivated' to tolerate even the most oppressive working conditions" (Banks 2007, 63). Today, to take advantage of such aesthetic motivations, a broader range of sectors have restructured work to no longer look like the collective activity of work at all, having instead shifted toward the highly individualized "auteur relation to creative work" (Banks 2007, 52) where individual workers are asked to be motivated by their *drive* and their *passion* for the task rather than an uncouth desire for adequate pay and entitlements. For McRobbie (2016, 34–35), this nascent governance system of workers is a *creativity dispositif* that now

> oversees novel forms of job creation (in times of both unemployment and underemployment), the defining features of which are impermanent, short-term, project-based or temporary positions; it orchestrates an expansion of the middle classes in the light of the policies adopted by most national governments in

recent years to increase the number of students attending universities and art colleges and at the same time it supports the creative activities of this *arriviste* middle class, allowing them to act as guinea pigs for testing out the new world of work without the full raft of social security entitlements and welfare provision that have been associated with the post–Second World War period. . . . The seemingly exciting compensation for work without protection is the personal reward of "being creative."

The creativity *dispositif* romanticizes precarity, individualizes struggle, and depoliticizes the site of work by making ambiguous just where autonomous creativity (for its own sake) ends and heteronomous work (for someone else) begins.

Along similar lines, game production researchers have examined the ambiguity between work and leisure, with a particular focus on the enjoyable, disciplining, and productive nature of play. Concepts such as playbour (Kücklich 2005), passionate play slaves (de Peuter and Dyer-Witheford 2005), and immaterial labor (Dyer-Witheford and de Peuter 2009; see also Lazzarato 1996) elucidate how commercial videogame firms capture and exploit the creative and passionate labor of both gameworkers and players (and successfully turn the latter into the former) so as to make gamemaking feel less like a job that deserves compensation for every hour worked and more like a lifestyle that is inherently rewarding. This, in turn, depoliticizes the sites of videogame production, individualizes labor issues, and facilitates the exploitation and underpayment of workers (Bulut 2020; Dyer-Witheford and de Peuter 2009).

Since the mid-2000s, the videogame field's process of intense in/formalization has converged this preexisting ambiguity of play and labor with the broader art-commerce ambiguity of the creativity *dispositif* through the *platformization* of cultural production: "the penetration of digital platforms' economic, infrastructural, and governmental extensions into the cultural industries, as well as the organization of cultural practices of labor, creativity, and democracy around those platforms" (Poell, Nieborg, and Duffy 2022, 5; see also Helmond 2015). *Platforms* here refers to a wide and eclectic range of digital and online software services such as YouTube, Facebook, Uber, Amazon, and Google that situate themselves as a seemingly neutral middleman that allows "users" to interact: YouTube facilitates the relationship between video producer and audience, Facebook between the business owner and the potential customer, Uber between a driver and a prospective passenger. Of course, platforms are anything but neutral and are instead highly political agents that drastically shape the very relationships they facilitate (Gillespie 2010; Matamoros-Fernández 2017; Srnicek 2017; Lorusso 2019; Poell, Nieborg, and Duffy 2022). Digital platforms play a fundamental part in the growth and ubiquity of the creativity *dispositif*, literally replacing firms' collective employees with individual, self-driven, seemingly autonomous users to whom they owe nothing. Uber's promises of autonomy and flexibility to drivers while refusing to recognize them as employees entitled to adequate legal protections until forced to by law has become a classic example.

In videogame production, platformization has made itself known most vividly through the rise of powerful, affordable production tools like the Unity and Unreal game engines, and ubiquitous distribution platforms like Valve's Steam and Apple's App Store. Both production and distribution platforms have facilitated and exploited the growth of independent videogame production since the mid-2000s (Boluk and LeMieux 2017; Nieborg and Poell 2018; Nicoll and Keogh 2019; Foxman 2019; Nieborg, Young, and Joseph 2020; Chia et al. 2020). Videogame platforms position themselves as facilitators of autonomous and independent videogame production, empowering a wider range of videogame makers to both create and distribute their work. In return, they take a cut of each sale.[1] It is no exaggeration to say that without access to such platforms, the Australian videogame field's transition to one dominated by independent studios and individuals following the collapse of the country's larger studios would not have been possible. Through the rise of indie modes of videogame production, the videogame field has been restructured so that North American companies can capture the value generated by aspirational and self-resourced gamemakers without needing to offer formal employment arrangements.

Gamemakers I spoke to, both in Australia and overseas, typically spoke positively of the ways in which platforms have empowered them to undertake more autonomous work. Yet questions about their working habits, financial security, and plans for the future highlighted extreme levels of precarity and volatility that gamemakers saw as the price of that autonomy. In Sydney, Flat Earth Games was a small videogame production company run by siblings Elissa and Leigh Harris—36 and 33, respectively—alongside several part-time collaborators. The team primarily worked out of a bedroom but sometimes used the available spare desks at another small Sydney studio. At the time of our interview, the team was nearing the end of

a years-long production process on *Objects in Space* and had been working particularly long and grueling hours. Leigh had explained to me how
exhausting it was to work in such a small team with limited resources, but
earlier in the interview had praised independent videogame production
over working for larger studios due to how exploitative employers in the
videogame field can be. I commented that this seemed like a contradiction.
For Leigh, with a reference to Karl Marx, the difference "has to do with who
owns the means of production":

> It's difficult because I am very tired and I've been working six or seven days a week
> pretty much all year and, yes, it's quite upsetting not being able to say yes to go to
> a friend's wedding or not being able to save money or even think about [buying]
> a house or anything like that. The way I can justify it is that I'm still contributing
> to an IP and that IP is owned by the company that we own. So we're still building
> something that has value. That's the way I justify it in terms of commercial liv-
> ing expenses. I don't know. I guess it's just if I didn't do this then *Objects in Space*
> wouldn't exist, so I don't have a choice.

This sense of ownership combined with a sense of having creative ideas that
must be expressed regardless of the personal cost was common. Independent
gamemakers typically felt like they had voluntarily opted in to their situation
and, in doing so, were avoiding the externally enforced poor working conditions and stifled creativity of larger studios even as they worked long hours
for little pay. While Leigh felt as though he owned the means of production
(even as the team relied on platforms such as Steam for distribution), this
"ownership" also meant the team was personally responsible for funding the
project, where once such an investment would have been at least partially
covered by a publisher. If the game ultimately fails to make a return match-
ing its costs, Leigh and Elissa must shoulder those costs personally.

For Australian gamemakers, this choice between self-imposed economic
sacrifice and externally imposed creative sacrifice was amplified by the specific, local history of the global financial crisis (GFC) detailed in the previous chapter. Matt Ditton, 40, worked at several larger studios in Brisbane
before the GFC and, after several stints in teaching and freelancing, moved
to Melbourne to cofound a collection of small companies with several other
veteran gamemakers. Ditton directly contrasted the current work arrangements of small independent studios with the work that was conducted in
the larger studios before the GFC: "From an on-the-ground perspective it
was easier prior to the GFC . . . but it was all based on debt and just making

shovelware for American studios. . . . The money wasn't great, but the stress wasn't what it is now. But at the same time, I actually think the work is more interesting now." Here we see McRobbie's creativity *dispositif* clearly articulated: easier, more regular—but also more tedious and less fulfilling—work is currently unavailable and is anyways dismissed as less desirable than the unpredictable, inconsistently paid, but more creatively fulfilling work that is now the only option. This is not to suggest that gamemakers such as Leigh or Ditton are misguided for holding these preferences, but rather it shows how they make a virtue out of necessity when faced with particularly bleak economic conditions.

For all the willingness to make seemingly voluntary sacrifices in order to pursue creative fulfillment, the precarious situation in which Australian gamemakers work comes vividly to the fore in both how they talk about their current role and how they talk about their plans (or lack thereof) for the future. For many, what was intended as a straightforward introductory question—"What is your job title?"—proved very difficult to answer. For instance:

> My current job title is—I guess I kind of—I'm most comfortable just calling myself a designer because I'm very cross-discipline but like in terms of a business title I'm a creative leader at a very tiny indie partnership. (Ben Kerslake, 39, Melbourne)

> I'm a programmer. That's basically it. Programmer, slash, incidentally a designer, I guess. As often happens in small groups like this I'm wearing multiple hats. (Nick Rudzicz, 39, Montreal)

> I—depending on—I don't know. It's a bit weird, my brother and I founded our company so we're both codirectors of the company and cofounders. Usually, the credit that I get is lead programmer, but it depends entirely on the context in which we're performing. For the most part we make a lot of high-level decisions together. (Elissa Harris, 36, Sydney)

> My position is . . . I just make games and do whatever I can myself and ask other people's help for the things I cannot do. I don't know what kind of position that is! (Mohammed Fahmi, 30, Jakarta)

Rather than specialist or specific roles, gamemakers working independently in smaller teams take on a wide-reaching and ambiguous range of creative, technical, organizational, and managerial responsibilities that do not easily fit within the specialized role titles conventional in the field's traditional larger companies. As Jennifer Whitson, Bart Simon, and Felan Parker (2021) show of Canadian independent videogame makers, this ambiguity of responsibility creates a situation ripe for self-exploitation as work comes to be defined less by concrete responsibilities or the amount of time worked, and more by the never-ending and vague list of tasks required to get the game done.

The future is often just as (if not more) unpredictable than the present for gamemakers. As with the senior designer at the start of this chapter, gamemakers rarely had a plan of where they expected to be five years from now or even where they would be once the current project wrapped up. Instead, answers to this question were presented as aspirations ("Hopefully, if this project does well . . .") or, tellingly, were redirected toward a desire for individual improvement and fulfillment ("I just want to get better and make cool stuff"). Terry Burdak, 32, was a Melbourne-based independent developer who works in a team with two cofounders and several part-time collaborators. The trio began working together at university on a final-year student project, *Paperbark*, which they were, at the time of our interview, working to turn into a commercial release. When we talked, Burdak and the team had been under a prolonged period of self-imposed crunch as they neared their release deadline. For Burdak, the imminent completion of a title that had been his professional focus for years made the future impossible to think about:

> Fucking no idea [where I will be in five years]. . . . Just so much is weighted on how well *Paperbark* goes. You know, if it tanks, if it goes well, if it goes really well, if it goes okay, if it doesn't go at all . . . how well the game goes determines the next project. But ultimately, you're hoping that everything you've been working toward pays off and you can just keep working on it and making it better. Realistically that's all you can really ask for.

The ubiquity of this type of response—anchored more in the *hope* for stability than any ability to plan for it—demonstrates how in lieu of any career certainty or job stability, independent gamemakers are driven by the individualist and idealized notions of creative entrepreneurism where the future is always up for grabs.[2]

While the workers of triple-A game studios undeniably experience constant precarity as an "existential condition" (Bulut 2020, 71), where even creating a critical darling or commercial hit can't ensure job security, those I spoke to at large studios nonetheless often had a clear sense of an at least hypothetical career trajectory and promotions ladder they could theoretically climb through planning with their supervisors and management. For instance, a junior designer might one day be promoted to a senior designer or a creative director. The portfolio careers of independent gameworkers such as those that are the majority of the Australian field, on the other hand, are less frequently defined by a foreseeable career path and instead are only rendered legible *as* career trajectories post hoc, as gamemakers jump between projects and teams, hustling and cobbling together a career and an income from a range of gigs and projects, some of which pay, some of which don't. Much like the triple-A gamemaker compelled to work evenings or weekends, independent gamemakers are driven by passion, a sense of self-responsibility, and the task-oriented nature of videogame production work. But for independent gamemakers this takes place in a context of even greater volatility, unpredictability, and personal risk. While independent gamemakers have a greater appearance of autonomy, their work is shaped by the same blurring of play and labor that normalize overwork in the triple-A space, albeit now with the added risks associated with sinking personal resources and a lack of the benefits and protections a larger employer would be legally obliged to offer, such as a minimum wage and sick leave. As Leigh said to me, "Survival and success often look awfully similar when you're trying to run an indie games studio."

Indie Entrepreneurism or Bust

To seek work in the cultural industries is, increasingly, to be entrepreneurial: to identify a gap that one can fill with one's unique skillset, and to invest large amounts of "sweat equity" into such work in the hope it will one day pay off. But the attractive go-getter connotations of entrepreneurism seem far removed from independent gamemakers who are driven by a desire to be creative and autonomous but also face chronic job insecurity and a lack of basic work entitlements such as superannuation or maternity leave. Kate Oakley (2014, 149) disrupts the positive and exciting framing of the entrepreneur, for cultural workers, as instead a *forced* entrepreneurship: "the need for people in rapidly changing industries to adopt worsening working arrangements lies behind much of the growth in entrepreneurship in the cultural sectors." For Imre Szeman (2015, 474) the entrepreneur thus represents

> the neoliberal subject *par excellence*—the perfect figure for a world in which the market has replaced society, and one whose idealization and legitimation in turn affirms the necessity and veracity of this epochal transition. The figure of the entrepreneur embodies the values and attributes that are celebrated as essential for the economy to operate smoothly *and* for the contemporary human being to flourish.

A normalization of entrepreneurism amplifies and reinforces the creativity *dispositif*, further dismantling the securities and assurances won by (some) workers in the postwar period as individual creative workers now embrace flexible work: jumping from one short-term gig to the next, setting up shop in cafés or bedrooms with their own computers running ostensibly free platformized software such as Unity, Photoshop, Garage Band, and Google Docs. This instills a culture of individualization that is about "new, more fluid, less permanent social relations seemingly marked by choice or options" (McRobbie 2002, 518). For Banks (2007, 43), much as we have already seen in the previous section, such "strong incitements to become more self-directed, self-resourcing, and entrepreneurial may enhance possibilities for workers' self-exploitation and, relatedly, self-blaming."

In the videogame field, the figure of the entrepreneur is most clearly manifest in the indie developer. Indie games rose in popularity through the 2000s, primarily through popular narratives of "self-made" white male auteur figures such as Jonathan Blow, Phil Fish, and Edmund McMillen working outside the then-dominant studio-publisher model. This was particularly popularized through the 2012 documentary film *Indie Game: The Movie*, which has become something of an easy punching bag for researchers and gamemakers alike wanting to highlight the hegemonic and narrow ways in which indie selectively represents only the most commercially viable subset of the diverse spectrum of independent videogame production. As digital distribution (and thus platformization) became the norm across the videogame field and the gatekeeping ability of the console manufacturers and publishers was weakened, smaller teams became able to distribute smaller-scale games. This was seen, much as indie is seen in other fields, as more autonomous and less restricted by commercial imperatives—more creative and less "selling out." More cynically, as independent creators from marginalized backgrounds have frequently pointed out, the games produced by the first wave of commercially successful indie gamemakers kept to a limited range of tried-and-tested retro genres that the primary demographics of indie gamemakers had themselves grown up with, such as side-scrolling platformers and arcade shooters.

Indie as a culture, identity, genre, and business model has undergone extensive critique (Lipkin 2013; Simon 2013; Ruffino 2021; Clark and Wang 2020). The early entrepreneurial model of indie creative *and* commercial success as shown in the exclusively white, cisgender, and male auteur figures of *Indie Game: The Movie* has been shown to be only a small sliver of the vast range of independent approaches to videogame production that have long existed beyond the triple-A industry (Anthropy 2012; Boluk and LeMieux 2017). Indie signifies the gentrification of independent gamemaking. Indie studios and individual gamemakers—and, paradoxically, the indie publishers that have emerged to support and be supported by them—are often romanticized as a countercultural movement, as having made a choice to refuse the conditions and stifled creativity of the mainstream industry, while simultaneously embracing a by-your-own-bootstraps individualized business philosophy that John Vanderhoef (2020, 17) has called an "antiestablishment neoliberalism." As Stephanie Boluk and Patrick LeMieux (2017, 33) note in their critique of *Indie Game: The Movie* and the limited conceptualization of independence it celebrates:

> The term *indie game* [valorizes] only certain kinds of precarious labor practices—the ones that paid off. The very concept of indie games circulates as a form of cultural imperialism that both colonizes profitable forms of independent production and sanitizes them for mass consumption. Adopting the term indie games from the much wider spectrum of creative and experimental labor, then applying it as a general descriptor for a specific form of game making, reduces all independent development to this particular aesthetic and mechanic genre of videogames and also reduces all independent developers to those white, North American men able to make a living developing games in the wake of the global economic collapse beginning in 2008.

Whereas indie game production was originally conceptualized antagonistically and broadly as "not triple-A" in the North American context (Lipkin 2013), "independent" now feasibly describes the overwhelming majority of videogame production positions in the world working in piecemeal, self-resourced arrangements with a reliance on digital distribution. The indie identity, as a particular position-taking in the videogame field, claims autonomy from the economic field while also maintaining a heteronomous ability to nonetheless ensure one is identifiable to particular consumer audiences as existing as an entrepreneur within that same economic field.

As Oakley (2014, 145) says of entrepreneurial cultural workers, indie gamemakers are indeed independent "but not as they please and not under self-selected circumstances." The forced entrepreneurship of creative workers exposes the autonomous myth and precarious reality of independent gamemaking. In the intensely in/formalized videogame field we see indie mobilized in much the same way as entrepreneurship is mobilized in the broader cultural industries, where a sense of self-chosen adventure and excitement masks worsening working arrangements, deteriorating access to social welfare, extractive platformization, and an absence of stable employment opportunities.

Tellingly, indie was commonly used by Australian gamemakers to describe the mode of gamework they undertake. Of the 288 survey respondents, in response to a question asking which terms best describe the type of game-making activity they undertake, 201 (71 percent) checked "indie" and 153 (53 percent) checked "independent"; 226 (80 percent) checked at least one or the other.[3] When interview participants described the strengths of the Australian field, the creativity allowed by the field's independence (as opposed to when Australian gamemakers were required by overseas publishers to produce "shovelware") was a common trend:

> I think especially in Australia's scene, given that the majority of game developers are indie developers, compared to the United States where developers are mostly working on big triple-A titles, we're starting to see people flex their progressive muscles and say, "I want to make a game that I want to play!" And so you're seeing all these games pop up that people do either on their spare time, or full-time because they've got funding, and it's pushing the envelope on what we see games can achieve. (Kim Allom, 27, studio manager, Brisbane)

This was a common refrain, and one that it is interesting to consider in relation to the history of Australia's videogame field where this transition to indie did not necessarily happen by choice but because it became the only feasible way to locally commodify videogame making practices in the absence of external employment opportunities.

The language of entrepreneurism reframes structural precarity as self-chosen adventure, obscuring both the conditions and motivations of game-work. For instance, in research with independent Canadian gamemaking teams, Whitson, Simon, and Parker (2021) note how gamemakers often used the language and posturing of tech industry entrepreneurism when talking about their ambitions or work practice to external parties such as publishers, investors, or government representatives, stressing a desire to expand, hire more staff, and generate more revenue. Yet, when asked to reflect directly on their craft or future ambitions as gamemakers, they instead articulate a desire to keep on keeping on at their current scale with their current colleagues. Or, rather, they wanted to continue to thrive at a particular, sustainable scale; they did not necessarily want to grow into large triple-A studios. That was not their idea of success.

This need to "talk the talk" of entrepreneurism to be perceived as professional and to access funding options, in turn, both exceptionalizes and hides sites of extreme precarity, both from popular imaginings of what gamemaking success looks like but also from formal statistics and legal framings. For example, I spoke in Melbourne to one studio cofounder who was particularly exhausted and downtrodden at the time of our interview. He was working from the local coworking space, The Arcade, surrounded by game studios that he perceived as having achieved various kinds of success while his own studio had toiled on game after game in relative obscurity with little to show for it. When we spoke, this gamemaker and his two cofounders were all individually undertaking freelance or contract work for other teams on other projects,

> just to pay bills and shit because our own IP that we've got is not generating enough revenue to pay wages. . . . So like it's a bit tough because the other two guys in the team are sort of right now especially doing a lot of contract work and part-time jobs and keeping themselves afloat, and I've been keeping myself afloat on the side as well.

Some of the cash that each team member made from individual work on the side was then filtered back into the studio. Actual wages for working at the floundering studio, however, were "sporadic":

> Because we're [company] directors we're not under the same stringency from the ATO [Australian Tax Office]. They're not like "you must be covering your employees' wages" and stuff. So when we're not doing [studio] work there's not really an expectation to be paid from [the studio].

Similar situations where a studio looked much more formal on paper than in the lived experiences of their owners or workers were common in interviews. "Employees" were not being exploited, necessarily, but "company directors" (that is, independent gamemakers who set up a company to undertake their precarious work) substantially underpaid themselves, in the hope things would pay off eventually. This situation becomes a nasty cycle where teams hide the true extent of their own precarity so as to mimic the external markers of success and stability they perceive in other teams and in so doing further obscured just how precarious most independent teams truly were.

This is not to imply that most independent gamemakers have simply been duped into thinking financial return for their labor is unnecessary or unwarranted. Many clearly articulated the exploitative nature of their current situation. Between her various roles, Leena van Deventer, whom we heard from in the previous chapter, noted that "the fundamental challenge of being a creative person is the neoliberal bullshit that's stopping you from actually getting work done." Like van Deventer, other gamemakers referenced neoliberalism and capitalism directly when discussing their work situation, or explicitly critiqued the labor practices of videogame companies they had worked at as exploiting gameworkers' passion. When Leigh said above that "it has to do with who owns the means of production," the reference to Marx's labor theory of value was deliberate, and Leigh implies his own independent creativity possesses a potential path to social equity—even as his work remains mediated by numerous external companies and platforms. Thus, even as the rose-tinted glasses of indie entrepreneurism obscure the true extent of precarity of the field, the sincere desire to be independent, to have some autonomy in how one undertakes videogame production, was nonetheless a major driver for gamemakers conscious of their own precarious situation. Indie provides a veneer of autonomy that romanticizes and obscures the individualized precarity of creative entrepreneurship in the videogame field without necessarily resolving the entrenched labor issues that have long faced gamemakers. Nevertheless, it is still the case that these independent gamemakers have a level of autonomy detached from the governance of the big, dominant studios, and some are striving to imagine different ways of structuring gamework communally and collectively.

Opting Out

In his blog post cited in the introduction of this chapter, gamemaker Robert Yang saw, much as some of my participants, the inability to make independent videogames in a financially sustainable way to be just part and parcel of pursuing a cultural practice under capitalism. If one were to be driven by the field's autonomous principles of hierarchization, by the desire to make art for art's sake, a disinterest in economic interests was inevitable and necessary. The scholars cited throughout this chapter so far see this as both a fundamental tension in industrialized cultural fields, and as the insidious ability of the creativity *dispositif* to defang collective responses to extreme precarity in an increasing range of sectors through the language of "being creative." Yet, it is insufficient to simply say that gamemakers such as Yang have been duped by a creativity *dispositif* into giving away their work for free.

Yang (2017; emphasis added) himself is articulate on his reasons for being economically defeatist:

> I don't expect to make a living off of my games. I give away my gay sex games for free because (a) they're short-form games in a market that demands "replay value" even though people don't even touch most of their Steam libraries, (b) I don't want to invest all my time and hope into commercializing it, just to earn like $5k a year if I'm lucky, which does not go far in NYC, (c) when an indie game has poor sales, then that often becomes the game's entire legacy forever. . . . To me, there's a certain peace of mind in not trying to make the next gay sex *Minecraft* blockbuster happen. . . . Why is it so important for us to make our living from selling our games? *Why can't we make our living from doing something else?*

As such, for Yang, choosing autonomy is a recognition, rather than a refusal, of the situations of extreme precarity and overwork outlined above that are required to make independent gamemaking a financially sustainable venture. Yang is not alone in this assessment, and other independent gamemakers also argue that the field's economic-centric markers of success do a disservice to gamemakers. In their own blog post, gamemaker thecatamites (n.d.) calls these market arrangements a sort of "business cosplay" and argues that:

> If [these market arrangements] are not challenged, and remain the default even in the rinky-dink small-scale spaces we create for our hobbyist projects outside the shadow of big capital, they will continue to act as the implicit limit to our sense of what's possible; will continue to act as the rake that we step on, again and again.

While the critiques of the creativity *dispositif* made earlier in this chapter are vital for understanding the conditions of work in the twenty-first century—both cultural and otherwise—it's important we don't reduce the myriad of reasons for which people undertake cultural activity to purely economic ones. Doing so imposes a capitalist realist (Fisher 2009) lens instead of critiquing the arrangement of contemporary capitalism, and it risks perpetuating the very circumstances we strive to critique.

While many aspirational videogame makers willingly work for either below minimum wage or no wage at all in the hope that "one day" it will economically pay off, some gamemakers I interviewed expressed, like Yang and thecatamites, a disinterest in striving to make a living from their videogame production work. Samantha Schaffer, in Adelaide, identified their own gamemaking practice as a hobby with no aspirations to turn this practice into a job:

> [When I was] employed, professionally I was a software developer and I have a degree in computer science so if I really wanted to, I could try to make games

professionally . . . , but I don't really connect with that side of it, so it's very much a hobby. I'm fortunate now to have the time to be not working and doing more creative stuff so I've been making a fair few games lately but generally speaking just every now and then. . . . Being able to churn out a Bitsy game[4] and be like "Well, that's over now, I could leave forever if I wanted to" rather than spending years on something big, was really helpful.

Likewise, Melbourne-based game design student Zachariah Chandler, 21, is unfazed by the commercial challenges of gamemaking and is content to get an unrelated part-time job to support his practice, rather than monetize it directly:

> The prospect of leaving university, going and getting some part-time retail job, setting up a Patreon, and churning out trash games that I enjoy myself does not seem like the end of the world or like some great hardship I have to fight through. It's almost gotten to the point now where it's like, oh, that's just the way it is. You're an independent developer. No one is a Notch [creator of *Minecraft*] anymore. You don't get to make billions of dollars off your videogame. You get to make $50 a week on top of whatever it is you're earning and cool, that's sweet, it pays for your Adobe Suite subscription or whatever. I don't have a problem with that because I have no pretentions of fame and riches or whatever. Who cares? Work is a lot more interesting when it is driven by necessity!

Gamemakers like Schaffer and Chandler who expressed such sentiments were, in their own minds at least, not accepting a lack of reimbursement for the sake of creative fulfillment but rather deliberately keeping their creative practice separate from their means of sustenance so as to avoid the notorious exploitation, anxieties, and deprivations of formalized gamework.

Like Schaffer, many such gamemakers used the word "hobby" to differentiate their noncommercial videogame production. In his history of hobbies in North America, Steven Gelber (1999) identifies hobbies as emerging in another time when the relationship between work and leisure was drastically shifting: the industrial revolution. Industrialization "quarantined" work from leisure and replaced "the fluidity of preindustrial time" with "discrete blocks of commodified time that could be sold for work or withheld for leisure" (1999, 1). The hobby, Gelber argues, emerged as a form of *productive leisure* through which "the ideology of the workplace infiltrated the home" (1999, 2). Hobbies "provide the satisfactions of a 'career' and confirm the legitimacy of the [capitalist] work ethic even for people in unpleasant jobs" (1999, 11) and "confirm the verities of work and the free market inside the home *so long as remunerative employment has remained elsewhere*" (1999, 4; emphasis added).

When remunerated employment *doesn't* remain elsewhere, however, one can see how the productive leisure of hobbies throughout the late nineteenth and twentieth centuries evolves into the creativity *dispositif* of the twenty-first century, where the capitalist work ethic of productivity encroaches the sphere of leisure to such an extent that any clear distinction between the two falls away and people strive to turn their passions into entrepreneurial business undertakings. The two now fuse together for many cultural workers in their constitution of personal and professional identities. McRobbie (2002, 520) makes this connection explicit: "The intoxicating pleasures of leisure culture have now . . . provided the template for managing an identity in the world of work." Where once one undertook a hobby to be productive beyond their formal employment, in the precarious hustle of today's portfolio careers, one more often than not strives to turn what would otherwise be a hobby *into* a form of employment in lieu of any other alternatives.

Nonetheless, as chapter 1 discussed briefly, and as videogame historians have extensively shown (Swalwell and Davidson 2016; Švelch 2018; Nicoll 2019; Reed 2020; Swalwell 2021), people have always made videogames in a hobbyist capacity beyond the most industrialized positions in the field, but the aggressive formalization of the 1990s obscured and delegitimized these positions. Hobbyist gamemakers did not stop existing through the 1990s, but they did become explicitly secondary to (and obscured by) the concerns and outputs of the field's dominant positions. For instance, modding and user-generated content have received extensive scholarly attention (see Banks 2013; Kücklich 2005) but are largely framed in the literature as activities undertaken by *players*, not gamemakers (at least until their creators' transition to commercialized modes of production). The extensive amateur communities that existed around tools such as Flash and RPG Maker in the late 1990s and early 2000s, meanwhile, are only recently beginning to receive the scholarly attention they deserve (Ito 2005; McCrea 2013b; Anthropy 2014; Salter and Murray 2014; Fiadotau 2020; Reed 2020). Following the videogame field's aggressive formalization, "choosing" to be a videogame hobbyist—to make videogames without hustling toward commodification—is an almost radically political act that, as Gelber (1999, 156) says of craft hobbyists generally, "evokes the mythical purity of the preindustrial artisan," as it requires a conscious rejection of trying to "make it" in the "videogame industry."

It is not a coincidence that those gamemakers I spoke to who were most adamant that they were deliberately refusing to participate in the ruthless

hustle of indie entrepreneurism were often from those marginal demographics who typically feel most excluded from or alienated by commercial videogame firms of all scales. Schaffer was explicit in this reason to remain a
hobbyist: "I like the low level of investment in it because the games industry
can be quite hostile towards femme people and queer people and that kind of
thing. So I didn't really want to go all in on an industry that might get mad
at me." While queer, transgender, and gender-diverse folk have always been
involved in the videogame field as creators, employees, critics, and players,
they have been particularly visible in the in/formalized field since the early
2010s (Keogh 2013; Harvey 2014; Ruberg 2020b). On the one hand, this
greater visibility has increased critical acclaim and recognition in terms of
the aesthetic innovations and interventions their videogames have made in
the field. On the other hand, visibility has intensified violence and harassment directed toward marginal gamemakers for producing videogames that
the dominant positions in the field are incapable of perceiving as legitimate
(Consalvo and Paul 2019). One catalyst of Gamergate, for instance, was when
Zoë Quinn placed their free videogame *Depression Quest*—released months
earlier on their own website—on Steam to reach a broader audience. That
Depression Quest was made in Twine, was text-only, was made by a queer,
femme-presenting nonbinary gamemaker, and was released for free infuri-
ated a dominant gamer audience that saw this as a newcomer incursion on
a dominant position in the field (the Steam marketplace). The subsequent
harassment, abuse, and death threats of a diverse range of gamemakers, journalists, and researchers led many marginal gamemakers to decide commercial videogame production and distribution was no place for them—but they
did not necessarily stop making videogames. Like Yang, many chose cultural
autonomy and economic failure as an alternative path forward.

How, then, as Jack Halberstam (2011, 1) asks in the introduction to *The
Queer Art of Failure*, do we find alternatives "to cynical resignation on the one
hand and naïve optimism on the other" when considering tactical responses
to the ubiquity of capitalism such as those that define the noncommercial
ambitions of hobbyist gamemakers? For Halberstam (2011, 2), "failure" as
an alternative to too-straightforwardly economic "success" as determined
by hegemonic, heteronormative, capitalist society "begs for a grammar
of possibility . . . and expresses a basic desire to live life otherwise." Failure
becomes, in part, "a refusal of mastery, a critique of the intuitive connections
within capitalism between success and profit, and as a counterhegemonic

discourse of losing" (2011, 11–12). Marigold Bartlett and Sam Crisp (2013), in the presentation at Freeplay Independent Games Festival cited in the previous chapter, connect Halberstam's notion of capitalist failure with the then-recent expansion of the videogame field by marginal hobbyists:

> By celebrating failure, we can shift our perception, and instead of looking at games which don't sell or don't get critical acclaim as games which must be doing something wrong, we can realize that these games are the only ones which can truly offer us emancipation. From a certain perspective, they're the only games doing something right. . . . Voices that are queer, feminist, or trans, who are implicitly seen as failures by society's notion of success, are on the forefront of transgressive game design and criticism. (Bartlett and Crisp, 2013)

For Gelber (1999, 19), the fact that some people willingly do in their spare time as hobbies what others do for a living points to hobbies not as an escape from work but as "a return to traditional nonalienated forms of labor" in which "participants determine the form, set the pace, and are the sole beneficiaries of the fruits of their labor." Yet, Gelber is ultimately skeptical that this points to a "return to a golden age of labor" and instead sees such hobbyist activity as "exercises that serve to ideologically integrate work and leisure by permitting workers to engage in worklike behavior in a non-coercive environment." We can think here, too, of McRobbie's notion of the creativity *dispositif* as encouraging rather than coercive—reframing unpaid work and hardships as part of the adventure of creative expression. Similarly, Aleena Chia (2019) has shown how videogame businesses directly and deliberately benefit from the "vocational passion" of their hobbyist player-base, and Bo Ruberg (2019) has shown how the dominant positions in the videogame field directly benefit from and absorb the social and cultural capital of the newly legitimized but still marginalized queer videogame creators on whom the responsibility (but not the commercial benefit) falls to "make games better." Hobbyist gamemakers might be conscious and articulate of the coercive and exploitative nature of commodified gamemaking work, but this does not necessarily mean they avoid exploitation by videogame studios and platforms that still benefit from their activity—a complex situation that will be explored further in chapter 7.

Yet I cannot help but think of the clear difference between those aspirational gamemakers I interviewed who were trying incredibly hard to make gamemaking their primary income—commonly stressed, overworked, exhausted, and pouring personal funds into uncertain ventures—and those who had consciously opted out of that race, at least partially, to make video-games in their own time, around other work—content, curious, communal. To me, these were not exploited and downtrodden gameworkers, but game-makers who had explicitly and deliberately distanced themselves from an alienating system that would never work in their favor anyway. As Banks (2007, 165) says of "the efforts of thousands of artistic, community-oriented and socially motivated practitioners," I feel it is to "disparage and, perhaps more importantly, to empirically misrepresent" the activities of videogame makers to suggest "that the fruits of their labor have served only the capi-talist mode of accumulation which contains (and often constrains) their efforts." Perhaps these hobbyists are then not escaping the nets of the cre-ativity *dispositif* or neoliberal capitalism, but, as one of McRobbie's (2016, 23) students justifies her own entrepreneurial activities, finding "a means of creating a space within a system that is so all-encompassing that it is dif-ficult to imagine an alternative. To have seemingly circumvented unhappy work." Or, as Jaroslav Švelch (2018, xxxiii) evaluates the videogame hob-byists of 1980s Czechoslovakia through Michel de Certeau, hobbyist game-makers are not finding top-down strategies to dismantle the systems that don't work in their favor but bottom-up tactics as an "art of the weak" to find ways to "make do." Or, in Halberstam's sense, such gamemakers seem to be determining alternative measures of success beyond the economically rationalist measures historically dominant in the field.

Of course, even (especially) among marginal demographics, not every-one can afford to simply give up on commodifying their cultural activity. Chandler, after voicing his own noncommercial ambitions, was careful to stress that he was in a particularly privileged position to be so nonchalant: "I don't have to worry about finances because my parents are doctors and live on a big farm. If everything goes to shit I'm not going to die, right? That's not going to be the case for others. . . . So it's like, I don't have a solution to that." This is a crucial reminder not to romanticize those who "choose" alter-native, autonomy-driven forms of videogame creation as somehow purer or more legitimate than those who prioritize financial subsistence. We must be careful not to trivialize or downplay the situations of quite extreme poverty that many marginalized independent gamemakers work from, especially in countries like the United States that lack sufficient social safety nets. Chandler, for instance, in addition to being able to fall back on his parents for accommodation and food also does not have to worry about excessive student debts or a health system that connects access to affordable care to employment contracts, as a hobbyist gamemaker would in the United States. With job shortages and flat social wages and increasing disparity between rich and poor, being able to not monetize your hobby into a hustle is increasingly a privilege few can afford. Such a position-taking is simply unavailable for many dispositions.

To be sure, almost every gamemaker quoted in this section would certainly choose to survive purely on their gamemaking craft if it were feasible to do so without accepting the precarity and exploitation that comes with the current structures of commercial videogame production. Instead, from their own disposition, the videogame field does not currently present positions in which it is possible to undertake the form of videogame production they wish to undertake and to also make an economic income. But neither would these gamemakers be served by, for instance, the return of large publisher-dependent studios to Australia that have historically been plagued by exactly the misogynistic and fraternal cultures of exclusion such gamemakers are striving to avoid. As Greig de Peuter (2014, 276) argues, opposing the neoliberal labor politics of the cultural industries requires us to go "beyond opposing precarity, and, indeed, beyond developing policy mechanisms enabling workers to better cope with flexible labor markets—to go a step further to propose and experiment with political-economic infrastructures of cultural creativity that provide an alternative to the dominant social relations of production." To account for, and ultimately to support, the full spectrum of gamemaking practice in the videogame field is to account for the economic, cultural, and social values that motivate different people to make videogames in their full diversity and contradictions, neither reducing them purely to economic metrics nor romanticizing them as ever fully autonomous from the demands of survival under capitalism.

Conclusion

The precarious and piecemeal nature of contemporary gamework, driven by individual desires for fulfilling work and dependent on digital platforms, aligns with broader neoliberal trends across the cultural industries. But at the same time, the videogame field's unique history of aggressive formalization complicates matters. Under capitalist industrialization, other cultural fields saw a previous dominance of autonomous principles of hierarchization weakened by the rise and penetration of market forces, and this has been cultural studies' concern with the industrialization of culture since the discipline's origins. For the videogame field, however, first emerging alongside neoliberalism's rise to ubiquity, the current age of intense in/formalization is also the first time that principles of autonomous hierarchization have been strong enough for videogame production to be perceived as happening within an autonomous cultural field, and not just within a commercial industry, at all. It is insufficient to simply dismiss the articulations of gamemakers' creative and other noncommercial ambitions as having been duped by a creativity *dispositif*, even as such a *dispositif* has undeniably restructured what work looks like in the videogame field. Many of the gamemakers I spoke to, just like Yang, thecatamites, and Bartlett and Crisp cited above, were articulate on the capitalist systems and ideologies of passion and creativity that work to suppress the conditions and pay of gameworkers globally. For these gamemakers, this was more an argument for opting out of the hustle of making gamework economically feasible to, instead, try to take positions that were more autonomous from, more disinterested in, the need to make an income.

Crucially, and as will be expanded upon in chapter 7, it is alongside the partial legitimization of this broader diaspora of independent gamemakers, beyond the managerial surveillance and ruthless individualism of triple-A studio workers, that a nascent collective politics of gamework is beginning to emerge, and through which the structure and nature of the videogame field is being rapidly redetermined. As Anna Anthropy (2012, 18–20) argues in *Rise of the Videogame Zinesters*, "carving new paths to game creation and distribution is valuable" because it undermines "the industry's claim to being the only route to game creation" and forces "the industry to try to reconsider its totalitarian attitude toward the people it employs." This was vividly demonstrated at the 2018 Game Developers Conference in San Francisco when a diverse collective of commercial and hobbyist, independent and employed gamemakers protested a talk given by the executive director of the International Game Developers Association (IGDA) that was largely perceived to be anti-union. This grassroots collective grew over the course of 2018 into Game Workers Unite (GWU)—not a union but a collection of communities advocating for unionization and collectivization throughout the game industry (Frank 2018). GWU's growth and its ramifications will be considered in depth in chapter 7, but here it is worth noting that it is no coincidence that the growing push toward unionization in the video-game field coincides with a diversification of just who is visible and has the authority to speak at videogame events as a perceived legitimate game developer. Detached from the surveillance culture of large studios, marginal gamemakers are reimagining what legitimate videogame work looks like, and are beginning to agitate for solidarity across the field in a way that an employee at a large studio, concerned about aggrieved managers, cannot. While de Peuter (2011, 421) rightly notes that workers' "earlier sources of organizational power and economic security" in a range of sectors are being undermined by the "de-standardization of employment, de-unionization of labor, dis-aggregation of production, [and] de-industrialization of econo-mies," the situation is more complicated for gamemakers, who have histori-cally never had *any* source of organizational power or economic security to be undermined in the first place. It is alongside the partial legitimiza-tion of this broader field of independent gamemakers, beyond the manage-rial surveillance and ruthless exploitation of triple-A studio workers, that the nascent collective politics of gamework is beginning to emerge, and through which the structure and nature of the videogame field is being rapidly redetermined.

Perhaps the politics of contemporary gamework is best viewed through Mark Bank's prediction over a decade ago that neoliberalism might facilitate "conditions under which individuals may actually choose to reject those individualizing systems that place them at the capricious mercy of the mar-ket" (2007, 166). Through the frequently articulated political consciousness of Australian gamemakers, their oft-expressed desire for stronger solidarity and better working conditions instead of a return to the traditional studio-publisher model that left the entire national field in the lurch following the GFC, I find, like Banks, that it is important not to "discount how, in myriad global contexts, cultural workers . . . are immensely valuable in keeping alive the possibilities of a life beyond total commodification—however par-tial and precarious that life may currently appear." It would be a mistake to completely discount the importance and value of the autonomy and creative freedom that many of these workers truly do enjoy, even while we acknowledge the contingencies these are based upon and the political-economic coordinates from which they arise.

4 Enrolling Students into the Field

In that increasingly common and prolonged precarious limbo that early-career academics enter after completing a PhD, I worked for two years teaching game design at a private multimedia college in Brisbane. The kind of place that might be called a "polytechnic college" in the US. The students at this college were particularly vocationally minded. My students had enrolled in a bachelor of game development program because they wanted to work as developers in the videogame industry. At least at the start of their studies, very few of the students knew what such a job would actually entail, and fewer still had ever tried to make a videogame before. They assumed, much as I assumed 15 years earlier when I briefly enrolled in and then dropped out of a game development degree myself, that so long as they loved playing games, someone else could teach them the specific skills needed to get a job making games—and indeed that a job was the only path into videogame production at all. They were generally oblivious to the fact that, as outlined in the previous chapter, most videogame production teams are barely getting by, that few teams in Australia will ever be in a position to hire even one graduate, or that if they want to one day get paid for making videogames, they would likely need to create their own job.

This created a number of challenges for us teaching staff that will be familiar to any reader who has taught in a game development program before.[1] Students would often be eager to learn the technical skills of particular software environments such as Unity or Unreal but were highly skeptical of the equally vital "soft skills" of cultural theories, creative practice, and critical thinking. They would boast of their knowledge of—and try to produce imitations of—massive commercial blockbusters such as *Dark Souls* or *Grand Theft Auto*, but turn up their noses at much smaller but more innovative independent and artistic titles more easily imitated with their available skills and

resources. With each new cohort, extensive time and effort would be commit-
ted by the teaching staff, often external to the college's formal curriculum,
to educating the students about the realities of work in the videogame field
and how unlikely they were to walk into a job after their degree. Even the
notion that making videogames was itself a creative practice and not simply a repertoire of technical skills was difficult to convey to some students.
These challenges always struck me as bizarre. While all creative students
surely commence their studies with a necessary optimism bordering on
naivete in regard to their own chances of success, I can't imagine a prospective student for a music degree being oblivious to the challenges of making
a career as a musician, or believing that they might be able to be an excel-
lent musician simply because they enjoy listening to the latest hits despite
never having touched an instrument or engaging with music theory. One
improves as an artist by making art badly until one can make art compe-
tently, but our prospective game development students typically thought
they would learn how to make videogames well and *then* they would start
making videogames.

Where our students picked up the mistaken idea that their years of experience as videogame players would straightforwardly convert them into com-
petent videogame makers was hardly a mystery to the teaching team. On the
walls of the corridor outside the small campus's main computer lab were two
marketing posters advertising a previous year's open day: one for the film
production degree, one for the game development degree. The film degree's
poster showed an assortment of equipment that one might see on a film set:
a director's chair, a camera dolly on rails, microphones, stage lights, a clapper
board. Over this assortment of objects related to the craft of filmmaking were
the words "Spoiler alert! You get the job." The game degree poster, on the other
hand, did not showcase the tools and equipment necessary for game production. There were no lines of code, software interfaces, motion capture suits,
drawing tablets, spreadsheets, or trigonometry equations. Instead, there
was a couch, an open pizza box, a PlayStation 3 console, three pixel-art
hearts in the corner of the poster, and chunky pixel text that spelled out
"PWN the competition"—embarrassingly outdated Internet lingo meaning
to beat the competition. The two posters side by side demonstrated a stark
contrast in how the college, its potential students, and those students' parents envisioned the difference between studying film production and studying videogame production. Film was depicted as first and foremost a creative

craft that required honing particular skills with particular tools; videogames were depicted as a consumer product that the students consumed. Neither the poster nor the prospective students had a comprehension of videogames as crafted works requiring, as films require, specific skills, tools, tastes, and design methodologies. The poster for the film degree was targeting prospective students interested in making films. The poster for the game degree was targeting prospective students interested in *playing* videogames.

This chapter examines how formal videogame development education perpetuates or challenges the dominant structure of the videogame field, considering in particular what position-takings it legitimizes, and how it encourages or discourages those of different dispositions to enter the field at all. Schools are "consecratory institution[s]" (Bourdieu 1993, 124) that are, at once, where newcomers to a field can experiment with new positions in direct competition with the established positions and where the established positions of the field have their dominance sustained through academic canonization. While a formal education is, of course, not the sole means through which a new cultural producer might take a position in a field, it is a common means through which the field as a space of possibles is presented to potential newcomers. It is through educational institutions that newcomers to a field come to perceive some position-takings as more favorable to their own dispositions and others as less so.

It is only relatively recently that the videogame field has "professionalized" in the sense that a formal qualification is seen as a dominant pathway toward employment as a videogame maker. Up until the early 2000s, pathways into videogame careers were often an unpredictable combination of hobby and happenstance. Traditional pathways typically included either starting as a self-taught modder or working in the notoriously exploited position of game tester in the hope of finding a path into a design role (Deuze, Martin, and Allen 2007; Bulut 2020). Since the early 2000s, however, as the required team sizes of commercial videogame production grew exponentially, and as existing gamemaker labor pools were rapidly burned through by grueling and exploitative conditions, the need for "a constant supply of workers" (Kerr 2017, 17) saw gamemaking transition into a professional identity one can train for. This is unsurprising if one considers the trajectories of aggressive formalization already mapped out in earlier chapters. If it is already difficult to imagine the ability to make videogames outside of a formal job in a videogame company, then it follows that one cannot access the skills to make videogames without a formal education in order to obtain that formal job. As the videogame field intensely in/formalizes, however, and pathways to videogame production other than formal employment are increasingly seen as legitimate, just what role a formal game development education plays in the field is deeply contested—and endlessly debated among gamemakers, journalists, and educators (e.g., Yang 2018; Wright 2018; Warner 2018). In game development education we can clearly see the contests that shape the frontiers of the field of videogame production. Between the varied foci of students, educators, and institutions are tensions between gamemaking as vocation versus gamemaking as craft; tensions between gamemaking as software development versus gamemaking as creative practice; tensions between traditional studio-publisher models and precarious, entrepreneurial indie models of production; tensions between the subjectivities of gamers produced discursively by companies and the dispositions required of aspiring gamemakers. Ultimately, by looking at videogame development education programs we can see just what positions in the field are presented as more or less preferable to the field's newcomers, and who is encouraged to take these positions.

To explore these tensions, I draw from insights provided by my game development educator, student, and alumni participants, and I contrast these perspectives with how Australian tertiary (or higher) education institutions presented their game development programs in the public-facing material available to prospective students. Here, I am greatly indebted to my research assistant, Dr. Taylor Hardwick, who collected and compiled this data. We began with an official list of Australia's 139 registered tertiary institutions, which the Australian government categorizes as either "public university," "private university," or "other approved higher education institution." Of these, public-facing information from each institution's website was collected from any program or major meeting either of the following two criteria:

- The program or major title includes at least one of the terms *game, interactivity, interactive media,* or *play.*
- The program explicitly references game development as a potential career outcome.

In total, 120 programs across 42 institutions met the above criteria, of which 81 (67.5 percent) met the first criteria, meaning that 39 programs (32.5 percent) did not directly reference games in their program name but did advertise game development as a potential career outcome for graduates of the program.[2] Of the identified programs, 110 (91.6 percent) provided a bachelor qualification or lower.

The first section of this chapter contextualizes the emergence and growth of formal game development education within broader neoliberal shifts in tertiary education toward prioritizing the "job-readiness" and "employability" of students. In Australia, over decades, students and parents have become increasingly anxious about future employment prospects as the cost of education rises and social welfare safety nets deteriorate. At the same time, for universities, the drying up of public funding avenues and an increased dependence on enrollment fees for covering operation costs (and exorbitant vice chancellor salaries!)[3] has led to institutional realignments that directly exploit these anxieties by prioritizing employability as the major marker of an education program's value. It is in this context that game development programs first emerged to, primarily, provide students a *pipeline* into videogame production jobs—jobs that, as we have seen, no longer represent the reality that most videogame production activity happens under. There is a clear tension here between the employment-directed pipeline that has traditionally defined videogame development programs and the nature of self-driven work in the intensely in/formalized videogame field.

The second section considers just what gamemaker dispositions game development programs thus attract and foster under such employment-centric conditions. In the context of hoping to enroll students with vocational ambitions (or at least anxieties), most Australian game programs align themselves with a dominant "gamer" identity through the language used and videogames referred to. As the gamer identity has been exhaustively shown to be highly gendered, this has a particularly limiting effect on who feels welcome in such programs, as well as what sorts of positions in the field students are likely to perceive as feasible.

The third section then considers the difficulties faced by both educators and students in transitioning these "gamers" into "gamemakers": a different position that demands a different relationship to videogames through different skills and values. Where students often start their courses expecting to be provided an incrementally expanding skillset that will allow them to turn ideas into videogames, educators instead wish to impart more holistic knowledge around creative identity and practice. Finally, in this ambivalent context, the chapter turns to what the students and their educators imagine their future will entail following graduation, especially in the context where a great deal more students are studying videogame production than there are employed gamemakers. Ultimately, students are shown to be torn between embodying three competing identities as they strive to take a position in the videogame field: the prospective employee, the autonomous and disinterested artist, and the hustling entrepreneur.

The Pipeline

It is no coincidence that formalized education pathways for gamemaking emerged at the same time as the team sizes required to produce commercially viable videogames were growing exponentially. At the height of the field's aggressive formalization in the early 2000s commercial videogames became increasingly technically complex and content-dependent, and so videogame studios required more and more workers skilled in a wider range of specialized technical disciplines. At the same time as studios required larger workforces, endemic poor working conditions ensured few remained at a single studio (or, indeed, in the field) for long. Studios desperately required a much larger pool of potential workers from which they could continuously hire.

As such, many of the earliest videogame development programs emerged as partnerships between large studios and nearby universities, providing a synergy between the needs of employers (for employees) and the needs of universities (for enrollments). For instance, Abertay University in Dundee, Scotland, has since the launch of its first game development degree in 1997 had a close relationship with local studio Rockstar North (originally DMA Designs) which developed the first *Grand Theft Auto* title in the same year. DMA cofounder David Jones was "instrumental" to setting up the university's first game development degree (Abertay 2017), and the university and Rockstar North have a close relationship to this day. The earliest tertiary game development programs in Australia, meanwhile, were explicitly designed to meet employer needs. Academy of Interactive Entertainment (AIE) was established by founders of Micro Forté studio in Canberra in the late 1990s to meet their own employment needs, and then expanded to meet the employment needs of other Australian studios (AIE 2021). Farbs, a 41-year-old solo gamemaker in Canberra, detailed this very direct pathway while telling his own story of how he entered videogame production in the late 1990s. While completing his studies at AIE, "the Micro Forté people came downstairs and said, 'We have job openings, who would like a job?' I put my hand up and got a job." This is a particularly exceptional case not of a university partnering with videogame companies but of videogame companies cutting out the university entirely to set up their own institution, controlling each end of the education-recruitment pipeline. Nonetheless, it exemplifies the employer-oriented modes in which videogame development programs first emerged.

University game development programs and local large studios thus become symbiotic in a way vividly and cynically detailed by celebrity game designer Warren Spector in a 2008 interview:

> We [game development studios] need so many more bodies now. We don't have the time to train [them], so they need to get that training some other place—and it happens in schools. On top of that, and one of the things we've discovered— and this is me being utterly cynical—in the US at least, the education system is less about educating students than making money. It's just horrifying. The reality is, videogame studies have become so popular that it'll make a lot of money for universities. So I get what I want—which is a larger talent pool from which to draw with a consistent baseline of knowledge, and universities get more students, which means they make more money which means they're happy. Which is kind of a win for everybody. . . . Sadly, the games education movement is kind of in its infancy. Most of the [teachers] are either people who can't get jobs, and if they could, they would—or they're people who love games, but don't really have any professional experience (Gillen 2008).

Tellingly here, "a win for everybody" encompasses both employers and universities but seemingly not the students who have been suckered into a system of supposedly (though I suspect not truly)[4] unqualified educators. What Spector is describing, aligning with broader suspicions among gamemakers toward formal game development education, is a situation where universities and employers are beneficiaries, but students are merely the product.

In such intimate arrangements between educational institutions and videogame companies, the student cohort effectively becomes a pool of human capital that local studios can tap into as required. Education here is presented to students as a streamlined pipeline through which students are taught the skills required of a videogame developer, and then directed into waiting videogame development jobs. As Alison Harvey (2019, 758) has explored, the education-as-pipeline metaphor "evokes a vision whereby if enough force is imposed at one end of the pipeline—be it pumping entrants in or 'priming' students for employability—students will inevitably be propelled toward success . . . it affirms a singular, normative direction for students, graduates, and employees to take."

This is not a situation unique to videogame education, however, and the pipeline to industry has come to be a prominent metaphor for shaping and marketing tertiary education. Where once tertiary education was largely seen to provide a more general level of knowledge and ability that employers could then build on, through the later decades of the twentieth century companies have tried to "break free of their social obligations to employees" and now "prefer to hire workers on a 'plug-in-and-play' . . . basis, rather than having to invest in expensive and intensive training before new recruits can 'add value'" (Brown, Hesketh, and Wiliams 2003, 114; see also Greene 2021, 10). Over the same time, at least in the UK and Australia, university funding has shifted away from reliable public investment and toward a dependence on the individual fees of students (Pietsch 2020, 237). Together, the demands of employers for ready-to-go graduates requiring no further investment or training, and the dependence of universities on attracting the enrollment fees of students who are themselves preoccupied with eventual employment opportunities, leads universities to narrowly focus on markers and metrics of employability or job-readiness, rather than a more holistic approach to the multifaceted reasons one might undertake further education.

Language of pipelines, job-readiness, and employability, turn the multifaceted reasons for undertaking a tertiary education and the diversity of experiences, directions, and pathways through professional lives into a homogenous pool of human capital simply waiting to be pumped into the needs of a specific industry. Focusing on individual students' job-readiness or employability forces students into an individualized competition where one needs to be *more* job-ready and *more* employable than their peers (who receive the same education) by networking, undertaking side projects, or further self-education. Subsequently, the inability to obtain employment following graduation, regardless of whether relevant jobs actually exist, becomes framed as the fault of individual students who failed to identify opportunities to make themselves sufficiently employable (Brown, Hesketh, and Wiliams 2003, 110).

Of course, some disciplines of tertiary education have historically been more vocational than others: few students study accounting, engineering, or veterinary science without intending to commence a career in accounting, engineering, or veterinary science. For the more traditionally open-ended programs of the humanities, arts, and social sciences (HASS), however, where cultural production programs most squarely sit, the pressure to shift toward job-readiness and to direct students toward identifiable employment gaps has been particularly disruptive. Whereas HASS graduates are just as likely to obtain a job as graduates in science, technology, engineering, and maths (STEM) disciplines (British Academy 2020), a supposed lack of prospective career outcomes of an education in HASS has been a long-running stereotype and public anxiety. The open-ended and generalist nature of HASS education fails to fit into the metaphor of the pipeline—of students directed from Degree X to Job X—and so are seen by employability-concerned students and parents as less attractive, and thus by university administrators and neoliberal governments as of less value to the corporate university.

As both prospective students and their parents became increasingly anxious about the need for tertiary education to lead directly to a job, HASS departments began rebranding their degrees in ways that drew attention to the "job-ready attributes" and "transferrable skills" they provided students. One response has been the reshuffling at many institutions of HASS disciplines to fit under a "creative industries" umbrella, which strives to better articulate the innovative value of the humanities and arts to the economy (Cunningham 2014, 10–11). This has allowed a restructuring of tertiary arts and humanities programs away from holistic arts graduates toward job-ready creative industries graduates. As one anecdotal example, my own university, Queensland University of Technology (QUT), abolished its arts faculty in the early 2000s to replace it with Australia's first creative industries faculty. This falls within the university's broader rebranding at the time to be a "university for the real world," a deliberate move to contrast QUT with Brisbane's other major university, the sandstone[5] University of Queensland (UQ). The implication to potential students (and parents) was clear: UQ can offer you the sandstone buildings and scholarly debate and campus lifestyle, but QUT knows what employers want. To this day, each undergraduate subject across the university requires at least one assessment of "authentic learning" that is "based on or related to real-world issues and problems." Of course, the communication and critical thinking skills of the traditional research essay are not considered "real-world" skills here, but rather the skillsets that would be perceived by potential employers as those that would add value to their companies but which they do not want to invest in developing themselves.

This is the context in which formal videogame development education became established as a pipeline through which videogame companies gain access to graduates as a reserve army of gamemaking labor. Just as videogames are a cultural medium native to the era of neoliberalism, the videogame development degree is native to the era of the neoliberal university, along with its emphasis on explicit and direct employability pipelines. But if game development education exists to serve the industry, what happens when that industry no longer exists? In 2016, the Game Developers Association of Australia (GDAA) estimated, through an unclear methodology, that approximately 5,000 students are enrolling in programs at least partly focused on game development skillsets each year, despite the local industry at the time only employing approximately 900 people (*Game On* 2016, 13). The 120 game development programs we identified in our own review is the equivalent of one program for every ten formally employed gamemakers in Australia. Further, as we have seen in the previous chapters, the Australian field primarily consists of small, grassroots teams not looking to substantially grow, and who don't require large intakes of graduates each year the same way a large triple-A studio might. What happens to a talent pool of job-ready graduates when there are vastly more graduates than jobs at the other end of the pipeline? If game development education is first and foremost an employment pipeline, it is drastically oversupplying.

The notion that there are now too many game development students to meet the needs of videogame employers is a common claim of those gamemakers critical of game development programs and suspicious of the profit-led ambitions of the universities that offer them. But whereas one might think it unwise to train to become an accountant, engineer, or veterinarian if there were ten times more accounting, engineering, or veterinary science graduates than jobs, the same is not necessarily true for creative fields such as writing, music, or acting. That is, despite the lack of poets making a living from their poetry, students still perceive some value in undertaking a poetry degree. This raises a much larger unresolved question when it comes to game development education, one that cuts to the heart of this book's central concern: do videogame producers exist in the cultural sphere, alongside dancers, poets, filmmakers, and artists? Or do videogame producers belong in the technological sphere, alongside computer scientists, information technology professionals, and software engineers? No straightforward answer exists for such a question, of course, but it is an epistemological tension that defines the frontier struggles of the videogame field; that underpins how different institutions approach videogame development in terms of pedagogy, course requirements, and graduate attributes; and that ultimately determines whether or not one sees the ratio of game development students to available jobs as a problematic oversupply of an employment pipeline.

The funneling of HASS programs into employability pipelines and job-ready outcomes thus only tells part of the story when it comes to the development of formal education pathways of game development. Also at play here is the ambivalent position videogames have always held between STEM and HASS policy, skills, education, and funding (Cunningham 2014, 34). Of the 120 Australian game development programs we identified, 37 (31 percent) were in a STEM-aligned department and 57 (48 percent) were in a HASS-aligned department, with those in each emphasizing different learning outcomes and potential career paths. Of the rest, 20 (17 percent) were in a games-centric department and 4 had unclear disciplinary homes. Surprisingly, only two programs explicitly framed themselves as collaborations of HASS and STEM departments across the university. While videogames are often advocated as the medium that marries art and technology, in Australian institutions game development programs seem required to make a decision between situating videogame production as *either* art *or* technology, as either a STEM or a HASS faculty takes ownership of a games program and molds it to their existing resources, staff, and programs. While this is almost certainly due to the mundane practicalities of how universities operate, that Australian game development programs are so broadly split between STEM and HASS departments points to the broader ambivalences around what institutions imagine videogame makers to be—cultural producers or software developers—what skills they imagine videogame producers require, and what identities and employment opportunities will be available to them. It speaks to just what dispositions an institution attracts, what positions within the field are presented as available to students, and what sort of position-taking students are encouraged to take.

Calling All Gamers!

At the start of this chapter, I described an open day recruitment poster at my former college that appealed to potential students first and foremost as gamers, not as gamemakers. Such a move was consistent across the public-facing material of Australian programs. Charles Sturt University introduces their Bachelor of Computer Science (Games Programming Specialisation) by explicitly "Calling all gamers!" and claiming to provide said gamers a "chance to turn your passion into a career." As we will see below, this speaks to a general sense of obscurity and mystery around exactly how one might go about acquiring the skills to produce a videogame, and indeed what such skills even are. Instead of focusing on those few prospective students who may have had some amateur experience with videogame production, institutions target the much larger pool of prospective students who are passionate fans of playing games. Playing and making identities and practices become conflated.[6]

Before elaborating on the obscuring of videogame production skills, it's important to first understand that *gamer* is not a synonym for *player*. As has been extensively explored by game studies scholars, the gamer is a particularly hegemonic and gendered videogame playing identity that speaks, primarily, to the young male audience cultivated by the aggressively formalized videogame field since the mid-1980s as a prominent and stable consumer demographic. There is not room here to adequately explore the social construction of the gamer in detail (see Shaw 2014; Kirkpatrick 2015; Chess 2017) but suffice it to say that when an educational institution is "calling all gamers," they are not simply calling anyone who plays videogames but specifically those enthusiasts who "live and breathe" videogames, who have a particular passion for consuming particularly commercial genres of videogames, who have a particularly limited and market-shaped notion of what videogames are and how they are made, and who have a particularly masculinist notion of the central, deterministic role of the player within videogame expression (Keogh 2018, 167–192). A passion for and experience of playing a particular kind of videogame—challenging but surmountable, systemically complex, technologically sophisticated, produced in a commercial context—has long been naturalized as the most authentic mode of videogame consumption, and consequentially is also presented by the public information of most game development programs as a preferred disposition for those who wish to study videogame production.[7]

A hegemonic and masculinist notion of the gamer was both a product and a prerequisite for the field's aggressive formalization, ensuring a predictable and stable consumer base existed for the narrowly commercial titles of this time. Consequentially, gamers notoriously have a limited and selective understanding of videogame production that is highly influenced by marketing lingo and focused on technological jargon (Arsenault 2017; Nicoll 2019) with little comprehension of the scale, required resources, or creative challenges of producing a videogame. For the gamer, videogame production is imagined less as an iterative creative practice always mediated by tools and skills—for lack of a better word, a *craft* (Keogh 2022)—and more as a highly technical and expert use of advanced computer software to bring already-formed ideas to life. Indeed, this limited understanding would seem to be why formal education has become a popular path into videogame production, as it promises not simply to teach the required skills but to reveal just what those skills even are. A Murdoch University program, the Bachelor of Information Technology (Games Technology), addresses this mysticism of game development directly:

> Have you ever wondered how your favourite video games are developed? As a software developer and computer programmer, you'll help turn an idea into a playable video or mobile game. With increasing opportunities in this growing industry, you'll gain the skills needed to work in both the international games industry and the information technology industry.

This program positions itself as not only the sole pathway into videogame production employment but the sole pathway into the competencies, capitals, and skills required to navigate the field. Indeed, employment in the industry and position-taking in the field are presented as the same thing. For the gamers that such material is targeting, as the previous Charles Sturt University program goes on to say explicitly, universities present themselves as "your key to the field of games."

Tellingly, in the above quote from Murdoch University, after the secrets of game development are revealed to students, they will be able to "turn an idea into a playable video or mobile game." Videogame production is thus presented to prospective gamer-students as both secretive but also ultimately straightforwardly learnable. Students I interviewed likewise expected it to work this way. When I asked students why they chose to study game development, they frequently began their response with a statement like "Well, I've been playing videogames my whole life" and went on to speak about their passionate lifelong engagement with videogames as a gamer. However, many students would then reflect that the actual process of videogame production is very different from what they imagined when they started. In Brisbane, 21-year-old Ash Muir was a part-time solo gamemaker who had graduated from a videogame design program two years before our interview. Muir reflected that when he began his studies he "kind of expected what I would expect out of just playing videogames: just raw fun. . . . So what I thought was that videogame development was, uh, I guess the equivalent of livestreaming. There's never a day where you're not playing games, right?" Similarly, 18-year-old second-year student Ethan Tilley reflected that "while playing games the past 12 years" he "didn't think it would be this difficult and this much of a struggle to get something working." Most vividly, 26-year-old third-year student Nicholas Duxbury gave the example of realizing "bullets don't just come out." A gamemaker can't simply place elements into a video-game and expect them to work; they have to design the videogame's techni-cal, visual, audio, and ontological attributes from the ground up in complex ways. This level of complexity shocked Duxbury: "When I was young and first getting into games that's exactly how I thought it worked. You just placed these things together and it makes a game." Muir, Tilley, and Duxbury all gesture toward the notion, much like Murdoch University, that when they commenced their studies, as avid gamers, they thought they would simply unlock the skills that would allow them to translate their ideas into products. But over time they came to realize that the process of videogame production is much more iterative and complex. One does not simply drag-and-drop bul-lets into a videogame; one has to first invent physics.

Teachers similarly struggled with the disconnect between how new stu-dents approached videogame production as straightforward and fun and the realities of how complex, iterative, and resource intensive videogame production actually is. Aaron Williams, a 27-year-old teacher in Brisbane, described how this disconnect led to exaggerated expectations of new stu-dents as to just what sort of videogame they might be able to produce:

> People come on board and they're like "I want to make *Dark Souls*," or "I want to make something like *Super Meat Boy*." "I want to make *Gone Home*." Cool. That was made by people who had a lot of industry experience, who worked within the triple-A sphere, so they knew what went into creating a large-scale project with a lot of people. . . . A lot of students come on board with ambitions of making "*Gone Home* but bigger." And it's like, no, you can make "*Gone Home* but smaller." A lot smaller.

In other words, how gamers understand videogame production to work—as they have largely deduced from gamer culture and the marketing material from publishers rather than from direct observations or experiences of videogame production—is disconnected from how production within the field, through the gradual development of a creative practice, actually functions. As such, when the marketing of videogame production programs focused primarily on attracting gamers, educators found themselves putting extensive effort, especially in the program's earlier classes, into shifting students' relationship to videogames away from that of a consumer position and toward that of a producer position. Or, as one anonymous teacher put it, into helping students "unlearn" their misconceptions of how videogames are made before they can actually begin learning how to make videogames.

To stress, the issue here is not simply what new students don't know but what they mistakenly *think* they know about videogame production and the process of becoming a videogame producer via their position-taking as gamers with "gaming capital" (Consalvo 2007). Educators felt this was particularly pressing in the Australian context, where graduates had very little chance of finding employment in a larger studio that may look more favorably on narrow technical skills over a broad creative portfolio and open-ended mindset. As one Melbourne-based educator put it bluntly, "If you are a more traditional triple-A gamer nerd, you're kind of in trouble in Australia . . . but if you come in with your own weirdo perspective, you can actually do a lot."

Counterintuitively, it is thus the students who have spent the least amount of time and energy participating in a dominant gamer culture that educators typically find the easiest to teach videogame production, as they don't require the same processes of unlearning before they are willing to take the positions in the field actually available to them. At the time of our interview in 2018, Grace Bruxner, 20, was a student in a game design program at a Melbourne university. Bruxner's small experimental games were already receiving critical praise in the videogame press, and she had already gained part-time work at a local studio in quality assurance. Bruxner described herself as previously being "interested in games, but I didn't like playing them" and stressed that she "was never much of a gamer." Instead, Bruxner enrolled in her game design program because, as an artist, she wanted her audience to engage with her work in a different way:

> I found with digital art and 2D art people weren't engaging with my stuff in the way that I wanted them to. . . . But one thing I liked about games is you're sort of forcing people to look at your game for an extended period of time and really engage with it. So maybe that is an ego thing. I just really want people to engage with my work a lot and really look at what I was doing.

Students like Bruxner are the ones with "weirdo perspectives," as the above educator described them. They don't come to their studies with the traditional gamer expectations and are thus better positioned to take advantage of the program as they do not require the same unlearning in order to fully grasp the space of possibles available to them. Often, they have enrolled in a games program in order to enhance a preexisting art practice, like Bruxner, and thus are better equipped to understand the iterative and nonlinear process of striving for legitimacy within a cultural field. But such students also risk marginalization when contrasted with the gaming capital of their peers who are prioritized both in the official literature and industry-inflected marking criteria of their institutions. While Bruxner was ultimately pleased to discover her university had a proactive student selection process that helps ensure the program maintained a gender equity among the student cohort—exceptionally rare for game development programs in Australia—she was nonetheless "apprehensive about it being male dominated" before commencing: "I was prepared to be ignored or disrespected for my opinions on games."

Ultimately, Bruxner succeeded and has since obtained critical acclaim and commercial success with her *Frog Detective* series of games. But as Harvey (2019; 2022) reminds us, the games education pipeline is particularly leaky for women and other minorities with its call to gamers and its focus on the fraternal bravado needed to produce the most commercially feasible genres of videogames. Even if educators think the "non-gamer" students are best positioned to take advantage of a formal videogame production education, when tertiary programs are "calling all gamers," few non-gamers (and, consequentially, few women, few trans folk, few nonwhite folk, few queer folk, and few poor folk) decide to enroll in the first place, and fewer still continue to graduation.

You *Will* Make Games!

How does one become a cultural producer? The simplest answer, for Bourdieu, is by producing cultural products that are recognized by other producers, by critics, and by audiences as the legitimate product of a cultural field. A formal education is one path through which many come to produce cultural products, but a formal qualification is not necessarily required to earn a living as a musician, an artist, or an actor. One can be recognized as a musician, an artist, an actor, or indeed a videogame maker if one develops, over time, a craft that is itself recognized as the craft of a musician, artist, actor, or videogame maker. Such a craft, however, is not simply applying previously gained skills to the production of new artifacts. As Glenn Adamson (2007, 4) notes, "Craft only exists in motion. It is a way of doing things, not a classification of objects, institutions, or people. It is also multiple: an amalgamation of interrelated core principles, which are put into relation with one another." These "interrelated core principles," however, are not simply determined by the individual craftsperson but also by the broader field within which they operate. As Bourdieu (1993, 63) notes, a "long, collective labor" leads "to the progressive invention of the crafts of [the field]." Or, as Karen Patel (2020, 9) similarly notes of what she calls "aesthetic expertise," "embodied cultural capital which, when recognized as legitimate, functions as symbolic capital (honour and prestige) and can be synonymous with an authoritative position in the field." One becomes a cultural producer, then, when one's activities and practices are recognized by others within the field as that of cultural production.[8]

As such, the profession of cultural producer is "one of the least professionalized there are" (Bourdieu 1993, 43). This is a stark contrast to many vocations that have very strict, legal, and commonsensical requirements of formal qualifications: you probably don't want to live in a house built by unqualified builders or undergo surgery with a surgeon who has not been to medical school. As already explored earlier in this book, however, the very notion that videogame production *is* a cultural field remains a contested one due to the ability of formalized, commercial videogame production to define itself as the only space in which a position as a videogame producer can be taken. If the students recruited into game development programs are themselves predominately gamers who perceive the videogame industry *as* the entire videogame field, it makes sense that they would in turn understand the role of videogame maker as one that, like the builder or the surgeon, requires specific qualifications and skills *before* one is able to make games when, in reality, as with musicians and artists and actors, one becomes a videogame maker by making videogames until one is recognized as a legitimate videogame maker.

The assumption that one needed formal training as a videogame maker *before* one could enter the field was clear in how few students I interviewed had experimented (or felt it would be possible to experiment) with making games before enrolling to learn game development—a situation that would surely be odd in most other creative disciplines. Some had experimented with level editors, amateur tools, or with nondigital game design but typically saw these activities as disconnected from the skills they assumed would be required to make legitimate, commercial videogames. Institutions reinforce this sense that formal education alone can reveal the process of making videogames, promising prospective students that as part of their studies they will, actually, make games. University of Canberra's Bachelor of Games and Interactive is the most explicit: "All students that complete the qualification will be given the opportunity to apply their skills and knowledge to the development of creative works. (You *will* make games!)" The parenthetical aside implies that while *other* programs won't actually help you make complete games, in this program you will. We will unlock the secrets of gamemaking for you.

As we saw in the previous section with Muir, Tilley, and Duxbury, students who have a primary relation to videogames as consumers, not producers, enter game development programs under the pretense that they will gain the ability to turn ideas into games once the skills to do so are revealed to them. This is at odds with understanding videogames as a cultural form and their production as a creative, iterative practice. Even in the unlikely situation where a new music student has never before picked up an instrument, one can assume they have a basic understanding that the activity of playing music differs from listening to music. The creative writing student has probably at least tried to write a story or poem, even if they never showed it to anyone.

Educators were commonly frustrated by this situation. They felt that one of their major responsibilities as educators was to help students appreciate what the process of becoming a videogame maker even is to begin with. Williams, the educator quoted in the previous section, pondered how this situation is perpetuated not only by university marketing but by a more general invisibility of the extensive labor, consideration, and iteration that goes into a videogame's production:

> On a film project—I'm looking at my Blu-ray of *Mad Max: Fury Road* right now—we can perceive that it required people to take a shit ton of vehicles out into the desert and crash them. That was really hard, and it took a long time. A lot of work went into that . . . We can grasp an understanding of it [even if we don't understand the filmmaking process]. Whereas when it comes to game development, it's also a shit ton of hard work [but] I think for a lot of students coming on board they don't fully grasp that in its entirety. Because it still comes down to this image of a person sitting in a computer chair looking at a monitor, right? That—in terms of

their understanding of what that image constitutes an activity being—is relaxing. It doesn't communicate hard work. If you [were making a film and you] wanted that shot in the desert you had to head out to the desert and grab that shot. If you want to set your game within a desert, you have to construct all of the necessary assets to effectively communicate that you are in a desert. And that's not just getting a really good painting of a desert and placing a really good character controller inside of there, right? You have to consider how's this going to feel, how can we correctly approximate the feeling of being in this environment? . . . It's fucking hard! It takes a really long time, and I think for a lot of students coming on board it takes a while to sort of develop that understanding of "Oh, I'm not just going to sit at my computer and magic is going to happen. I'm going to need to work hard at this, and it's going to take a long time."

Just as Duxbury came to realize that you can't simply drag-and-drop bullets to create a videogame, and as Muir came to realize the process of making videogames is not the equivalent of playing videogames all day, here Williams outlines a much more pervasive confusion where the intangible, digital nature of videogames obscures even a basic layperson comprehension of the skills, craft, and labor of videogame production.

New students, and the marketing of the institutions that helps to attract them, thus have the process back-to-front. They think they need to learn the skills so that, as Williams puts it, they can sit at their computer and let the magic happen. But in reality they need to begin making videogames—probably bad and derivative ones—in order to begin the long process of getting better at making videogames and slowly developing a legitimate position within the field. Educators thus found themselves spending effort and time getting students to think of themselves as *already* videogame makers before the creation of any one legitimate videogame. Tony Parmenter, 40, teaches at the same Brisbane college as Williams. Parmenter reflects:

What I came to realize, and I say this explicitly to students who I'm teaching, is that I'm not here to get you a job in the games industry. I'm here to help you learn how to make games. I'm here to help you become a game developer. And if I do my job right, by the time you graduate, you will already be [a game developer] because you will already be making games. More than one game. You will already have things to your name. You will already have things that other people have played. You will already have things online. You will already be trying to talk to people and get feedback from them about the things that you made. You may not be getting paid for it yet, but you have the skills and you are doing the thing. And that's worth something.

Teaching game development means teaching students how to take a position in the field of videogame production—or perhaps more so, it means shifting students away from thinking of videogame developer as simply a job one obtains after one gains the necessary qualifications, and instead teaching students just what positions are available to be taken, in the present tense, by producing videogames now. To put it simply (and in words that I would regularly use with my own students), one does not simply learn how to make videogames and *then* make videogames. One makes videogames badly and, in the process, becomes better at making videogames.

Williams explained the challenges of getting students to think of their own practice in this way, in part because of the popular narratives surrounding videogames that emphasize a creator's eventual commercial success and not the extensive noncommercial work that preceded it:

> The thing that always shits me when I hear people talk about *Super Meat Boy* and talk about the significance of *Super Meat Boy* is, like, you're negating the fact that Ed McMillan [one of the developers of *Super Meat Boy*] made 30 to 50 things beforehand that were all made for nothing, released for free, and had very little attention in the beginning. . . . But I don't think we go through those stories, I don't think we look at those small, weird, experimental trash art games that developers start off with. That you *have* to start off with. . . . You start off making these small, weird ideas that go nowhere and do very little but [are] where you identify who you are and what you want to make so that you're prepared to tackle that larger project, so that you can put more stringent restrictions on what your bar of quality is. But you need to do the work. You need to put in the effort to do small things, to throw shit at the wall and see what sticks, before you can reach that point. But I don't think we communicate that as an industry globally. As an industry I don't think we communicate that there is a starting point for this.

Thus, the teachers and the program marketing are themselves in agreement that it is crucial that students actually *will* make games. But where they differ is in the types of videogames that they insist students should be making: the commercial, polished videogames of an industry (an end point), or the small, rough videogames of a novice first entering the field (a starting point). The institutions market game development as a skill that will be revealed. The educators instead present game development as the practice of game developers and see the games that students make during their studies as the first steps toward a position-taking that, over time and with much practice, might become legitimized.

In other words, game development educators are interested, primarily, in *producing videogame producers*, in teaching students how to take a position in the field, or in teaching students "how to teach themselves" as one anonymous educator put it. Educators are priming students to undertake the act of position-taking in the videogame field, to understand that videogame production even *is* a cultural field that requires position-taking, that this is more than simply an industry where one gets a qualification and then subsequently gets a job. As an anonymous educator put it:

> So I think the best students realize they aren't students. They're just out there; they're cool; they have friends, and of course those are the people who get hired because they're already known as dependable. Part of what it means to be successful in this kind of highly networked, contractor, entrepreneurial-whatever-artistic mix is just being a cool person out there.

Game development students are, in this educator's telling, quite unlike software engineering or information technology students who gain a suite of skills, formalized in a qualification, and then get employed to use them. Instead, they are like novice cultural producers who are given some introduction to the skills, networks, ideas, movements, and tastes required to start producing cultural works and who in the future might make better cultural works. Whether or not they get paid to do so is another question.

PWN the Opposition

At the annual Game Developers Conference (GDC) in San Francisco, the two-day Education Summit brings together game development educators to share knowledge about pedagogy, industry partnerships, and career pathways. At the 2019 Education Summit, I presented a talk called "Are Games Art School?: How to Teach Game Development When There Are No Jobs" (Keogh 2019a). The talk was inspired by the debates that regularly play out on Twitter and in videogame production mastheads as to whether or not it is ethical for educational institutions to enroll so many game development students when, in most cities around the world, there simply aren't enough game development jobs for them. The title was an intentional provocation against the general assumption, detailed earlier in this chapter, that game development education should exclusively be about funneling students down a pipeline toward employment. I instead suggested there might be other ways in which a game development education could be valuable. My argument, echoed throughout this chapter, was that we don't (or at least shouldn't) stop offering poetry programs simply because there are no poetry jobs, and we shouldn't stop offering music programs despite the small number of music graduates who will ever become full-time musicians, so why should game development be any different? The crucial difference, I argued, was that poetry and music students typically know, vaguely at least, that they are receiving an education to enter a cultural field with its inverted economics of disavowal and disinterest, whereas game students, as we have already seen, often too straightforwardly believe they are receiving a qualification for a technical job. Most music students surely optimistically hope they will be the lucky one who actually makes it, but a game development student might not comprehend that luck will have anything to do with it at all. "Teaching game development when there are no jobs," I argued, means teaching game development students to be the right *kind* of videogame makers to survive when employment opportunities don't exist: as entrepreneurial cultural producers—or, what amounts to the same thing, as artists.

As it would turn out as I undertook this book's interviews, I was far from the only educator that felt this way. We've already heard from Parmenter, who stresses to his students that "I'm not here to get you a job in the games industry. I'm here to help you learn how to make games. I'm here to help you become a game developer." An anonymous educator was much blunter on the point that it was not their responsibility to get students employed by a videogame company and echoed Robert Yang's comments quoted in chapter 3 that not commodifying gamemaking activity is an acceptable outcome for their students: "If 100 percent of our graduates didn't work in games but either got something out of it or made smallish games for free in their spare time and that was a useful hobby for them, and they become fucking, like, garbage collectors or accountants or whatever I would say mission accomplished." Educators widely insisted that their responsibility was to teach game development, not to get students employed in game development. I suspect most educators in making such claims imagine themselves reacting—much as I was when proposing my GDC talk—to debates in the field among gamemakers that regularly question the ethicality of game development programs and the ability of game development educators.

Such frustrated responses by teachers make even more sense when one considers them to be counternarratives to what their institutions have promised students, particularly in the context of the previous chapters, which have painted a picture of working in the contemporary videogame field as highly precarious. In contrast to the unpredictable nature of finding work in the videogame field, prospective students (and, just as importantly, the parents of prospective students) are reassured by institutional marketing that careers exist on the other side of their studies and that they will be employable for those jobs. Much like policy and trade association reports, Australian educational institutions do this by regularly drawing attention to how much money videogame production generates globally:

> *Angry Birds. Candy Crush. Minecraft. Call of Duty. Grand Theft Auto.* Thanks to each of these, the gaming industry today is worth billions of dollars. . . . This degree will equip you with the skills you'll need for a successful career designing and creating the next wave of popular video games and virtual worlds. (Macquarie University, Bachelor of Game Design and Development)

> The immersive media wave is growing, with virtual, augmented and mixed reality set to explode. Exciting opportunities are emerging everywhere—from marketing, entertainment and digital art, to training and education. And then there's gaming, which now generates over $134 billion annually. (University of Adelaide, Bachelor of Media [Immersive Media])

In these highly typical justifications for why one should undertake a videogame development education, the impressive economic value of global videogame production is boasted while any mention of the disproportionate concentration of this revenue in a small handful of North American, Chinese, and Japanese companies, or of the relative dearth of employment opportunities within Australia, is conveniently ignored.

Institutional framings of game development education obscure the reality students will face after their studies further through a vague focus on the opportunities a student might be able to take advantage of, rather than a more explicit outlining of clear career pathways:

> *Game of Thrones* fans, *Fortnite* addicts and Pixar lovers, turn your passion into a successful career in the exciting world of film, television, gaming, and digital design. . . . you'll acquire the skills, mindset and contacts needed to reach the top of your game in your dream career. (Flinders University, Bachelor of Creative Arts [Visual Effects and Entertainment Design])

Today, having the right skills and evidencing qualifications are insufficient to ensure a graduate is employable. As this university alludes, students don't only need skills but the "mindset and contacts" required for success. As a human resources manager told Philip Brown, Anthony Hesketh, and Sara Wiliams: "Academic qualifications are the first tick in the box and then we move on" (2003, 120). In a time of self-enterprising portfolio careers, a student must be *more employable* than their peers who are obtaining the same education, and so must exit their studies not simply with a qualification but with the right mindset and established professional networks. In the above university's instance, this is promised through formal industry partnerships and contacts, reiterating Daniel Ashton's (2009, 292–293) finding that videogame production students often place more authority in industry representatives than in their academic educators.

Students striving to identify a pathway into the videogame field thus find themselves caught between the overly optimistic but strategically vague framings of videogame production by the institution, and the overtly pessimistic counterbalance provided by their educators. These competing pressures and expectations were felt and internalized by students in a variety of ways. Some were clear-eyed, verging on pessimistic themselves, about the lack of job opportunities, and put this down to the warnings from their teachers. This included Zachariah Chandler, in Melbourne, whom we heard from in the previous chapter:

> I'm pretty sure the first lecture I went to, like the first thing they said to us was "Guess what? None of you are going to get a job ever." And I took that completely at face value. Like, yeah, it's an arts degree. It's probably worse than the graphics design and the programming degrees on their own because they're an art form. No one pays artists. No one cares. . . . I think it's been a repeating motif among the lecturers. I don't think it was just said once. I think it's been hammered in pretty well.

This sense of defeatism in terms of employability carried through into the careers of gamemakers after they graduated. In Melbourne, Alexander Perrin, 26, and his colleague founded their own two-person company after their studies. When I asked Perrin why they took this route, he replied, "Probably because it was half-drilled into us by all the teachers that [getting a job] just wasn't going to happen." In these cases of students hearing and adapting to the warnings of educators who themselves are trying to counterbalance the misrepresentation of employment opportunities presented by their institutions, we can clearly see how, as Harvey (2019, 761–762) details in the UK context, trying to prepare students for reality as a gamemaker can also lead to students internalizing a "labor bravado" that embraces precarity and uncertainty, and makes game development education "a sort of formal-ized school of hard knocks" where little economic return for autonomous creative gamework is naturalized.

The grim realities of how unlikely they are to find employment in the vid-eogame field lead many students to adopt (and many teachers to encourage) an entrepreneurial mindset that, in addition to producing videogames, insists students network within their local community and hustle on side-projects external to their formal assessments—in a way not actually dissimilar from Flinders University's above promise to provide students "the skills, mindset and contacts" required for success. Benjamin Drury, a 23-year-old student in Brisbane, deflected my question asking what sort of position he hoped to be employed in after his graduation. Instead of having concrete goals of specific companies or positions he wished to be hired for, Drury would "rather spend more time working on getting connections. . . . I don't really care who I work with, as long as they're cool people and they're making a cool thing." Bruxner in Melbourne, meanwhile, explained how she had been "consistently hus-tling" throughout her studies "because I went into the course knowing how difficult jobs are."

> I had no expectations of getting a job. . . . I just know it's a difficult industry, and I still feel a lot of students don't. I had a conversation with someone a few months ago, my friend had just lost his job and we were just talking to another student and she's like "Oh, you're going to get a games job?" as if it's just something you can just go and get.

Even as institutions' and educators' framings of videogame production are starkly at odds, both ultimately frame videogame production as an unpredict-able but passion-driven vocation that demands an entrepreneurial position-taking to develop the networks and mindsets required for success—or at the very least for survival.

As Bruxner also suggests, however, many students certainly remained unaware of the difficult situation facing them after their studies. When asked what their plans were after they finished their degree, many were simply pin-ning their hopes on the internship offered in their program's final year to turn into a paid position, or they thought they would find a job at a local indie company to get experience before applying for triple-A positions overseas—a career pathway that is certainly uncommon.[9] Importantly, however, a disin-terest in future employment should not imply such students are necessarily naive. Many students simply didn't want to think about future employment and were instead just embracing student life as its own important period of their life.

Ultimately, and unsurprisingly, many game development graduates aren't employed by existing videogame companies. A 2019 survey of game development graduates by the Higher Education Video Game Alliance (HEVGA) with participants overwhelmingly (89 percent) from the United States found that only 54 percent of respondents were working at videogame companies.[10] But if we can safely assume most graduates are also not making a living off independent work, as the previous chapter would suggest, then where are all the graduates going?

This isn't a question I can definitively answer, but it is worth noting one further strategy educational institutions take to market the employability of their videogame production graduates: highlighting the flexibility and transferability of videogame production skills. While each program is primarily interested in attracting students who, through their passionate consumption, want to obtain employment as videogame makers, they also often tacitly admit how unlikely this actually is. In addition to the excitement and value of videogame production jobs, many of the courses also note the transferrable skills imbued by their program, or the extensive range of economic sectors now looking to take advantage of game design methods and software:

> The games industry is experiencing substantial growth and the ubiquity of games means that there are not only more jobs than ever available in the entertainment games space, but that companies in other fields are looking to skilled games graduates to create digital experiences for their business needs, such as simulation, training, or education. (Murdoch University, Bachelor of Creative Media [Games Art and Design])

> Games developers design, create and produce computer and video games and other graphically based software in a range of industries. . . . This degree also prepares you for work outside of games and digital media to give you broad career options. You can work in health, defence forces, education and automotive, and could join our graduates who are designing everything from simulators to medical imaging. (Federation University Australia, Bachelor of Information Technology [Games Development])

Game development programs advertise a diverse range of potential job outcomes of their programs beyond the videogame industry, such as software developer, technical architect, security architect, UX designer, web designer, mobile app designer/developer, and visual effects artist. In a less grounded but similar vein, program descriptions also draw attention to a general sense of unpredictability in terms of the future—an anxiety many students feel personally—but reframes this as a means of potential, adventure, and opportunity: "You'll graduate with the expertise needed to find work in this flourishing creative industry and, more importantly, the knowledge that you can adapt to whatever the future holds" (University of Canberra, Bachelor of Arts [Digital Media]).

Claims that students will possess "transferable" skills sits squarely alongside the language critiqued earlier in this chapter of job-readiness and employability. As universities become more financially dependent on the career pathways of students, HASS disciplines in particular become pressured to speak about their students' learning outcomes less in terms of general knowledge and more in terms of concrete skills that can be exploited by a potential employer (Bridges 1993). The traditional humanities education, with its organic and multifaceted pathways for students, is usurped by a need to ensure "the practical competence or capability of students" (Bridges 1993, 44). "Transferrable skills" thus becomes a language through which traditional humanities and social science education contexts can speak the language of employability and make a case that the "skills" of the humanities and social sciences (critical thinking, communication, problem solving, and so on) have a value for the broader economy. While an accounting student's accounting skills have clear value for an accounting firm, a poetry student, if they wish to be employed, needs to be able to make a case for some sort of learned skill that is transferrable out of the poetry context. For game development programs, gesturing toward a general transferability of game development skills provides a way to reassure anxious students (and, perhaps even more so, their parents) that one way or another, there will be *some* sort of job available on the other side of the degree—even if the institution can't say exactly what that job might be.

The following chapter will consider those gamemakers who transfer their skills into other sectors in more detail. Here, though, it is worth noting that just how this transferability of skills into other jobs and sectors could be achieved was unclear to current students, and typically wasn't something they had thought much about before I explicitly asked. Students studying more programming-aligned courses (more often those embedded within STEM faculties, such as computer science) had an easier time seeing how they might seek employment beyond the game industry, considering how the programming languages and software environments often overlapped. Students majoring in more specific roles such as animation or audio could also see how the same skills could easily fit in other areas of media production that similarly use the same tools and processes. However, the majority of students in more nebulous "game design" tracks struggled to imagine how game design skills might serve them beyond game development jobs specifically.

Ultimately, between the marketing of the programs, the preexisting expectations and consumerist identities of students, and the attempts of teachers to prepare their students for the realities of survival in a precarious and unpredictable cultural field, student gamemakers are torn between three competing professional identities: *employee*, *entrepreneur*, and *artist*. They strive to become employees by focusing on building the skills perceived to be most desired by imagined employers (in or beyond videogame companies) and by building their job-readiness before entering the pipeline. They strive to become entrepreneurs so as to create their *own* jobs at the other end of that pipeline, complementing their game development skills with business literacies, bolstered portfolios, professional networks, and self-driven mindsets. They strive to become artists who can build a creative identity through the iterative development of a craft and by accruing the necessary cultural and social capital in place of unavailable economic capital. The competing demands, dispositions, and available position-takings of each of these professional identities remain unresolved in videogame development education as a pathway into the videogame field, with different programs placing more or less emphasis on each, but always torn between all three. In each instance, students are effectively told that success is up to them, and that they need to be *more* employable, *more* entrepreneurial, and *more* artistic than their peers—an individualized competitiveness very much in line with my former college's poster that promised students they would "PWN the opposition."

Conclusion

In Melbourne, I interviewed Christian McCrea, a 39-year-old educator who had been involved in the development, delivery, and directing of game development programs at several universities. I asked McCrea about the perception held among gamemakers that educational institutions are exploiting students to profit off enrollment fees while not making students job-ready for videogame production work—never mind the fact that even if they are job-ready, there are too many students for the needs of local companies anyway. McCrea, like many educators, pushed back on this:

> More important than job-readiness is why do the job-ready not go for the job? The Australian games industry would be stronger if they did. We'd be making more money as a country if they did. . . . Why are these very talented people walking away? Sometimes it's a really obvious answer. They hate the culture of game development work. They don't want an unstable work life. . . . Sometimes it's personal but often I think it is systemic. . . . So historically games industry luminaries have said, "Here's a skills problem" and I've always thought, well, you've got a pipeline problem. You've got a flood that hasn't been tapped correctly. You've got skills out here that exist in the world, provable skills, but they're not applying [for jobs]. There's no skill lacking. . . . That skill and talent is being burnt out.

In McCrea's reframing, the problem is not an inability of educational institutions to provide the graduates that videogame companies need, but a failing of videogame companies to produce a culture that adequately welcomes, fosters, and retains the skills of Australia's junior gamemakers. McCrea's redirecting of the problem to the feet of videogame companies themselves is an important reminder of Brown et al.'s (2003, 110) point that evaluating a student's job-readiness is itself a form of victim blaming that demands the student adapts to the demands of employers, rather than asking what it is employers are or are not doing themselves to attract, invest in, and retain graduates.

Christian continued, providing examples of various highly talented graduates he knew who either left videogame production entirely because of the toxicity and precarity of the field's culture, or who were working away quietly on their craft in "hidden nooks and crannies of skill, talent, and ideas" beyond the purview of local companies. The pipeline metaphor of tertiary education, Christian emphasized, needed to be considered more critically and literally:

> What's a pipeline in the real world? A pipeline is a private contract built over public land. It's two companies, privately owned, wrecking public land between them. . . . The university is a private corporation, and the company is a private corporation. What's the thing in the middle being wrecked? What's being driven over the top of? There's a web or pool of skills and talents and interests that's there, that is in the world, but which has no outlet. . . . [There is] a huge web of game development knowledge and skill [in Australia]. There are people who worked on multiple triple-A games who can't find work. There are many many many talented developers in Australia who can't make the rent. Adding more students to them is not

a problem. It doesn't actually hurt. You're making something bigger. But like, again, if you think about it as a pipeline you're only thinking of two ends of a transfer. That's crazy. That's not how value is represented. . . . It's about the field. You just talk about the field rather than the sector.

It was in this interview with McCrea that the seed of this book's focus on the broader field of videogame production first came into focus for me. McCrea's call to step away from the pipeline metaphor, to think of the role of videogame development education more holistically than simply pumping students into the industry, serves as a broader call for us to better articulate, as this book is striving to articulate, the nonlinear pathways into, through, and out of the field of videogame production.

Formal videogame development education programs, with their contesting of employee, entrepreneurial, and artistic student outcomes, exemplify the broader conflicts over the frontiers of the field of videogame production in its current, intensely in/formalized state where a wider range of positions and position-takings are contesting legitimacy than ever before. Formal videogame development education programs reinforce and reproduce the dominant structure of the field by focusing on the employment pipeline first and foremost, and working to primarily attract and legitimize students of a gamer disposition while discouraging and disavowing potential students of other gameplaying dispositions. But, despite this, they are also a site where newcomers can experiment with new positions that challenge the existing structure of the field. The trick, for researchers, educators, and students themselves, is to consider the whole space of possibles presented by the videogame field and the various pathways available for taking a position within it, not just those at either end of the industrialized graduate-employee pipeline.

5 Embedding Gamemaking Skills

In 2019, in the Netherlands, I spoke to an educator teaching in a game development program at a vocational college in Rotterdam. Just like the Australian educators in the previous chapter, this educator was preoccupied with just what sort of graduate identity they were fostering for their students, and what sort of employment opportunities awaited them. Their program, the educator told me, was considering a strategic name change from "bachelor of game development" to "bachelor of Unity development," spotlighting the specific Unity software that graduates would have expertise in rather than the genre of cultural work they would be skilled at producing. This surprised me. I had always personally considered it important to be "software agnostic" in the classroom. If one were to teach students how to become gamemakers, as we have seen in the previous chapter, it was more important, I thought, for students to learn basic principles and learn *how to learn* a new software framework than to learn the specific software that happens to be the standard at the time of their studies.

Yet I saw the logic in this starkly opposite approach. Rather than a narrow expertise in developing videogames, it was hoped this potential name change might increase graduates' employment opportunities in the broader range of sectors that increasingly rely on game engine software such as Unity to produce interactive 3D simulations, such as marketing, education, architecture, manufacturing, and freight logistics. While the students were primarily interested in the creation of videogames for entertainment or cultural purposes, educators at the institution were conscious that for most students, employment would most likely come from deploying their skills in another sector beyond videogame production. As we saw in the previous chapter, this college was hardly alone in this concern: Australian game development programs regularly advertise the "transferability" of game development skills—an implicit admission that obtaining employment to produce original videogames full time is unlikely for many students.

As videogames become increasingly normalized as popular culture (that is, as they become recognizably autonomous as a cultural field), and as the number of videogame enthusiasts gradually begins to outnumber the naysayers, videogames are finding themselves in demand across more sectors of the economy and society for reasons other than entertainment. Where once the supposedly highly persuasive nature of videogames was cause for extreme levels of concern among researchers, the press, and the public, today we're told in countless TED talks, education conferences, and morning news segments that playing videogames can change the world. Whether or not videogames truly are more persuasive or educational than "noninteractive" media is beyond the scope of this book.[1] Nonetheless, it is uncontroversial to note that the excitement and enthusiasm for videogame products, design methodologies, and technologies have risen dramatically over the past decade. Their combination of (supposedly) highly persuasive interactive design and (relatively) easy-to-use tools for producing real-time and responsive 3D environments have made videogames newly attractive as both texts and technologies to a wide range of sectors. Videogame makers are now in high demand beyond the videogame field.

The demand for skilled gamemakers in a range of sectors beyond the cultural industries has grown alongside the number of aspiring gamemakers and graduates seeking alternative ways to sustain themselves through independent gamework. Consequentially, a common trend across my fieldwork sites was small, independent game production studios contracting out their skills to commercial clients. Perhaps they would produce a videogame to be played on displays in a shopping mall to advertise a new food brand, a VR simulation for a logistics company to train new employees in workplace health and safety protocols, or perhaps just a minimally interactive corporate webpage for a local small business. While producing an original videogame for the entertainment market is highly fraught and requires large investments of time and money with no guarantee of any return or recognition in a crowded and unpredictable marketplace, taking on contract work for a client provides specific objectives, a concrete scope, and, typically, a predetermined financial return. If autonomous cultural work requires a (partial) disavowal of economic capital in pursuit of the field's symbolic measures of success, such client work represents the other end of the field: work that requires a (partial) disavowal of symbolic capital in pursuit of economic capital. As one gamemaker we'll hear from below told me, "It's a lot less creatively fulfilling, but it does keep the lights on."

As is a common mantra throughout this book, this situation is hardly unique to the videogame field; producers exist in most if not all cultural fields who use their skills for "noncultural" purposes in other sectors to achieve a reliable income while also—or instead of—undertaking autonomous creative work. A musician may produce their own original music while also undertaking contract work producing commercial jingles. Those same commercials might be directed by film school graduates applying their cinematography knowledge. Illustrators and artists become graphic designers; new media artists design corporate websites; professional copy is written by creative writing graduates. Actors and models appear in TV and print ads while hoping for a breakthrough in their theater and runway work. Cultural workers, and their creative skills, have long been embedded within and providing service to a much wider range of sectors of the economy than the cultural industries narrowly defined.

While a field of cultural production strives for complete autonomy from market forces through its internally consecrated markers of success, demanding an "interest in disinterestedness" (Bourdieu 1993, 40) from its constituents, Bourdieu also reminds us that "there are economic conditions for the indifference to economy." A cultural producer's striving for autonomy always occurs within the context of the broader field of power, never fully detached from the forces of economic and political profit. That is, the heteronomous principles of hierarchization persist as cultural producers find themselves to be still subservient to the field of power even as they strive for autonomy. Very few cultural producers in a field can ever afford to become fully disinterested in economic success, to focus on producing "pure" culture. The autonomous and heteronomous principles of hierarchization are a formative tension in any cultural field—the "art versus commerce" struggle of the individual creator played out on a structural level. Bourdieu goes so far as to say that the cultural field "is at all times the site of a struggle between the two principles of hierarchizations" (1993, 40). If this book is to delimit the frontier of the videogame field, then those videogame makers working beyond the entertainment context, prioritizing the heteronomous principle over the autonomous principle, represent a crucial site of struggle where the very boundary of the field is constituted. Put simply, we cannot adequately explore the cultural field of videogame production as a field striving for autonomy (art for art's sake) without also accounting for those videogame producers driven by heteronomy (making a living from their art skills).

This chapter considers the creative-commercial tensions of these gamemakers who contract out their videogame production skills. While cultural industries research often focuses on how autonomous cultural production differs from other economic sectors (Banks 2007; Oakley and O'Connor 2015; Hesmondhalgh 2018), *creative* industries researchers and policymakers account for heteronomy by investigating the creative workforce and skillsets that exist beyond the cultural industries strictly defined (Hearn et al. 2014; Cunningham 2014; Bridgstock and Cunningham 2016). Such researchers might argue that the situation of extreme precarity outlined in chapter 3 is a selectively pessimistic view of the conditions of *creative* work. It's certainly true with the gamemakers we will hear from in this chapter that those who decided to pursue client-based work typically felt less precarious than those trying to make a living solely from the production of original intellectual property. However, at the same time, client work was not typically the form of videogame product they wanted to be focusing on but simply what they felt they *had* to do in order to get by. Many articulated desires to move away from client-based work in the future once they had saved enough of a "war chest" for an original venture to not be a massive financial risk. In other words, they desired to be driven more by the videogame field's principles of autonomy but were unwilling to make the extreme financial and personal sacrifices that independent developers make to do so. In Bourdieu's terms, they do not possess the economic capital that would allow them to be disinterested in the accruement of economic capital.

The first section situates Australian gamemaking teams working in this space within broader debates in cultural and creative industries research as to just which industries—and just which workers—should be accounted for by researchers and policymakers when evaluating the size and quality of cultural or creative work. If it is true, as Stuart Cunningham (2011, 32) claims, that "there are more creatives working outside the creative industries than inside them," what does this mean for how we articulate and demarcate the videogame field? This section works toward an ultimate understanding of such gamemakers as *embedded within* and providing a *creative service for* other sectors. The second section, then, looks at how the gamemakers who have chosen to work for clients in other sectors articulate the creative sacrifices they have made for financial security. Most see their client work as a stopgap to returning to eventual creative autonomy rather than a long-term solution, and this complicates more positive evaluations of creative service opportunities for cultural workers. Finally, the fact that gamemakers are employed by clients in other sectors suggests that there are (or at least, are perceived to be) particular or unique creative skills associated with videogame production that such gamemakers "transfer" into other fields. The final section of this chapter thus asks just what, exactly, are gamemaking skills, and are they truly as transferrable as the education institutions of the previous chapter claim them to be?

Gamemaking as a Service

In chapter 1, we were introduced to Chaos Theory Games, a small studio in Sydney started by four young friends initially hoping to produce the large-scale blockbuster role-playing videogames they themselves loved to play growing up. It didn't take them long to realize, however, that the scale of videogame they could feasibly produce with their available resources would have to be much smaller and would have much lower chance of a financial return large enough to ensure the company's sustainability. As 24-year-old managing director James Lockrey told me, "It became very obvious to us very early that we weren't going to hit fantastic success and build a stable career out of this reliably." Instead, because they wanted to "actually earn a salary," it was a "natural evolution" to begin using their game development skills "in the capacity that we do now, which is building games for business and working for the education and advertising sectors." The Chaos Theory Games website lists a wide range of previous projects, including a water management simulator produced for a local council, entertainment games produced for private clients, and games and augmented reality apps for marketing campaigns for brands such as M&Ms and the Natural Confectionery Co.[2]

In Melbourne, Opaque Media Group works on a range of high-fidelity simulation and training software for a wide range of military, government, and private clients, predominately for virtual reality (VR) platforms, and predominately made with the Unreal game engine.[3] Also in Melbourne, GOATi Entertainment has been working on a long-term original project, *22nd Century Racing Series*, while also deploying their proprietary game engine technology originally developed for this project, RevGen, through contracts for government and private clients. They also undertake outsourcing work for other game development companies.[4] Bondi Labs, with a team split between Brisbane and Melbourne, produces training and assessment simulations for logistics companies, providing expensive commercial licenses for their "software solutions."[5] In Hobart, Secret Lab—who we will learn more about in the following section—splits their time between specialist technical support of independent videogame studios, open-source tool development, writing software guidebooks, and client contracts.[6]

Each of these teams came to their current work through an initial ambition to pursue autonomous videogame production; each primarily works with videogame development software and deploys videogame design philosophies; many work from within videogame coworking spaces, attend videogame production conferences, and are otherwise involved in their local gamemaking communities. Yet they are selective about when they publicly present themselves as "videogame development" companies to prospective clients. At Bondi Labs, 30-year-old customer solutions manager Josh Hall explained to me that "probably a few years ago we would have [called ourselves] a 'serious games' company, [but] more recently we pulled back a little bit and just say 'software solutions' or 'technology.'" GOATi describes themselves on their website as "a Melbourne-based entertainment company" that specializes in "real-time rendering engine technology, accurately simulated vehicle physics, real-time traffic AI simulation and the building of bespoke vehicle-based projects." Opaque, according to their website, is "a software development and consulting team dedicated to emerging digital technology." At the time of writing, Chaos Theory's website describes the team as a "game and app studio." But according to 24-year-old creative director Nico King, the team is considering removing the word "Games" from their company name entirely since "for the work that we do, it can be a sticking point for some clients." Secret Lab is "an independent games and creative technology studio." While those members of these teams that I spoke to agree that it is their expertise and skills in videogame production that they primarily offer their customers, the work being produced by these companies is just as often not videogames: sometimes it's VR or augmented reality (AR) projects, sometimes it's web design, sometimes it's writing books.

How are these gamemakers positioned within the videogame field? Are they in the videogame field at all? Similar questions are being asked more broadly in debates around how best to count the size and economic contribution of the cultural or creative industries. At the turn of the twenty-first century, while game studies was deadlocked in a debate as to whether or not games were stories, another debate over terminology and disciplinary remits was unfolding in the broader area of cultural production between "cultural industries" and "creative industries" approaches. The battle lines and stakes of this debate have been more comprehensively outlined elsewhere (O'Connor 2009; Turner 2012; Hearn et al. 2014; Oakley and O'Connor 2015; McRobbie 2016; Hesmondhalgh 2018, 175–182; Cunningham and Flew 2019; Mould 2018). Suffice it to say, "cultural industries" speaks to a defined range of industries that "deal primarily with the industrial production and circulation of texts" and which are "most directly involved in the production of social meaning" (Hesmondhalgh 2018, 14–15) and a cultural studies concern for the distributions of power and wealth therein. "Creative industries," meanwhile, tries to measure in economic terms the broader significance and innovations of creative work so as to translate the significance of this work to neoliberal policymakers increasingly disinterested in the intrinsic value of the arts or humanities. In a 2019 reflection on the much-cited initial definition of "creative industries" provided in 1998 by the UK's Department for Culture, Media, and Sport (DCMS)—to which he contributed—John Newbigin (2019, 21) candidly admits, "The term 'creative industries' was as much a branding exercise as an attempted definition; it was a political initiative, aimed at raising the profile of an eclectic jumble of generally IP-based, culturally rooted businesses that governments and banks had conspicuously failed to understand or take seriously as part of the economy." Advocates for a creative industries approach nonetheless argue that tracking creative work instead of cultural industries more accurately represents and measures the experiences and value of the majority of creative workers. As Greg Hearn et al. (2014, 1) argue in the introduction of a collection focused specifically on *Creative Work Beyond the Creative Industries*, "Creative occupations exist across the entire economy. The creative worker's habitus cannot be discovered by looking only in film studios, games companies or artists' garrets." Here, Hearn et al. are insisting that researchers of creative workers must look past the most autonomous and legitimized positions of the field—indeed, look past the field entirely—to account for the much broader range of creative jobs and skills "embedded" (Cunningham 2014) throughout the economic field. This suggests that a cultural industry's focus on the precarity and (self)-exploitation of those striving to build autonomous careers within fields of cultural production is in fact a selective, pessimistic, nonrepresentative, and perhaps even privileged depiction of the experiences of cultural workers, and consequentially overplays the precarity of (largely middle-class) creative workers compared to those of other sectors (Cunningham 2011, 38). Instead, as Cunningham argues, "a great many creatives, we must assume, have managed precarity by working outside the creative industries." Essentially, a cultural industries approach broadly emphasizes the value and difficulty of striving for autonomy within a cultural field, and the threats to and exploitation of this autonomy. Meanwhile, a creative industries approach draws more attention to those cultural producers most driven by the heteronomous principle and the need to make a stable living, and the innovations and contributions they make to a broader range of economic sectors. To truly describe the state of a cultural field's frontier and its formative tensions of autonomy and heteronomy, aspects of each approach are necessary.

In the creative industries approach, the movements and impact of creative workers beyond their own narrowly defined cultural industries become easier to trace. But at the same time, the "imaginative, dynamic, transformative, and glamorous aspects of culture [are] pressed into the service of an innovation machine. Questions of value other than innovation and other economic impacts [are] dropped" (Oakley and O'Connor 2015, 2–3). When people talk about the "creative industries," few are talking about literature or theater. Susan Luckman (2015), for instance, has been critical of creative industries research for not paying adequate attention to arts and crafts and other analogue cultural forms, as a focus on innovation and economic growth sees it instead fixated on the lucrative digital industries of urban centers. Kate Oakley and Justin O'Connor similarly critique the inclusion of "software, computer games, and electronic publishing" (2015, 3; see also Kerr 2017, 6) in early definitions of the creative industries, ensuring a large number of technical roles greatly inflated the employment numbers and economic contribution estimates of the creative sector. Oakley and O'Connor (2015, 5–6) are particularly critical that the shift in focus from "culture" as collective output to "creativity" as individualized input obscures just what skills and identities are being evaluated: "'Creativity' when used outside of the cultural practices to which it has traditionally referred, can be applied to any professional activity that requires situated skills and intelligent judgment."

Similar critiques have been made by Mark Banks (2007), Angela McRobbie (2016), and Olli Mould (2018) as to how "creativity" becomes a catch-all to justify unclear hours, ambiguous responsibilities, and self-driven overwork in an ever-widening range of sectors. Essentially, that creative industries researchers and policymakers have identified a greater number of creative workers beyond the cultural industries than within them might not necessarily mean more *cultural producers* work beyond the cultural industries than within them—it could just mean the category of roles that can be counted as creative has expanded. Yet, while a consequence of the conceptual shift from culture to creativity might be that "lines drawn between a 'creative sector' . . . and other highly skilled sectors can only be arbitrary" (Oakley and O'Connor 2015, 6), creative industries advocates might argue that dismantling such arbitrary lines is entirely the point.

Responding to such critiques, researchers at the Australian Research Council Centre of Excellence for Creative Industries and Innovation developed the creative trident framework (see Table 5.1) to provide a rubric through which to map creative and noncreative occupations to creative and noncreative industries. This distinguishes between specialist creatives employed in creative industries, support workers (noncreatives) employed within creative industries, and creative workers embedded in noncreative industries. While the creative trident doesn't assist necessarily in helping us determine just which jobs or industries are creative or noncreative, it does nonetheless allow a conceptual differentiation between creative occupations (in and out of the creative industries) and creative industries (including both creative and noncreative occupations). Combined, three spikes of the trident provide the total

Table 5.1

The creative trident framework (Higgs, Cunningham, and Pagan 2007)

Category of employees	Employment within creative industries	Employment within other industries	Total employment
Employment in creative occupations	Specialist creatives	Embedded creatives	Total employment in creative occupations
Employment in other occupations	Support workers		
	Total employment in creative industries		Total creative workforce

level of employment in "the creative workforce" (Higgs, Cunningham, and Pagan 2007).

This framework helps us to better situate gamemaking teams like Chaos Theory, Secret Lab, Opaque Media, and Bondi Labs. These teams best fit in the rightmost spike of the trident as workers in a creative occupation embedded in noncreative industries. As such, I primarily refer to these gamemakers as *embedded gamemakers*. However, it's not quite that simple as these gamemakers are typically *not* employed in the industries in which they work so much as they provide services for clients in these industries. Where the companies that employ these gamemakers, such as Chaos Theory or Secret Lab, fit between creative and noncreative industries remains contested. Indeed, at the time of my interviews, several videogame companies and trade associations were trying to popularize the term *applied games* to replace the term *serious games*, to better define their activity not as producing videogames with a serious intent but as *applying* videogame development skills *from* a position in the videogame field *to* noncreative sectors. Nevertheless, as the work these gamemakers do primarily contributes to and is financially supported by noncreative sectors, even if their employment is technically external to those sectors, this model remains useful for thinking of such gamemakers as embedded gamemakers that provide a creative service to a range of industries that are themselves not necessarily creative.

The ongoing tensions and debates between cultural industries and creative industries approaches to examining and analyzing cultural work are particularly useful to help us situate embedded gamemakers within the videogame field. It is insufficient to say embedded gamemakers take a position beyond the boundary of the field, as to claim that they cross the boundary presupposes where the boundary even is and, in doing so, makes assumptions that can only reproduce the field's dominant structure. Instead, we must render the struggle to define the field—the struggle which *is* the field—visible by accounting for how embedded gamemakers navigate the principles of autonomy and heteronomy in their own position-taking within (or without) the videogame field.

Doing What You Love, Strategically

A common trend for embedded gamemakers I spoke to was how they articulated their work in the client space as a compromise that allowed some balance of both heteronomous values (a reliable income, a broader social impact) and autonomous values (creative fulfillment, peer recognition). Secret Lab, in Hobart, is exemplary. Cofounders Paris Buttfield-Addison, 32, and Jonathan Manning, 31 (along with a third cofounder who has since moved on) began Secret Lab in 2008. Manning described the venture as emerging from that "'Hey, cool, let's make videogames' kind of rush of enthusiasm that you get immediately after graduating and all the options are open to you and you have just enough funding to be able to support doing that." After launching a game in the early days of Apple's App Store, the team was contracted by an American start-up to undertake iOS development and software support. As Manning tells it, this was a "much, much better and more lucrative offer" and so "videogames kind of became the second tier to that." Nevertheless, "we'd always seen Secret Lab as a primarily game-focused thing, even when that didn't really necessarily end up being what we made." When the team moved back to Australia around 2011–2012, they strived to return to game development, which, as Manning explains:

> kind of ended up happening in bits and pieces. We worked on little bits and pieces for somebody else's games; we made products that had game-like elements; we made gamification systems for existing products. . . . We never really considered ourselves to be actively in the process of making videogames, we just made software that was games. That kind of felt different in our minds.

Then, in 2015 the team got "an in into the games scene" through a collaboration with American independent development team Infinite Wall to support development of *Night in the Woods*. This work ultimately saw Manning on the main stage of the prestigious Independent Game Festival (IGF) awards in 2018 when *Night in the Woods* won the Seumas McNally Grand Prize.

At the time of our interview in 2018, Secret Lab had funding for original intellectual property through the state funding body Screen Tasmania. They continued to provide support and develop features for other independent gamemakers both in Australia and overseas. They undertook contract programming and consulting for iOS software development. They even wrote technical manuals and ran software developer conferences. Instead of committing all their resources (that is, money and time) to producing enough of an independent project to maybe attract the interest of a publisher or investor, client work is typically more reliable for Secret Lab. It provides a well-defined list of deliverables, a concrete timeline, and a known income. This compensates for the financial unreliability of videogame production and ensures, according to Manning, that Secret Lab is still able to spend at least some of their time undertaking videogame production:

> When you're making a videogame, especially if you're making your own videogame, then the question of whether you're going to be able to make enough money to make another game or to continue operating as a business is much more up in the air. Whereas client work is more reliable. You are told what to do within a certain set of parameters and you can get that done and move on to the next job. And at the same time, you can develop skills. Most of my Unity skills come from doing just random indie jobs or solving certain things. In fact, we made a game for [an airline] which was designed to keep children occupied on long flights and so we did that in Unity and developed skills in that area. And of course, the downside is [client work] is a lot less creatively fulfilling, but it does keep the lights on. So yes, it's almost entirely a financial decision.

For Buttfield-Addison, Secret Lab chose to work in this capacity because they know how precarious videogame production can be: "We're very aware of the way we think the [videogame] industry works, and we apply our interests and skills very strategically to get what we want." But, he stressed, the solution for Secret Lab isn't simply about prioritizing commerce over creativity but rather to be "very strategic about doing what we love." If the team did just want to make a lot of money, then, as qualified software developers, Buttfield-Addison was confident they could each "go over to Google or whatever":

> It's always going to be there if we want it, realistically, just because the skillset we have is so in demand outside of games. . . . We could make actual money if we weren't staying with games, and we know that. It's kind of always in the back of our head, but it doesn't drive us. But it's also kind of like a safety net, or this idea of a safety net, that in the future we can move to that, but it hasn't come up yet.

But money is "not really the primary motivator" for Secret Lab, Buttfield-Addison stressed. Instead, by simultaneously working between consulting, tech, and videogame production Secret Lab strives for a balance of both financial and creative autonomy.

In Melbourne, Alexander Perrin and Joshua Tatangelo, both 26, cofounded the studio 2pt Interactive after graduating university. 2pt worked on a range of "games and interactive digital playthings" according to their website, some independently and some for commercial clients.[7] Whereas Secret Lab was happy with the middle ground between artistic and commercial projects, for 2pt client work was only ever a way of (as Bourdieu would say) accruing the economic capital necessary to become disinterested in accruing economic capital. Perrin explained:

Initially we set out to do client work just so we could actually have some money. We both knew we wanted to [work together] but none of the game projects we really wanted to do for ourselves would be quick enough to put together where we could actually live in the interim. So like we never had enough time to make something that we would want to make so we decided to go the other route and try to get some capital.

As Manning said for Secret Lab, Tatangelo articulated 2pt's client work as a conscious sacrifice in creative autonomy:

When client work aligns with our kind of vision or allows us a chance to forge some of our direction into it, I find that stuff really satisfying. Sometimes client work is quite dry and there's no room for that. It's just people have seen one thing and they want that again and it's not the most satisfying thing. . . . It can very quickly become something we just try to get done. But we're very aware we could be in a far worse situation, so we try not to let that get us down too much if the job isn't 100 percent creatively fulfilling. We just try to take it like, okay, that's rent money and once that's over we'll get back to [our own work]. It's this balancing act but it's kind of nice because it means when we do get time to do our own stuff it feels like more of a luxury. I feel like we appreciate that time a bit more.

In the stories of both Secret Lab and 2pt, embedded gamemakers aren't simply choosing between creative *or* economic pursuits. Rather, in order to find a sustainable way to take a position in the videogame field, they constantly negotiate the demands of autonomy (accruing symbolic capital only recognized by others within the field) with the demands of heteronomy (accruing economic and political capital only recognized by those external to the field).

With some client work, the desire for autonomy would be redirected away from creative fulfillment toward a sense of making a social contribution. While Chaos Theory Games in Sydney also pivoted to client work specifically because of the lack of financial feasibility in purely autonomous creative work, each member of the team insisted their work was still driven primarily by noncommercial motivations such as the ability to work on projects that might lead to social change. Technical director Will Bagley, 24, explained:

It's often hard to see a branding project that's supporting a brand that you don't necessarily agree with and go out there and sort of help them sell their product. We don't go, "Yes, [soft drink brand] managed to up their sale by 5 percent because of our game!" But if we made something and it's like, "Hey, the Great Barrier Reef Foundation made $50 million because people started getting excited about it because of this game that we made for them" then that would be really exciting.

Here, the passion to be creative is shifted to being socially responsible, and this in turn connects to broader rhetorical and strategic moves of the serious games industry to have videogames popularly reimagined as a social good, as opposed to a social ill. While Chaos Theory still made creative sacrifices in order to run a more economically feasible business, they also, like Secret Lab, felt like they were willing to make economic compromises in order to maintain some level of intrinsic fulfillment in their work. The principles of autonomy—the pursuit of noneconomic capital intrinsic to the field—are not entirely absent in their work. Instead, as Buttfield-Addison puts it above, each of these teams of embedded gamemakers is attempting to take a position in the videogame field that allows them to be strategic about doing what they love.

Many embedded gamemakers were emphatic that, one day, they would like to leave client work behind and focus exclusively on original videogame production. The path back to original content is a difficult and intimidating one, however, for the very reasons they began client work in the first place: committing the upfront investment of time and money, with no reassurance of ever breaking even, is difficult to justify. Emre Deniz, the 31-year-old CEO of Opaque Space within the larger Opaque Media Group, was explicit about this tension:

> Three months of dev work for us with the defense sector generally averages [hundreds of thousands of dollars] worth of contracting. That eclipses what a lot of the indie dev teams [in Melbourne] have to work with for even a twelve-month period. . . . Everyone in that row of people [pointing through glass wall] wants to be working on games for a consumer audience but, you know, we don't have the war chest right now to be able to facilitate that.

The metaphor of building up a war chest of savings before venturing forward on the unpredictable and arduous path of developing original intellectual property was a common refrain. It speaks directly to the acute awareness of these gamemakers of the high levels of risk and precarity in independent videogame production as outlined in chapter 3. These companies and individuals would prefer to be creating their "own" games autonomously, but they are unwilling to make the excessive financial sacrifices required to undertake such a venture. Instead, they first want to be in a position where their savings can offset the risks of working on original IP, ensuring everyone still gets paid and the company doesn't collapse.

However, even if an embedded team accrues the funds to commit to original work for a period of time, other complications emerge. Clients are gained through the slow building and retaining of relationships. Committing to an original project requires saying no to potential clients for a time and potentially losing future jobs from that client as well. Buttfield-Addison explains this predicament thus:

> We're hoping to spend some time in the next six months working on our own game. It's really important to us. . . . But things keep coming up which are very valuable or interesting to us so we just keep deferring our own games to do them. . . . We could sit down and spend [tens of thousands of] dollars on finishing this small game of our own, but then the local power company might offer us [hundreds and thousands of] dollars for an educational game for kids. And if we don't pick that, because Tasmania [is a very small state], we might completely burn our bridges as far as any opportunity in that direction in the future. So we go, "Okay, we'll put our game on hold and we'll do this thing for some external company for a reasonable amount of money that will keep us going for another couple of years." It's really hard to juggle that . . . the lowest thing on the rungs is making our own games because it doesn't directly result in money.

Common across these interviews was a sense that while autonomy-driven original work was both desired and preferable, it was a financial and professional risk embedded gamemakers were rarely willing to make. They hoped to undertake it one day, but the war chest never filled up sufficiently to offset the extreme levels of risk and self-exploitation common among the more autonomous gamemakers we heard from in chapter 3. Of all the teams in this chapter, at the time of writing in 2022, 2pt is the only team to have transitioned into full-time original videogame production.

This is a point that is sometimes obfuscated by the creative industries literature's emphasis on communicating the value of creative workers and industries to the broader economy. While Cunningham's (2014, 43) observation that cultural workers often "manage precarity over a career life cycle by moving outside the Creative Industries" is reaffirmed by the experiences and decisions of these gamemakers, there's more to the story. Embedded gamemakers have not simply chosen to leave videogame production for greener economic pastures but are constantly negotiating the art-commerce nexus, trying to figure out how to obtain creative autonomy without giving up economic stability. The political struggle of art and commerce—of autonomy and heteronomy, of economic interest and economic disinterest—that the cultural worker embodies cannot be simply reduced to whether or not the cultural worker has been able to find dependable employment. We must also consider what *sort* of employment the cultural worker is ultimately pursuing. An exaggerated emphasis on how economic capital is gained and circulated obscures the equally important ways in which cultural and social capital are gained and circulated across the field. Indeed, just as Bourdieu (1993, 38) notes that if the heteronomous principle of hierarchization were to reign unchallenged the field would disappear, if any of these embedded gamemakers were to entirely deny principles of autonomy in their work, they themselves would disappear as gamemakers. The point here is not simply that embedded gamemakers still *want* to be doing creative work but that their everyday experiences as embedded creative workers, their business and career decisions, are defined by how they continuously navigate the art-commerce struggle, the principals of autonomy and heteronomy, in ongoing ways. The experiences of embedded gamemakers don't simply provide a solution to the precarity of independent videogame production but rather further demonstrate how all producers within the cultural field of videogame production navigate autonomous, creative disinterest with the economic demands of survival as they strive to take positions recognized, still, as existing within the field at all.

Transferable Game Development Skills?

We have now seen how some gamemakers address the precarity of gamework by deploying their gamemaking skills for means other than the autonomous production of videogames. The accounts of the gamemakers detailed above seem to confirm the promises made by education institutions and trade associations as to the transferability of gamemaking skills and the value they add to the broader economy. But this fact alone brings us no closer to understanding what even *are* the gamemaking skills that gamemakers seemingly transfer from autonomous videogame production within the videogame field outward to other sectors. Does videogame production foster the growth of unique skills that can't be obtained anywhere else but which can then be transferred beyond the field? Or does it foster more generalizable skills that *can* be learned and applied to videogame production but which can also be learned and applied elsewhere? When gamemaking skills are claimed to be transferable, is this advocating for a unique value of videogame production that deserves external support? Or is it simply acknowledging the ability of cultural workers to "make do" between autonomous and heteronomous motivators?

Most straightforwardly, the technical skills of using software environments and coding languages were understood by gamemakers as being particularly transferable. Game engines such as Unity and Unreal are now used for interactive 3D simulation in a wide range of sectors (and, tellingly, no longer refer to themselves as game engines on their websites but as real-time 3D creation tools), yet gamemakers are nevertheless those most trained and experienced in their use. At the same time, game programmers use programming languages such as C#, C++, Java, and Python, all of which are used extensively in software development more generally. Similarly, artists and audio engineers use the same graphic design, modeling, animation, and composition software as those in other sectors. When individual gamemakers were asked about future alternative career paths, just like the students we heard from in the last chapter, those gamemakers in more technical and programming roles were the ones who could most easily imagine jobs they could do beyond gamemaking. For the generalist game designers, however, imagining sectors in which their more nebulous skillsets would be in demand was a much more difficult task.

Perhaps this is because "skills" as a concept does not adequately capture the critical capacities and knowledges more typically associated with cultural production. As we saw in the previous chapter, a language of skills has encroached education and employment discourse since at least the early 1990s, alongside and as part of the broader shift in universities toward graduate employability. Uncertainty over just what skills were being transferred to their clients was common for the embedded gamemakers spoken to throughout this chapter. Embedded gamemakers saw their work as still inherently a creative endeavor, even in its more heteronomous form. They believed gamemaking required periods of ideation and iteration that couldn't be predetermined, and the quality of the final products couldn't be measured in purely quantified metrics. This often clashed with clients' ideas of videogame production as a straightforward and technical process. As Lockrey at Chaos Theory explained:

> We do work for a lot of agencies who I think see us as a primarily technical resource to solve a problem in an amount of time: "You are an expert, and you know how long it's going to take with a little bit of margin for error, and you get

it done by that time" kind of thing. There are some other clients who are maybe a bit more familiar with the creative process and thinking in a more iterative way of not getting it right the first time and that's where I think game design really comes into it: thinking about those problems and solving them creatively. It's sometimes hard to communicate that value and it's especially hard to quantify how long is it going to take to design a good game because when it comes down to client work you really do end up having to present them with a budget and a timeline. . . . Something that's particularly challenging in games to put into a production schedule is how long it's going to take to make this fun, how long is it going to take to make this art style look good and fit? It could end up being way under; it could end up being way over. Usually, it's one or the other.

For some clients, the skills offered by embedded gamemakers are purely technical, such as the American company that saw Secret Lab's iPhone games as evidence of skills in iOS software development. For others, there was something specific about videogame design that was worth paying for. This speaks to a pervasive challenge in the videogame field, one referred to numerous times throughout this book: the tension between videogame production as a cultural enterprise, and videogame production as a technological enterprise.

Ultimately, there was little consistency as to just what specific, discrete skills embedded gamemakers transferred into their clients' sectors. Instead, what was consistent was how they framed their overall capacities differently depending on what a prospective client was looking for. While, as we saw above, many of these studios don't call themselves game development studios, when talking to potential clients they make strategic choices as to whether or not to present their services as inflected by game development skills, experiences, or knowledge. As Deniz explained when I asked how Opaque Media presents themselves to prospective clients:

> I specifically use [game development] as a point of differentiation. . . . We say we employ game design because we want them to see us as game developers that are doing very valuable and interesting things that they're interested in specifically. So, when their outcomes align with us, presenting ourselves as game developers tends to breed a new perception of how they view game development and how it can benefit their organizations or agencies. . . . We don't shy away from being game devs.

For Bondi Labs, however, Hall explains that the decision to present themselves as a game development company or not is made on a case-by-case basis, informing decisions such as where they first meet with a potential client. Bondi Labs are based in The Arcade, Melbourne's videogame production coworking space. For a "certain level of customers or clients or executives," Bondi Labs will organize formal business meeting room space in the CBD, in spaces available through the Victorian government. But for other clients:

> Like if I'm talking to learning development coordinators, they actually love coming to places like [The Arcade]. Because this is where all the cool shit happens, right? They come and play games and it just blows their mind, really. So depending on who it is, we'll pick and choose how we craft that day.

Essentially, whether embedded gamemakers frame their skills *as* gamemaking skills (as opposed to technical skills or creative skills or something else) comes down to their perception of just what sort of skills the client is after. As Hall says, "We try and manage conversation so that we don't start with games, but if we feel it's appropriate we'll definitely use the game angle, it does add a lot of value."

Critiquing the increasing push toward transferrable skills framings of education in the 1990s, David Bridges (1993, 51) suggests that what are called transferable skills (or core skills, or key skills) are less "an atomistic list of competencies" and instead "look more like the kind of competence, capability, or ability which lies at the heart of the sensitive, responsive, and adaptable exercise of professionalism in any sphere." Similarly, albeit more bluntly Len Holmes (1998) argues that transferable skills simply don't exist. When educators talk about developing transferable skills in graduates, Holmes argues, they are in fact talking about developing in the student a particular graduate identity that allows one to negotiate the "outcome of the individual's claim on the right to the desired social position and the evaluations made by the gatekeepers to such a position." That is, to articulate oneself as having transferable skills is to take a position on the field's frontier that is legible to those external to the field as a position that is internal to the field. Transferable skills, Holmes claims, are thus nothing more than a skill of "early-impression-making": less a concrete transferring of skills from one context to another, and more the ability to convince a potential employer (or client) that one's previous experiences provide relevant competencies. Gamemakers, when selling their services beyond the videogame field, present their skills as transferred from gamemaking only when it would be advantageous to do so. Just as for humanities and social science (HASS) education programs and graduates, for these gamemakers transferability itself becomes a selling point that selectively communicates to clients the creative and critical capacities required for (but perhaps not unique to) gamemaking.

The questions of what game development skills are, how transferable they are, and the value they add to the broader economy are ultimately the wrong questions. Skills are not simply transferred from videogames to other fields. Instead, embedded gamemakers strategically, selectively, and contextually present their skills, knowledge, and competencies as either having arisen from the field of videogame production or not when it is attractive to clients to do so. Some gamemakers, some students, some educators take *a position of transferability*, with one foot in an autonomous field of production being recognized by their more-autonomous peers, and one foot external to the field, recognizable as having value to external clients in the broader field of power. The very language of skill transferability speaks to what practices are legitimized as within the field, and what practices are illegitimized as without it.

Conclusion

By this stage of the book, it is hopefully clear that the provocation that the videogame industry doesn't exist isn't simply about replacing the word *industry* with *field* in a semantic shift that resolves or reveals nothing. The videogame field instead exposes a larger, more complex picture of numerous, diffuse sites of videogame production that are obscured when we only consider those positions that fit neatly within "the videogame industry": the numerous positions taken by videogame producers, informed by the perpetual tensions between autonomy (art for art's sake) and heteronomy (economic survival). Embedded gamemakers' refusal (or inability) to be disinterested in economic interests highlights the contested borders of the videogame field, where its autonomous values and modes of production blur with the broader field of class relations driven by the hegemony of economics and politics.

Ultimately this chapter and the previous one have been concerned with where lines are drawn around the field, or perhaps more accurately the act of line-drawing itself. By considering how embedded gamemakers take liminal positions in the videogame field, we can complicate existing creative industries literature that, in trying to communicate the economic value of cultural production, too easily reduces cultural production to its economic values. Whereas a creative industries approach might note how embedded gamemakers have successfully found ways in which to survive financially beyond the risks and precarity associated with the production of original IP, this doesn't account for the broader entanglement and negotiation of cultural, social, and economic values at play for both individual gamemakers and entire companies. Embedded gamemakers are rarely driven by purely commercial means, and few see client work as a long-term business model, even when it ends up being so. Embedding, it seems, is precarious in its own ways, with short-term contracts and perpetually looking for the next client always trumping any ability to make long-term plans. At the same time, embedded gamemakers complicate cultural industries literature that insists on the unique, special nature of cultural production in its limited autonomy from the economic field. Hearn et al. (2014, 1) are indeed right that "The creative worker's habitus cannot be discovered by looking only in film studios, games companies or artists' garrets." If, to understand fields of cultural production, we only focus on those producers that have successfully taken the most autonomous positions, we fail to account for the always-present heteronomous principles of hierarchization that provide a counterweight, always pulling the field in the opposite direction.

In this chapter, I have focused solely on independent videogame studios supported, at least in part, by working for clients beyond the videogame field. This has allowed me to critique the rhetoric of skill transferability as less a straightforward or linear transferal of specific skills from one sector to another and more holistically as the open-ended ways in which all gamemakers navigate the competing demands for autonomy and heteronomy as their own disposition demands. Skill transferability, as we can see through how embedded gamemakers position themselves differently when talking to different prospective clients, doesn't describe a process so much as demonstrate how the videogame field has successfully obtained such a level of autonomy that those outside it perceive it as a location from which value can be obtained. This, in turn, produces opportunities for gamemakers to translate the symbolic capital they have accrued within the field to economic capital beyond the field.

Embedded gamemakers are not the only gamemakers navigating such complexities. Samantha Schaffer in Adelaide and others I have not quoted directly undertook hobbyist videogame production in their own time, while working in (or striving to work in) day jobs that were not videogame production but which used the same skills and software, such as web design, computer programming, or architecture. Overseas, I encountered independent studios in Utrecht and Berlin, cities that similarly house only a small number of larger videogame studios, that also undertake client work like those Australian groups detailed above. In Seattle and Montreal, where larger studios are much more prevalent, independent teams still often balanced their time between independent and client work, but the client work was in these instances more likely to be provided by larger commercial video-game studios in the same city looking to outsource specific aspects of the production process. Few were able to talk about such arrangements openly, considering the strictly secretive nature of triple-A videogame production. Ultimately, embedded gamemakers are not a unique outlier in the videogame field but are exemplary of the struggles and position-taking of all gamemakers between autonomy and heteronomy; through their heteronomous work, they reinforce and elucidate the autonomous aspects of the field of videogame production. There is no autonomy of the field without heteronomy, and there is no heteronomy without a counterbalance of autonomy. It's the irresolvable struggle between them that delimits the field.

6   Scenes and Communities

In Melbourne, I met 29-year-old art director and freelance artist Marigold Bartlett in a downtown café, a couple of blocks from the small, single-room office her independent team had rented within a small coworking space. The group Bartlett was working with was Ghost Pattern, developers of *Wayward Strand*, whose cofounder Jason Bakker we heard from in chapter 3. Bartlett is responsible for the game's iconic, hand-drawn style. Beyond Ghost Pattern, Bartlett is highly active in the Melbourne gamemaking community, working on several parallel projects and contributing to numerous groups such as the Freeplay Independent Games Festival. However, when we talked, she expressed a frustration and exhaustion at all the "social stuff" associated with the hustle of her work:

> You have to be the best one; you have to be the one that people want to hire; you have to be the one that people think of when they need an artist. And as that market, as the industry, is expanding and flooding out—which is wonderful in so many ways because I'm all for everyone having opportunities—it's making it increasingly difficult to not have to consider all sorts of shit that isn't my work, or that I didn't think would be my work. The hustle. The Twitter presence and personality management. Like where you are at the right time. Who you're hanging out with. Who likes you and doesn't like you. It's terrible.

For Bartlett, the blurring of personal relationships and friendships with the more "hard-nosed networking" (McRobbie 2002, 520) required for finding short-term work in the precarious indie ecosystem makes the local video-game field in Melbourne sometimes feel "toxic" despite its vibrancy: "I love my friends, you know, and I'm open to new people, but you can smell it a mile away when someone . . . has an alternative motive."

While conducting my interviews in Melbourne, and through my own personal experience with the local field, I was conscious of a vague sense among local gamemakers that there were two different sides of videogame production in the city. Remembering from chapters 2 and 3 that "indie" fails to meaningfully distinguish between different modes of videogame production in the field's intensely in/formalized context, these different sides might instead reductively get gestured at as the "arty" and "commercial" sides of Melbourne videogame production. I wanted to know which side of Melbourne's videogame field Bartlett associated with these people whose alternative motives instrumentalized friendships. Was it a problem with the "industry" side of Melbourne or was it (and here I paused briefly to try to think of the best words to capture the sites of production I wanted to gesture toward) the "broader scene"?

Bartlett did not give a straightforward answer to the question but instead took issue with the question's very formulation. To introduce the central problematic of this chapter, Bartlett's articulation of how the structure of local videogame production is much more complicated than a straightforward binary of commercial gamemakers on the one hand and artistic gamemakers on the other is worth quoting at length:

> I've found that before the industry and the scene—I don't like using that word, scene, but it's convenient—decided to be friends, the arts people were really happy hanging out making cool shit, talking about cool shit, pushing really hard for gender diversity. We were all around Melbourne doing our thing and having a good time. And then only in the last year or so the industry has sort of opened up to us, and I think the scene has kind of opened up to the industry. Places like Bar SK [game bar and media art gallery] opening up, people having drinks together; me getting jobs at The Arcade [coworking space]; me getting jobs at established companies rather than for mates who were trying to make something cool and little. . . . The wants of that scene were to make good art and to make stuff that was very ethically considerate, inclusive, genre-defining, medium-pushing shit. When that stuff started to become commercially viable, which it has in the last two years, we found people with money and people with studios coming and saying, "Oh shit, this is cool. This has an audience. This is hip. We want to make this stuff. We're going to hire you, you, not you, not you, you, you, not you, and you." [They broke up] that scene with their money and their opportunities. I feel like that's when it's become political, and that's when it's become ugly, and that's when it's become really difficult to enjoy it. When it wasn't surrounded by money but we were all still able to get by, it was a delight.

What Bartlett describes here is not simply two distinct videogame production communities that each exist in Melbourne but instead how the two ends of the field—what Bourdieu might call the subfield of restricted production and the subfield of mass production—have come to be defined in relation to the other. The commercial and the noncommercial, art-for-art's-sake and the art-for-a-consumer—positions which Bartlett saw as previously having been quite discrete even within the same geographical site of Melbourne—now overlapped considerably as aesthetics and tastes previously seen as fringe were now seen, by commercial studios and publishers as well as government funding agencies, as sites of potential value generation. Within an increasingly autonomous field of videogame production, differently positioned videogame makers now vie for the same forms of capital, and each is anxious that the other's growing legitimacy might delegitimize their own position-taking.

Melbourne's field of videogame production has its own dynamics, which we'll hear more about below, but similar local tensions were articulated by gamemakers in every city I visited. In the South Australian capital of Adelaide, a long-running grassroots collective of hobbyists and artists expressed feeling either sidelined by or wanting to distinguish themselves from a rapidly growing local cluster of companies that primarily developed commercial mobile games for children. In Montreal, home to 10,000 employed videogame makers and some of the largest commercial studios in the world, smaller teams and individuals expressed frustration at an inability to make local governments enthusiastic about independent work, as the government was instead focused on the large employment and revenue generators of the city's massive, foreign-owned studios. In Utrecht, the once-fringe Dutch Game Garden coworking space and incubator was now seen by an emerging, younger generation of independent gamemakers as itself the commercially focused institutional core of the Dutch videogame industry, and alternative sites and collectives were beginning to position themselves as explicitly *not* the Dutch Game Garden. My single Singaporean participant describes their local field as consisting of "a few camps" that they distinguish as the "established companies" and the "hustlers."

A field of cultural production is, fundamentally, the perpetual struggle to determine which positions taken by producers are legitimately within the field. Or, more accurately, it is the perpetual struggle to determine the field itself in such a way that one's own position is considered legitimately within it, and in such a way that one's own accrued symbolic capital is recognized as legitimate, exchangeable tender within the field, and as exchangeable for economic capital beyond the field's borders. A field is temporal, as relationships and struggles and markers of success shift over time, but it is also spatial, and one's disposition within the broader field of class relations influences, in part, just what positions within a local field of cultural production one is more likely to inhabit, just which processes of position-taking are more or less attractive, or indeed feasible. Numerous factors determine not just who is able to be involved in a local field of cultural production, but *how* they are able to be involved: proximity of employment opportunities (of both quantity and type), access to education, modes of government support, the cost of living, social welfare, nightlife, public infrastructure such as transport and Internet. To trace the contours of the videogame field is to place videogame production in its local geographic and socioeconomic contexts. Just as importantly, and the point of this chapter, is to also treat these local contexts as having the same complexity, the same struggles and variety of positions, the same dynamism, as the global videogame field.

The importance of the local context has been an underlying theme throughout this book, and it is one of growing interest in videogame production and history research more broadly (e.g., Joseph 2013; Chung 2016; Kerr 2017; Švelch 2018; Jiang and Fung 2019; Swalwell 2021). There is no singular global experience of being a videogame maker; there is only a constellation of interrelated local videogame production contexts. Despite the high concentration of revenue in a small number of North American, western European, and East Asian companies, it's inaccurate to say a single global videogame industry reaches out from its few dominant sites and spreads across the world. Rather, videogame production emerges, haphazardly, in different shapes and sizes from different locales around the world, and these local sites of production themselves intersect and relate, asymmetrically, to form a complex network or tapestry which is too-simply referred to as a singular global games industry. Crucially, the same top-down, economy-first simplification risks being played out at the local scale where competing, contradictory, complex local understandings and formations of videogame production culture themselves intersect and relate asymmetrically—taking different positions in the ongoing struggle to determine, to *be*, the field of videogame production. Local videogame production anywhere in the world is no more homogenous than global videogame production.

To complicate and pluralize the local, I find the notion of scenes as it has been developed by popular music theorists particularly valuable. While I introduced the word in my interview with Bartlett, other interviewees throughout my fieldwork sites regularly used scene themselves to designate, as Will Straw (2004, 412) says, "particular clusters of social and cultural activity without specifying the nature of the boundaries which circumscribe them." Gamemakers spoke of scenes affiliated with geographic locations (the Australian scene, the Melbourne scene, the Montreal scene); affiliated with particular companies, groups, or coworking spaces (The Arcade scene, the Sokpop scene); affiliated with particular software tools (the Unity scene, the Bitsy scene, the Twine scene); affiliated with particular identities or movements (the queer scene, the indie scene, the hobbyist scene); or the entire videogame field as a whole (the games scene). While the word *scene* was used inconsistently (and, when it was used, often with a reluctance and discomfort, as if it was perhaps pretentious even as it felt the most fitting), it productively speaks to fractured, heterogenous, but nonetheless intricately connected sites of localized videogame production in ways that feel less homogenizing than alternative terms such as industry, community, or perhaps even field.

In this chapter, I want to unpack the tensions of videogame production in its local contexts by considering how multiple local scenes overlap and compete to produce local fields. My goal here is less to exhaustively detail the sociopolitical, historical, or geographic situation of any one city but instead to further dehomogenize how we think about videogame production and draw attention to how videogame fields are always sites of struggle between differently positioned producers, quite literally, in the competition for space, employees and collaborators, recognition, investment, funding, attention, awards, and festival speaking slots.

The first section considers how to situate videogame production between global and local frames of reference. While a top-down consideration of the global provides important insights into the extraction and concentration of capital by the field's dominant sites, a bottom-up consideration of the local articulates the complexity of those sites from which this capital is extracted. The next section provides case studies of two Australian cities, Melbourne and Adelaide, to highlight the different tensions inherent within each and to trace a preliminary picture of how a field is constituted locally and constituted by localities. Through a lens of scene theory, adapted from popular music studies, we will see unique conditions and challenges that influence the positions taken by gamemakers in each locale, but also common struggles between gamemakers differently concerned with autonomy and heteronomy as they work to ensure the field is understood in such a way that their own position is legitimized as existing within it.

The final section considers another complicating factor for comprehending the local: the dominance of social media networks for gamemakers' understanding of the field. For many gamemakers, the peers they most
commonly communicate and collaborate with do not necessarily share the
same local geographic space. This does not demand a return to global frames
of reference, however, but instead to *trans*-local considerations of how different local fields and positions intersect and overlap.

Videogame Production between the Global and Local

Studies of media industries and cultural production are always split between
global and local lenses. On the one hand, the intensity of globalization, the
internationally dispersed labor forces of massive media conglomerates, and
the pervasive cultural imperialism of Western stories and genres across the
world all demand a global scrutiny of asymmetrical power relations between
distributed workforces and audiences, and centralized distributors, investors, and platforms (Jin 2015; Curtin and Sanson 2016; Nieborg, Young, and
Joseph 2020). On the other hand, local cultures, traditions, histories, geographies, stories, and styles have long been shown by cultural studies researchers to mediate, remix, co-opt, and influence the products of global media
industries in complex and nonlinear ways (Appadurai 1996; Darling-Wolf
2015). To consider the local is to consider, as Arjun Appadurai (1996, 178) says,
"the relational and the contextual." Locality is "a complex phenomenological
quality constituted by a series of links between the sense of social imme-
diacy, the technologies of interactivity, and the relativity of contexts [that
expresses itself] in certain kinds of agency, sociality, and reproducibility".

To complicate things further, a sense of the global itself has become quo-
tidian in localized ways through our mundane "interaction with globalized
cultural forms" (Darling-Wolf 2015, 143). Now, terms like *translocal* (Ma
2002; Bennett and Peterson 2004) and *glocal* (Robertson 1995; Tay 2009)
highlight how media texts, their creators, and their audiences interact in
complex hybrid ways between local and global conditions, never easily
reduced to one or the other. Ultimately, albeit crudely, a global focus tells
us more about the flows, extractions, impositions, and concentrations of
capital by the most powerful conglomerations in a media industry, while
a local focus tells us more about the formation and negotiation of the cultures of production and consumption from which this capital is extracted.

Local videogame production is shaped, in part, by global factors: the power and regulations of specific digital platforms, the uneven concentration of potential investors, the locations of large studios, the distribution or concentration of crucial consumer markets. David Nieborg, Christopher Young, and Daniel Joseph (2020), for instance, extensively analyzed financial data from Canada's iPhone App Store to demonstrate the difficulty Canadian-made or Canadian-owned mobile games face when competing with those produced by incumbent, primarily American studios. Their findings suggest a general ineffectiveness of Canadian cultural policy in preventing US-owned digital platforms from increasing "the unidirectional flow of global capital" (2020, 9). Elsewhere, Dal Yong Jin develops the fruitful concept of "platform imperialism" to articulate how digital platforms—overwhelmingly owned by US companies—both expand and concentrate value extraction from global labor and reinforce imperialist dominance. Jin (2015, 39) goes so far as to say that "The U.S., which had previously controlled non-Western countries with its military power, capital, and later cultural products, now dominates the world with platforms." The reliance of videogame developers around the world on the platforms of Valve, Apple, Google, Microsoft, and Epic reinforces this point. Local videogame fields are constituted, in part, by companies that are globally distributed but with roots firmly grounded in (and with revenue overwhelmingly flowing back to) North America, western Europe, or East Asia.

When we talk of global actors in the cultural industries, often we are referring to those most powerful "large corporations operating transnationally but incorporated in the most powerful nations" (Darling-Wolf 2015, 143–144). While the videogame field has historically been considered a quintessentially global media industry due to the dominance of a small handful of multinational companies, the concentration of these companies in North America and Japan (and, more recently, in western Europe and China) risks analysis concerned primary with the political economy of videogame production focusing on the extractive power of the most powerful at the obfuscation of the multitude of gamemakers around the world these powerful companies extract their capital from. Such analyses are crucial for understanding the dominance and strategies of these companies. However, as Aphra Kerr's (2017, 30) detailed analysis of global videogame production makes clear, when one takes a truly global look to see what gamemaking cultures look like in different places, videogame production becomes defined by its variability rather than its uniformity, and thus "the industry and culture of digital games" must be placed "firmly within local and regional economies and societies."

Empirical studies with local videogame-making communities have already shown how the videogame field emerges *from* the multitude of local videogame-making cultures that exist in specific regions, countries, cities, towns, and neighborhoods. For instance, Daniel Joseph, in a foundational 2013 article, looks at how the Toronto indie community, much like those in Australian cities, developed in specific ways due to—and in spite of—the absence of the large foreign-owned companies present in other Canadian cities like Vancouver and Montreal. Through the lens of assemblage theory, Joseph (2013, 95) articulates how indie games are "enmeshed and entangled with a variety of objects at different scales—from the flows and pressures of the global videogames industry all the way down to the affective relationship between an artist and their artwork." Joseph (103) traces the indie darling *Sword & Sworcery EP* through its creators' relationships within Toronto's indie games and music scenes, demonstrating how "this is a game created outside of the major production houses, but still just as much a part of the global marketplace" whose makeup is "intertwined with the motives and reasons" of its creators. Joseph (101–102) argues that Toronto indie developers are not so much independent as they are interdependent: "tied up, entangled with the urban geography of Toronto itself. . . . There is no 'independent' community here without a city-sized assemblage capable of fostering close ties between organizations and persons."

Elsewhere, Kristine Jørgensen, Ulf Sandqvist, and Olli Sotamaa (2017, 459) take an oral history approach to look at how Nordic videogame production cultures have long been shaped by "both geographic features and socio-economic context[s]," such as how Swedish videogame production's emergence from a vibrant 1990s demoscene directly influences the focus of contemporary Swedish studios on PC development, and how Finland's current strength in mobile development aligns with the previous dominance of Finnish mobile company Nokia. In these cases, formalized national videogame industries emerged almost by accident from the collaborations of gamemakers for whom, at first, "creating games with their friends was a lifestyle. They just happened to get paid for doing their hobby" (466). Jørgensen et al.'s specific case studies and oral history approach well evidence the claim they make at the start of their article that similarly motivates this book: "The major industries [of the United States and Japan] supported by large home markets provide a very particular and somewhat limited perspective on the origins of the global game industry" (458). Local videogame production communities do not simply exist beyond formalized videogame companies but are the broader field of creative, affective, and social activity through which formal videogame production sometimes emerges to be understood *as* a videogame industry.

It is, however, not videogame production researchers but videogame historians who have most extensively examined local production cultures in ways that convincingly challenge top-down and homogenous presumptions as to where and through whose activity the global videogame field emerges. Videogame historians have long challenged the dominant marketing and fan narratives that tend to focus on a small number of American (Atari, Activision, Microsoft) and Japanese (Nintendo, Sega, Sony) companies, exposing a much wider range of moments of "difference and discontinuity in videogame history" (Nicoll 2019, 13). Examples include Jaroslav Švelch's (2018) account of how Czechoslovak hobbyist gamemakers in the 1980s built a grassroots informal industry in the shadow of the Soviet Union; Melanie Swalwell and Michael Davidson's (2016) account of how New Zealand videogame producers in the 1980s navigated local identity and global imitation through the case study of *Malzak*; Laine Nooney's (2020) examination of the uncredited professional women involved in the operation and success of Sierra Online in Simi Valley, California; and Benjamin Nicoll's (2019) account of the early days of South Korea's videogame field (today one of the largest and most lucrative national game industries in the world) as that of deliberate, opportunistic, and patriotic poaching of Japanese technology and intellectual property (IP). In each of these case studies, happenstance, local culture, regulation and funding policies, and both state and personal relationships and antagonisms all influence the structure of local videogame fields no less so than the actions of global companies and platforms. Across these accounts documented by videogame historians, we see how videogame production always emerges from somewhere. A field of videogame production doesn't just appear in a local community due to imposed global factors. It also, as these historical accounts show, *emerges from* formative local conditions, communities, and conflicts.

Two Tales of Two Scenes

The concept of scenes provides one way to account for this plurality of local cultures. While different communities or networks of people participating in a cultural activity are commonly referred to loosely as a scene, the term remains notoriously difficult to pin down for both those within a scene as well as for academics researching them. Scenes have primarily been theorized through sociological research of music subcultures. For Will Straw (1991, 373), a music scene "is that cultural space in which a range of musical practices coexist, interacting with each other within a variety of processes of differentiation, and according to widely varying trajectories of change and cross-fertilization." For Holly Kruse (2010, 625), scenes describe "both the geographical sites of local music practice and the economic and social networks in which participants are involved." But scenes are also always in flux, never stable, deriving "their effervescence from the sense that the 'information' produced within them is forever in excess of the productive ends to which it might be put" (Straw 2004, 412). Further, and perhaps most crucially for our current consideration of the videogame field, Straw (2004, 412) suggests that a scene emerges "from the excesses of sociability that surround the pursuit of interests, or which fuel ongoing innovation and experimentation within the cultural life of cities." Straw provides a number of examples where cultural scenes—such as the Montreal disco scene of the 1970s or the Beat Generation of poets after World War II— emerged in part as an overproduction of culture unable to be fully captured by the commodifying forces of formal cultural industries. Instead, the work of these scenes is mobilized as other forms of capital (social, cultural) that solidify into shared stylistic traits of locally specific scenes.

Considering a scene as "overproductive"—as extending beyond the commercial activity of formalized companies to pervade social spaces and draw new actors and aesthetics into its jurisdiction—goes some way toward explaining why those cities with a history of cultural production but with relatively few formal videogame production employment opportunities are also those cities whose videogame activity is most readily referred to as a scene (such as Berlin, Austin, New York, Toronto, Melbourne). As the barriers of entry to both videogame production and distribution have lowered over the past decade, there is in one sense in cities such as these an overproduction of videogame-making activity insofar as the number of people able and eager to create videogames has outgrown the needs of local employers and instead manifests as informal networks and communities of practice: shared spaces, friend groups, meetups, festivals, parties, resource sharing, game jams. Such a framing, however, risks centering formal videogame production companies as the core that all other gamemaking activity is oriented toward; it potentially implies these scenes are the leftovers of a global videogame industry after that industry has taken its fill. Rather than overproductive, then, scenes are perhaps better thought of as underindustrialized. In either formulation, they consist of a much broader range of actors and events than the small fraction that is more directly assimilated into the flow of economic capital. In the latter formulation, however, the broader range of actors and events is understood as coming before the industry, not as a result of the industry's presence. Local game scenes are not what is left over by a sated global game industry in a top-down sense. They are the broader field of informal creative, affective, and social activity that a local formalized industry sometimes emerges *from*. To consider local videogame communities as scenes is to capture the broader, often contradictory, social, affective, political, and cultural reasons that people produce videogames.

Few have applied the theoretical lens of scenes to local videogame production, with Christopher Young's (2018) study of the Toronto game development scene being a notable exception. Through a prolonged period of participation and observation in the scene, as well as interviews with scene participants, Young traces the numerous collectives, groups, and companies that play formative roles in shaping videogame production in Toronto. Young (2018, 69) works toward an understand of scenes as palimpsests: "a cultural activity that has been written upon several times by various stakeholders through the inscription of their cultural norms and practices, often with remnants of the erased inscriptions still visible across the platforms of the scene." In Young's detailed description of the Toronto game development scene, a number of organizations and stakeholders offer different spaces and activities for different parts of the city's videogame production community, such as social and networking events held by Dames Making Games and the Hand Eye Society, the annual TOJam game jam event, and semiformal networking and education events organized by global companies such as Unity and Unreal to help foster the take-up of their software platforms within the local community.

Young, in the Toronto context, follows the cultural activity of gamemaking, rather than any one specific locale or organization to constructively consider this wide spectrum of actors constituting *the* Toronto game development scene. In the following analysis of Melbourne and Adelaide, however, I find it conducive to consider these citywide palimpsest scenes as themselves constituted by a number of interlocking, overlapping, and competing local scenes. This is in no small part because of how these scenes and communities were often articulated by my own participants. If a scene is revealed by following the cultural activity rather than the place (Young 2018, 76), in the following examples we will see how competing local videogame scenes can disagree on what the cultural activity of videogame production even is. Just as a single city might not simply have a music scene but a jazz scene, a rock scene, a punk scene, and a rap scene, a single city might also have multiple competing videogame scenes.

To demonstrate how the shape of a local videogame field is structured by the interactions and struggles between local scenes, I will detail the local videogame fields of two Australian cities in detail. Melbourne and Adelaide offer two stories of Australian videogame production that, while sharing many parallels, are far from identical. In each story, we will see, as detailed by Bartlett in this chapter's introduction, and as witnessed by Young (2018) in Toronto, competing evaluations of the different position-takings within the local field, and competing understandings of what is and is not considered legitimate videogame production. In each example, different scenes will make themselves known as they emerge through different sites of activity, different forms and perceptions of cultural capital, and a more general and broad tension between those videogame makers striving for creative autonomy and those striving for economic sustainability.

As an important caveat, the following analyses are limited by both space and methodology. I do not provide exhaustive histories, political economic analyses, or cultural geographies of either site. A more expansive analysis of local videogame production would consider broader socioeconomic and geographic factors, infrastructure, cultural histories, and government policies. Here I am limited to what my interviewees told me and my own firsthand or secondhand knowledge from my own participation in these communities. As such, the following analyses should not be read as complete or objective evaluations of why videogame production is shaped the way it is in each of these cities. Rather, my sole objective here is to demonstrate how videogame makers themselves perceive and articulate their local videogame production contexts as neither homogenous nor stable, but as contested and dynamic.

Melbourne

Melbourne is the state capital of Victoria and Australia's second-most populous city after Sydney. It is commonly regarded as Australia's culture capital, home to many of Australia's most successful musicians, artists, sportspeople, literary figures, films, and television shows. Melbourne is home to Australia's oldest art museum (the National Gallery of Victoria, established in 1861) and a range of nationally and internationally significant cultural institutions, including the State Library of Victoria, the Australian Centre for the Moving Image (ACMI), and the Melbourne Cricket Ground. Each year the city houses cultural events such as Melbourne International Comedy Festival, the Australian Open (tennis), and, since 2016, Melbourne International Games Week. Beyond the big institutional names, Melbourne is known for its more nebulous music scenes, café culture, and street art.

Melbourne has long been the primary videogame production hub in Australia and was arguably in a better position to adapt to the drastic changes brought about by the early 2010s than any other Australian city. As we saw in chapter 2, countercultural and fringe videogame makers were present within Melbourne's broader, robust cultural field long before the collapse of Australia's commercial, foreign publisher–dependent videogame studios. The Freeplay Independent Games Festival emerged out of the Next Wave arts festival in 2004. Around the same time, Melbourne-based gamemakers were collaborating with artists and journalists on political games such as *Escape from Woomera* (see Swalwell 2007). Further, also in the early 2000s, government-funded agencies and institutions, such as ACMI and Film Victoria, were already showing some interest in and support for alternative modes of videogame production, such as Helen Stuckey's curatorial role at ACMI's Game Lab.

As the nation's videogame makers found themselves forced into indie business models and mindsets following the closure of nearly every large studio in the country, Melbourne fostered this transition relatively successfully through a number of cultural and political advantages. First, in addition to those studios focused on obtaining contracts with foreign publishers to ensure financial stability, Melbourne was already home to a number of independent videogame makers more interested in creative autonomy through generating new IP. Second, Melbourne gamemakers were already self-organized into broader communities of practice such as those around the Freeplay Independent Games Festival and the local International Game Developers Association (IGDA) chapter. Third, its state government screen-funding body, Film Victoria, was more proactive than their interstate counterparts in terms of providing levels of funding and support relevant to independent videogame producers, such as small pools of direct funding with assessment criteria not directly tied to commercial outcomes.

All of this ensured that, by the end of the 2010s, Melbourne was the undisputed capital of Australian videogame production, housing over 50 percent of all commercial Australian gamemakers (Interactive Games and Entertainment Association 2020). In part, this was due to the growth of Melbourne's field, but more so due to its resilience as the field contracted elsewhere in the country. Indeed, the two are closely related, as many videogame makers around the country found themselves with few local opportunities and moved to Melbourne to take advantage of the favorable funding opportunities and to participate in the vibrant local community. In 2012, I myself moved to Melbourne to commence my PhD, as it seemed like the logical, perhaps only, place in Australia where one could undertake a game studies PhD at the time.

The Melbourne videogame field today is a vibrant ecosystem of large corporate studios, entrepreneurial coworking spaces, artist collectives, student cohorts, bedroom coders, government funding bodies, fringe cultural festivals, and slick international consumer expos. Videogame production in Melbourne happens at a range of scales, in a variety of contexts, across networks of people whose direct relationship with each other might be positive, antagonistic, or nonexistent. At the time of writing in 2022, massive North American publishers EA and Activision each have studios in the city (EA's from the purchase and merger of independent studios Firemint and Iron Monkeys; Activision through the recent establishment of a branch of its Sledgehammer studio). Midsized independent companies such as League of Geeks (*Armello*) and Hipster Whale (*Crossy Road*) have grown out of grassroots beginnings to provide established, steady employment for 15 to 50 people each, typically focused on more commercial titles in the games-as-a-service and free-to-play spaces. Around these are a large number of smaller studios working on a wide range of premium and free-to-play titles, including Samurai Punk (*The American Dream*; *Feather*), the Voxel Agents (*The Gardens Between*), Mighty Games (*Shooty Skies*), Paper House (*Paperbark*; *Wood and Weather*), Mountains (*Florence*), and House House (*Push Me Pull You*; *Untitled Goose Game*). Around *these* are extensive communities of students, hobbyist gamemakers, interdisciplinary dabblers, academics, and hangers-on. From these communities emerge various collectives and collaborations that last anywhere from a few weeks to a number of years, sometimes disappearing after a single party, sometimes organically evolving into long-term commercial projects.

Within this nebulous and dispersed field, relationships and collaborations reach out beyond discrete teams and projects. As people move between projects, workgroups, parties, sharehouses, or romantic relationships, they inevitably develop and maintain networks with those working on other projects. Interteam community comes to replace the discrete community of the single workplace, short-circuiting the culture of secrecy that dominates cultures of videogame production in larger studios (O'Donnell 2014). This broader community consolidated with the founding of the games-centric coworking space, The Arcade, in 2013. Subsidized in its early years by the Victorian State Government and run by the Game Developers Association of Australia (GDAA), The Arcade provides (relatively) affordable office space for small videogame production teams and allowed teams and individuals to pull together and share resources and knowledge.[1]

For instance, Ben Kerslake, 39, had recently returned to Melbourne after a decade of working for both videogame and software companies in Shanghai. Kerslake now works on an independent project with a collaborator based overseas. Rather than work alone at home, Kerslake regularly sets up shop at the hot desks available in The Arcade. Kerslake explained that this was because, as a solo developer,

> Without the community, it makes everything very difficult. Because you can't externalize problems. You can't get help. That's just a hugely isolating problem. . . . For me [The Arcade offers] a lot of the positives of being in an office space and none of the negatives. A chance for me to meet with people and make new connections. . . . It's helped me prepare for the Film Victoria [funding process], because . . . I feel like half the people I meet here have been involved in that process either as an applicant or on the selection committee.

Other residents in The Arcade likewise highlighted the significance of cross-team collaboration and support that the space afforded as vital to their operations. Nicholas McDonnell, the 25-year-old managing director of Samurai Punk, saw the collaborations fostered by the shared physical space of The Arcade as foundational to the running of their studio:

> That's part of the reason we don't want to leave . . . because of the quality of these relationships. We helped another studio to grow and other studios here have helped us grow. So much of our existence now is tied to the people here, and so

much of our social culture is tied to the people here. It feels like if we ever left, we'd be taking part of our studio away.

Here, even formal companies feel connected to a broader community due to a shared openness, collaboration, and pooling of resources.[2]

The Arcade consolidated and made visible an otherwise nebulous and loosely affiliated network of small teams and individuals scattered around Melbourne, providing a professionalized space that advocates could point publishers, investors, and government officials toward as *the* Victorian video-game industry—or where researchers, such as myself, immediately turn to in order to locate research participants. However, this also came with its draw-backs for the broader Melbourne community not occupying The Arcade. As Tony Reed, 47, the founder of The Arcade and (at the time of our interview) CEO of the GDAA, explained: "The thing I didn't see coming was The Arcade becoming a clique. People in The Arcade felt they were special because they were in The Arcade, and people outside of The Arcade felt they weren't part of things because they weren't part of The Arcade. That really bothered me." The Arcade's success, for a time, effectively positioned it as the center of Melbourne's videogame field, as the physical site within which Melbourne's most legitimized videogame production was occurring.

That those who operated outside of The Arcade felt they "were not part of things" was especially true for those younger and more peripheral teams not interested in producing videogames in the commercially feasible genres that would be necessary to justify paying rent for an office or desk in a coworking space.[3] One gamemaker who worked in a small team external to The Arcade expressed that despite their own team's commercial and critical successes, they felt generally ignored by "that world." "[It] always seemed too inward looking and also just distastefully commercial. . . . I think because we never kissed the ring, we've never been acknowledged by them." Thus, also in the early 2010s, parallel gamemaking communities emerged in Melbourne, buoyed by the proliferation of informal and hobbyist modes of videogame production and the growing number of students emerging from dedicated university programs in videogame design and development from universities such as RMIT and Swinburne. Loose organizations and affiliations such as Glitchmark and Hovergarden, alternative coworking environments such as All Day Breakfast and Share House, the computer labs and student spaces of RMIT University's downtown campus, and the long-running Freeplay Independent

Games Festival became crucial hubs for these alternative collectives and communities who did not necessarily feel catered to by organizations such as IGDA Melbourne or The Arcade.

These alternative communities were explicitly countercultural and considered their own position-taking as very much against those position-takings of the field's more central actors. Lee Shang Lun, 25, was a cofounder of the group Glitchmark, which met regularly to discuss and share knowledge about game design skills and theory. Lee described the constitution of Glitchmark thus:

> The people that would go to something like [Glitchmark] were hungry for a community and for that kind of vocabulary and development of a scene or of a discipline. And so those people continue to create networks and communities that are interested in those same things, and you can see the effects of those individuals and those communities have had in fragmenting, fracturing in a very positive way in my opinion, the Melbourne independent game scene.

This sense of a fragmenting or fracturing of the Melbourne scene where different organizations direct their energies in different directions toward different ends, rather than inward toward a single space or goal, was similarly articulated by other Melbourne-based gamemakers. Another anonymous gamemaker, who had moved to Melbourne a couple of years before our interview, was "realizing increasingly that I have this particular view on what Melbourne is." They realized that rather than simply a Melbourne videogame maker, they were "part of a particular scene" and that they "don't know at least half the people in The Arcade." The previous anonymous gamemaker who said they had refused to "kiss the ring" of the organizations more central to the Melbourne field articulated their own understanding of the two sides of Melbourne's videogame field as instantiated through different physical locations: "In my mind there's two Melbourne game worlds. There's The Arcade and what I think of as Bar SK." Bar SK was (until its closure in 2020) a bar located in the trendy inner-city suburb of Collingwood. Founder Louie Roots had previously been part of a gamemaking collective in Perth, Western Australia, focusing on exhibition and party videogames. Both a local, public-facing bar and an exhibition space for "trash videogames and media art," Bar SK served as a physical location for subcultural Melbourne gamemakers, providing an alternative space and visibility that, for a time, countered the dominant visibility of The Arcade and larger studios.

While this subcultural side of videogame production in Melbourne is still overproducing in Straw's sense that much of its activity is not formalized into commercial videogame products, its increased visibility, acclaim, and authority inevitably had a direct impact on the shape and value of Melbourne's formal videogame production. Primarily, this occurs through the creative, experimental energy of the fringe creators contributing to a broader perception that Melbourne is a cool, vibrant site of videogame production, which in turn works to attract increased interest from employers, investors, and government. Ken Wong, the 36-year-old creative director and founder of small studio Mountains, had spent much of his career working in videogame studios overseas. Despite originally being from Adelaide, when Wong moved back to Australia he moved to Melbourne with the explicit intent of founding his own independent studio. Wong chose Melbourne in large part because of the access to talent: "There is a scene here, there's universities here" and, further, because "There's support here like The Arcade, that is a huge reason."

More than just providing the skills base and culture required for growing formal videogame production, some gamemakers felt the success and vibrancy of Melbourne's countercultural videogame scenes was shifting the kinds of projects the better-resourced studios undertook. As one gamemaker put it:

> Film Vic[toria] does come into it. There's only so much grant money. Both parties want the grant money. There's part of me that wants to be really healthy and say, "Yeah, we can all get along." But I think you see people being almost tokenistic about the games they're wanting to make now. So Film Vic have got a tricky thing on their hands because they might be unaware of or they might not look deep enough or they might just blindly say, "Yeah, that sounds perfect. I'll fund it," even if that person's last game might have been a really exploitative clicker, you know?

While ambitions and intentions are almost certainly more complex than this interviewee suggests, the sense of a clashing and overlapping of cultures and values in funding and employment opportunities was felt keenly by those gamemakers richer in symbolic capital but poorer in economic capital.

The growing legitimacy and cultural capital of Melbourne's countercultural creators was also a source of anxiety for gamemakers working in commercial independent studios. The autonomous positions taken by the countercultural gamemakers shifted the position-taking of the commercial gamemakers' own positions that strived to balance creative expression with the financial sustainability of their companies. A gamemaker in their mid-40s working at a studio dedicated to free-to-play mobile games was defensive about their studio holding such an ambivalent position:

> It's always really interesting finding that kind of pressure between creative and commercial. I think it's the biggest sticking point with games and I get very excited when you can combine the two, but obviously that's not always going to be the case. [Some people say] "I'm interested in it purely from a creative side" and, bless you, that's wonderful. I'm glad you don't have a mortgage. Good for you. Like, if you can just make games for the fuck of it what a position of privilege you are in! . . . If you don't have to commercialize it, then all power to you, but if you want to keep talent that's got the skills then you need to commercialize it. The older we get the more we cost to run, and we have families we need to support.

For this gamemaker, the fact the countercultural gamemakers could afford to be disinterested in economic return as they strove for and gave further power to the autonomous principles of hierarchization in the local field, was a sign of societal privilege. In particular, this gamemaker was suggesting that such gamemakers were economically well-off—possessing the economic capital that allows one to be disinterested in accruing economic capital. Indeed, the countercultural gamemakers I interviewed were, as this gamemaker themself suggests, often young with few external expenses other than rent and sustenance. This hardly makes them rich, but it does suggest, if nothing else, an advantage of (some) youth to disavow, or at least defer, economic interest, while such a choice no longer exists for older gamemakers with mortgages, families, and increasing health and life expenses.

One gamemaker at a larger independent studio residing within The Arcade similarly articulated the local field between those gamemakers most interested in making a financial profit (heteronomous principles) and those more interested in disavowing such profit for artistic goals ends (autonomous principles):

> There are studios that make mobile games that are hugely profitable, but I think their value is less on creating meaningful experiences and more so about maximizing profit. And there's also another side of games in Melbourne which is like "Games should just be an expression of yourself" and money is far less valuable than the statement.

While this gamemaker was quick to stress that "I'm not trying to say one way is better than the other," they also felt that the studio they worked at was "the greedy studio that wants it all"—a sentiment surely shared by most Melbourne videogame producers as they strive to legitimate their own position in relation to the numerous other position-taking individuals and communities that constitute Melbourne's videogame field. A rich tapestry of activity and constituents across Melbourne are all part of the Melbourne videogame field. They reflect a vast range of values, identities, and groupings that often intersect and sometimes overlap—either collaboratively or antagonistically or indirectly—but which are just as often conceptualized by their constituents as distinct worlds. To say that Melbourne has an indie game scene would be to homogenize complex, overlapping communities among Melbourne gamemakers in terms of differing perceptions of the resources, values, ambitions, and opportunities available to differently positioned gamemakers.

Adelaide

Approximately eight hours drive northwest of Melbourne is Adelaide, the state capital of South Australia. Adelaide is a much smaller city than Melbourne; it covers only 3,200 square kilometers compared to Melbourne's 10,000, and houses only 1.3 million people compared to Melbourne's 5 million. Nonetheless, the cities share a lot in common in terms of climate, culture, and football codes. Their videogame fields, too, differ greatly in scale but share much in terms of the relationship between their most dominant and fringe gamemaking positions. The struggles and tensions that have evolved gradually over the past decade in Melbourne have made themselves much more abruptly known in the Adelaide field, with several corporate actors setting up shop on top of a small-scale, grassroots community to reveal sudden and sharp distinctions.

Through the 1990s, Adelaide was home to Ratbag Games, founded in 1993 and producer of the successful 1998 PC racing title *Powerslide*. Ratbag came to an undignified end when American publisher Midway bought the studio in August 2005, before shutting the studio down entirely in December of the same year. Brisbane-headquartered Krome also ran an Adelaide studio for a short period, established in large part by workers let go by Midway, and then closed in 2010 as part of broader job cuts across the company. Since 2004, animation and game development studio Monkeystack has sustained itself on a combination of audiovisual and interactive, client and original work, not dissimilar to the studios detailed in the previous chapter, and today employs approximately 40 people according to CEO Justin Wight. Elsewhere, Mighty Kingdom has grown steadily since 2010, working on games for popular toy licenses such as Shopkins and Lego and, as we will see below, has taken a particularly central role in Adelaide's videogame field. Around these companies is a rich community of hobbyists and independents coming together around a loose collection of events, organizations, and groups such as ARGGG (Adelaide's Really Good Gathering of Game Developers), Adelaide Game Dev Breakfast, Adelaide Game Dev Talks, the Indie Games Room at the annual Anime and Video Games Festival AVCon, Adelaide Global Game Jam, and SA Women in Games.[4] Today, the best-known videogames out of Adelaide are from small, independent teams such as three-person studio Team Cherry's *Hollow Knight*, and single-person studio Team Fractal Alligator's *Hacknet*.

When I visited Adelaide in July 2018, the local field was in a state of flux. Games education institute Academy of Interactive Entertainment (AIE) had recently opened a campus in the city, along with an AIE-run coworking space, Game Plus. An established albeit small community of hobbyists and artists was finding their city suddenly full of highly visible newcomers strong in economic capital, as well as a whole new class of gamer-identifying students interested in a mode of videogame production very different from that favored by themselves. Unlike in Melbourne, I have very little firsthand experience of Adelaide's videogame field, and so I regularly asked my Adelaide interviewees if they could describe the local community—if indeed they felt there was one—in their own words. Damon Reece, a 23-year-old freelance narrative designer, gave an extensive and detailed answer that maps the different positions of Adelaide's field, with relationships and tensions that clearly parallel Bartlett's description of Melbourne:

> There is a community. It's—there's some weird things going on in the past year or so. So you've got your hobbyist indie-dev community who've been here for over a decade. It's good at passing the torch and having events, and people come and hang out, talk to each other, make friends. You've got groups like the IGDA who until recently were running Global Game Jam and Ludum Dare and stuff like that. A lot of stuff comes from the university clubs which I've never really been involved with, but you still see their effects, and that's sort of been like this low-key community centered around a gathering called ARGGG and the indie games room at AVCon. That's been here for ages. Then in the past couple of years AIE has come in and they've got all these game students who, you know, are straight out of high school and who aren't interested in participating in a pre-existing community. So they've got their own sort of weird clique full of gamer bros, and since AIE has the capital and AIE has the ear of, well, *had* the ear of the

government,[5] and the coworking space [Game Plus] and all that, things are sort of weirdly shifting toward that and it doesn't seem like they're interested in bringing the communities together. I feel like they're trying to selectively pick from the preexisting community. It's frustrating because it doesn't feel anywhere near as inclusive or diverse or friendly.

There is a lot to unpack here, but in Reece's detailed overview of the Adelaide field are the various positions competing for legitimacy—for recognition *as* Adelaide's videogame field—that would reappear throughout my Adelaide interviews: small-scale artists and hobbyists, an influx of "gamer bro" students, and growing commercial actors positioning themselves *as* the field of videogame production in Adelaide.

The joint arrival of AIE and Game Plus was regularly brought up by Adelaide gamemakers as being a major disruption in the local field. AIE, as discussed in chapter 4, is a specialist school for game development education, set up from the start as a deliberate pipeline of skills to be tapped by Australian videogame companies. Game Plus, a not-for-profit initiative of AIE, runs coworking spaces in Sydney, Canberra, and Adelaide that provide similar benefits for local commercial gamemakers as The Arcade does for Melbourne gamemakers (relatively affordable rent, visibility, community). The coworking space operates as a value-add for AIE to its prospective students, with AIE students and graduates having access to Game Plus spaces, events, and tenants. While The Arcade in Melbourne was often mentioned by gamemakers around Australia as evidence of Melbourne's strong gamemaking culture and community, Adelaide gamemakers were more ambivalent about the influence of Game Plus on their own local field. Game Plus is one block from AIE's campus in downtown Adelaide. In one corner of the coworking space, between the large hot-desking main room and the corridors to the individual studio offices, are several large computer labs used by AIE students for classes and assessment work. Students can access Game Plus at any time of day or night, just like the professional gamemakers, giving them the opportunity to network with the broader local community and role-play at working in a "real" studio. In addition to computer labs, AIE graduates have discount access to Game Plus spaces through incubator programs, keeping them tied to an ecosystem in which AIE is a central actor even after their graduation.

As an explicit and dedicated space for videogame production, Game Plus has increasingly become home to many of the city's videogame production events, despite technically being a members-only space. For some Adelaide gamemakers, that a space densely populated by the dominant type of gamer-student detailed in chapter 4 has become so formative to the local field has a negative impact on the city's broader videogame production culture, giving it a feeling of being more masculine, nerdy, and commercial and less artistic, experimental, or inclusive. For instance, Chris Johnson, 30, worked as a software developer at a small tech company residing in Game Plus. Johnson has been deeply involved in Adelaide's videogame production community for over a decade. He noted that the involvement of AIE in Game Plus meant that as a worker in the space "it feels a little bit like we're the product here. The students want connections to industry and, hey, industry is here in the same spot." Johnson felt the direct pathway from AIE student to aspiring developer all under the one roof of Game Plus shaped the overall culture of the space:

> It just creates this monoculture that spreads out, and it frustrates me. . . . Like, it's ten o'clock [in the morning] and this kid in the corner, must be like twenty or something, just came out of AIE, works for this game studio that's pretty much just a monetization studio, there's a can of Coke on his desk. Then I come past at lunch time and see another can of Coke. I come past again at three o'clock: third can of Coke. And it's just terrible. . . . [Another developer came into the coworking space at 2am because he was managing a sale in a US time zone] and some other dude is just playing *Overwatch* all night. So, in some ways, I feel like a bit of an outsider [here].

While on the surface it might seem petty to complain about an individual's caffeinated drink of choice, what Johnson is reaching for is an articulation of a clash between different gamemaker position-takings, where a "gamer bro" consumer identity clashes with fringe, autonomy-driven videogame production identities.

Samantha Schaffer, a 25-year-old hobbyist developer who worked external to Game Plus, expressed similar concerns about the space. They articulated how they try to keep their own personal networks at an arm's length from Game Plus:

> I definitely feel a bit wary about bringing people not in games into those kinds of spaces. . . . It is still very heavily skewed male so . . . I don't want to bring my cool [artist] friends to [Game Plus] and then someone says something sexist that they don't even realize is sexist, and then I feel bad for subjecting [my friend] to this.

Much like The Arcade in Melbourne, Game Plus provides some Adelaide gamemakers with community, resources, and visibility. But for others, it reduces the varied positions of the Adelaide videogame field to one particularly dominant and commercial mode of videogame production. Coworking offices, as physical instantiations of the field, seem fated to become central sites over the struggle to determine who is most legitimate within local fields of videogame production.

Also brought up frequently by Adelaide gamemakers as a significant factor in the drastic changes facing the local field was studio Mighty Kingdom. Mighty Kingdom's founders and directors have been highly vocal in the Adelaide videogame field, often lobbying the state government for industry support, and talking up the city in the press as an ideal location for both national and international studios to set up shop. Together, Mighty Kingdom and AIE successfully lobbied the South Australian government to invest in the establishment of Adelaide's Game Plus campus, and Mighty Kingdom became, according to Mighty Kingdom's general manager, Dan Thorsland, the coworking space's "anchor tenant," committing to a "fairly long-term lease which gave [Game Plus] the confidence to come and open up here." As Thorsland tells it, and as is reinforced by a cursory search for mentions of the studio in the press or at local gamemaker conferences, Mighty Kingdom is unapologetic about their attempts to formalize and grow the economic value and sustainability of Adelaide's videogame field. In 2021, after rapidly expanding to over 100 employees, the studio become Australia's largest independent videogame studio.

As Thorsland tells it, growing the company and striving to be profitable is itself crucial for supporting the local gamemaking community as it provides employment opportunities and stability for other local gamemakers. Thorsland is frustrated by those small local independent studios and individuals—what he calls "boutique game developers"—with no interest in growing beyond their current size, regardless of whether or not they are commercially successful:

> If you're a boutique game developer and you have a great passion for what you've done, great. . . . But if all you want to do is just benefit yourself and then cash it out and get rich . . . I have no time for folks like that. What you need to do is you need to support the industry around you and keep that door open for other professionals. . . . Get out of your bedroom, get out of your safe little Arcade, get off your government drip feed. Seed funding is good but get it in the fucking market. . . . Be ambitious and grow as big as you can, at your own expense at times.

For Thorsland, being a responsible member of the local videogame field means striving to grow businesses that can offer employment opportunities to others. It's a striking counterperspective to those "boutique game developers" themselves who, for the most part, would see growing a company larger, hiring other people to work for them, and striving to make a larger profit the more intrinsically selfish position. But at the same time, the precarity and unreliability of independent start-ups such as those detailed in chapter 3 does give credibility to the idea that producing stable employment opportunities benefits and stabilizes a local field, giving newcomers to the field an alternative to forced independence.[6]

Rather than make any sort of definitive moral judgement over who is right or wrong in terms of what is best for Adelaide's videogame field, what is more interesting here is the different ways in which the field as a space of possibles, between artistic and economic motivations, is perceived by differently positioned videogame makers in Adelaide. Just like in Melbourne, not all Adelaide videogame producers share the same motivations or principles as to how the local videogame field should be grown, or which positions within that field should be considered the most legitimate. But as can be seen through the contradicting perspectives on the increasingly difficult to avoid Game Plus, all of Adelaide's gamemakers are, one way or another, mediated by the entire network of related positions that is the Adelaide videogame field.

Videogame Making between the Local and the Translocal

In the above overviews, I deliberately omitted considerations of online networks and interactions to focus discretely on the physical spaces and networks of Melbourne's and Adelaide's local fields. But Australian videogame makers are also highly active across a number of social media platforms within local, national, and international communities of videogame producers—mainly Twitter, but also Facebook, Discord, and others. Just like their geographically centered communities, these online communities are not homogenous but dispersed across a wide range of clusters and groupings that are, at once, local and global. Social media ensures Australian videogame makers remain in regular contact with gamemakers in other Australian cities, as well as with gamemakers across the world (though primarily in North America and western Europe). The complexity of local videogame fields is made more complex still by the online networks and relations shared by geographically dispersed but nonetheless closely connected gamemakers.

As both Holly Kruse (2010) and Christopher Young (2018) demonstrate in their own analyses, online spaces and communities fundamentally

augment—but never straightforwardly replace—physical spaces and relationships. In his own analysis of the Toronto game development scene, Young
(2018, 83) examines how through Twitter in particular "the overlap between
geographical and online documentations of the local offers an interesting
view into the activities of the scene and how not only my participants and
people I meet gain value from the scene, but also how others who I am
less familiar with or have never met engage with the scene." Similarly, in
their work with independent Canadian videogame makers, Felan Parker
and Jennifer Jenson note that their participants consider themselves to
be part of an "imagined 'global' indie game community" due to a general
understanding that indie videogames originate as a primarily online phenomenon through online forums such as The Independent Gaming Source
(TIGSource), IndieGames.com, and Game Jolt: "Everyday online engagement
is for many developers a fundamental part of being indie" (Parker and Jenson
2017, 872; see also Browne 2015). Consequentially, among Canadian independent videogame makers, Parker and Jenson (2017, 881) find that "identifica-
tion with local communities and the generalized, 'global' ideals of indie-ness"
trump any sense of national identity as a Canadian videogame developer. As
such, Parker and Jenson consider videogame production less as global or local
but as *trans*local in the way that physical local community "provides ground-
ing and encouragement" while online community "provides a greater sense
of imagined community and helps to position different individuals and
scenes in relation to one another and the wider game industry" (2017, 886).

For Australian videogame makers, there *was* a sense of being an Australian videogame developer, perhaps due to the shared national experiences of
geographical remoteness and sector-wide collapse. That Australian gamemakers operate in starkly different time zones from most other English-speaking
gamemakers on social media might also lead to a more discrete feeling of
being part of a national community, even online. Nonetheless, the situation of Australian gamemakers is certainly similar to that of Canadian gamemakers. Participants often brought up stories of friends and communities in
other cities central to their own networks and practice, sometimes directly
collaborating in remote teams of independents distributed across the country
or even the world. Persistent social media connections can also have a down-
side, however, for those Australian gamemakers living beyond the central
hub of Melbourne. Alisha Stone, 26, is the creative director of a four-person

studio (and also a web developer at a separate day job) in Hobart on the remote island state of Tasmania. Stone comments, "Twitter has that weird effect of sort of connecting you but also making you realize you're not connected. . . . All these people going to conventions [that] you can't go to all the time, which sucks. But at the same time, it also helps you focus and make you realize what is the important thing that's worth working on." On the one hand, gamemakers around Australia are able to develop everyday connections to gamemakers around the country and overseas in order to access crucial, distributed networks of collaboration and promotion in lieu of possessing adequate resources at a single workplace; on the other hand, this connection makes Australian gamemakers acutely aware of what is happening offline, in physical spaces, in the local communities that they are removed from.

Online connectivity augments the scenes a gamemaker is able to feel associated with, and thus alters that gamemaker's position within the videogame field both locally and globally. Some gamemakers I interviewed felt more connected to communities overseas than in their own physical locale. Sometimes these relationships were fostered entirely in online communities that came together around the use of a particular software tool or around a particular genre or aesthetic (see Reed 2020; Grimes 2015 for online game-making scenes).[7] Jake Strasser in Melbourne, for instance, explained that while their studio, House House, "definitely like to be involved and want to try to help foster things and be involved in some ways" in Melbourne, they also "find we've got absolutely stronger relationships internationally, particularly the Wild Rumpus people from London. That feels like the most important kind of creative little bubble that we have." For Strasser, this was in part because Wild Rumpus, a group that organizes public videogame events, was the first group to become interested in and champion House House's first game, *Push Me Pull You*, after encountering it online. And so, exemplary of the translocality that Parker and Jenson describe, a British collective first showed an Australian game to the press and public at a party in San Francisco. Here, the translocal relations between Melbourne and London for House House don't completely override their local relationships (the team, after all, was a group of friends in Melbourne before forming their studio) but augment them, highlighting even more ways in which both relationships within a local field and *between* geographically dispersed local fields are complex, dynamic, and multifaceted.

Conclusion

In this chapter, I have detailed how local videogame fields are no less complex and contested than are the national or global videogame fields they constitute (and through which they are constituted). Videogames are produced through complex relationships between the global, the local, and the translocal. They rely on international networks and distribution chains controlled primarily by giant North American, Japanese, and (increasingly) Chinese media companies. The economic capital of the global videogame field is disproportionately concentrated in a very small number of countries and companies, but that capital is generated by and extracted from the activities of gamemakers all over the world. It is generated within local scenes and communities whose loose and ambiguous networks of members are taking positions in local fields, national fields, and global fields of videogame production simultaneously. In each of these fields or subfields, gamemakers' same positions have different value as position-takings that, in turn, differently impact their ability to generate either the symbolic or economic capital required for their ongoing participation in the field locally, nationally, or globally. In considering videogame production between global and local forces, we must ensure we don't homogenize the local—the *locals*—that any individual gamemaker finds themselves caught between as they choose which events to attend, which friendships to foster, which gamemakers to collaborate with, and which online communities to participate in.

It is worth stressing again, however, how superficial this analysis has been. By focusing solely on the fact that tensions and struggles exist between different positions in local fields I have not paid much attention to the conditions that have led these local fields to being structured in that particular way: socioeconomic conditions, infrastructure, Internet access, education access, funding access, employment opportunities, and other variables would all need to be better accounted for to provide a more thorough account of Melbourne or Adelaide gamemaking. Yet, despite this, the point remains clear in the articulations of the Melbourne and Adelaide gamemakers heard from here that in neither of these cities—nor in any other city I visited in Australia or elsewhere—was there a consensus as to what the local field was, or who was active within it.

When considering the local context of videogame production, these constitutive internal tensions and contradictions must be embraced, not resolved. In this chapter, I've found the concept of scenes to be one valuable way to capture without resolving this ambiguity of relationships that produces local videogame production. If the territorial ambiguities and revolving roster of participants of a scene means that a scene centers first and foremost on the cultural activity itself rather than the place (Young 2018, 76), then the numerous conflicting interpretations of differently positioned gamemakers as to just what constitutes the cultural activity of gamemaking gives rise to numerous conflicting and overlapping scenes. One could argue that the contradictions and tensions outlined above are merely constitutive of *the* singular Melbourne or Adelaide game scene. But to do so would be to flatten the wide range of competing understandings that exist within each of these cities of what gamemaking even is. These competing understandings of different local scenes, their perpetually unresolvedness, interact with the externally imposed global conditions of audiences, platforms, policy, and socioeconomic conditions to give shape to a local videogame field.

What has been most vivid across the Melbourne and Adelaide case studies here is a sense that a videogame production culture existed in each city before commercial videogame companies exploited that culture for its skills, energy, and reputation in order to industrialize and formalize into commercial studios. The final chapter of this book, then, will turn to how the dominant positions of the field that we think of as the videogame industry have always actually emerged from and relied on the broader field of positions which their dominance obscures.

7 From Videogame Field to Videogame Industries

In May 2021, as I was completing the first draft of this book, the Australian federal government announced a 30 percent refundable tax offset for videogame production businesses spending at least $500,000 in Australia. The announcement was met with jubilation from Australian gamemakers and trade organizations, such as the Interactive Games and Entertainment Association (IGEA), who had lobbied for such an offset for years (Maxwell 2021; Walker 2021). As we saw in chapters 2 and 3, the independent teams that currently dominate the Australian field persist at a small scale in a sort of perpetual entrepreneurism that can't provide significant or stable career opportunities for many. The tax offset, for many Australian gamemakers, looks set to provide a missing piece of the puzzle required to stabilize and grow the Australian field. Local companies can risk growing and taking on more staff with the money no longer committed to taxes; international companies may decide Australia is now an affordable location to open a large studio, bringing with them crucial upskilling, stability, and graduate roles that the current small teams are unable to provide. Symbolically, for many Australian gamemakers, the announcement of the offset, providing videogame production a comparable level of support as other screen industries in the country, felt like long-awaited recognition from a federal government that for nearly a decade had shown no interest in the sector whatsoever.

Two months later, the IGEA and the federal government's Global Business and Talent Attraction Taskforce jointly released a showreel of Australian-made videogames, showcasing the talent and ability available in the country for foreign companies looking to take advantage of the tax offset. The showreel presented a vast range of titles, from triple-A projects predominately made overseas but in part by Australian contingencies such as *World of Tanks*

(Wargaming) and *Call of Duty: World War II* (Sledgehammer), high-fidelity sports games such as *AO Tennis 2* (Big Ant) and *Real Racing 3* (EA Firemonkeys), and several critically successful independent titles such as *Paperbark* (Paper House), *Florence* (Mountains), and *Dead Static Drive* (Reuben). For the showcased foreign-owned studios, the tax offset means potentially heightened job security, with their international owners now having one more reason to keep their Australian studios open, rather than closing them and opening a cheaper studio elsewhere. For the showcased larger Australian-owned studios, the tax offset means hiring more staff to undertake larger projects won't require quite as much of an up-front financial investment, and so more ambitious projects can be pursued with greater confidence. For the showcased smaller independent teams, however, the tax offset will have very little direct impact. Many of the teams responsible for the showcased games consist of very few workers (often fewer than five) with shoestring budgets well below the $500,000 necessary to be eligible for the tax offset in the first place. Others will have spent the necessary amount but still only employed two to five gamemakers on short-term contracts—hardly the employment booster that either the Australian government or the IGEA is trying to encourage with the tax offset.

There is an irony here that some of the videogames used to advertise Australia as a great place to make videogames would not themselves have been eligible for the government support program striving to grow Australian videogame businesses. But, of course, assisting small independent studios—the "backbone of Australian game development" (Apperley and Golding 2015, 61)—is a distant secondary priority of the tax offset. While its existence could encourage local teams to scope more ambitiously and employ more people, its primary goal is to convince large multinationals to set up shop in Australia rather than somewhere else, and to hire dozens or even hundreds of Australian gamemakers. But tax breaks alone don't attract large studios: tax breaks *and* a local talent pool attract large studios. There's no value for Ubisoft or Activision to set up a studio on the opposite side of the world from the rest of their operations if there is no local labor to be recruited into that studio. As Jason Della Rocca (2013, 133) reminds us, even in triple-A hubs such as Montreal, complex videogame production ecosystems are a necessary precursor for the likes of Ubisoft and Activision to show interest in entering a local field in the first place. What is being advertised in this showreel is not the critically acclaimed videogames made in Australia but the Australian videogame field itself—that is, the available labor-power that could now be exploited for a discount rate by a multinational company. In order to build videogame development jobs and companies in Australia—what we would typically call a videogame industry—there needs to already exist an active field of videogame production.

In this final chapter, I want to use the contested nature of the current moment to show how the dominant positions of "the videogame industry" don't only obscure the rest of the videogame field but have in fact always relied on the positions they obscure for their dominance. One of the key takeaways from this book, I hope, will be that alternative and noncommercial modes of videogame production are not the fringe of the videogame field but its foundation. As the Global Business and Talent Attraction Taskforce's showreel exemplifies, the broader, informal cultural activities of a videogame field is a required precursor for the growth of a videogame industry. The field produces the skills, the communities, the aesthetic and design innovations that videogame companies are then able to selectively privatize and commodify (Boluk and LeMieux 2017, 8). If a cultural field is the uneven distribution of cultural, social, and economic value between the field's differently positioned agents, how do the dominant positions ensure this value flows overwhelmingly toward them? And how might the field come to be distributed more equitably?

In the first section, I demonstrate how the broader field of videogame production is tapped as a resource through which the field's dominant commercial positions are able to present themselves as sites of creative innovation and progressive politics. Drawing on Marxist theories of surplus-value and immaterial labor, here I argue that the field's dominant commercial positions no longer simply disavow the broader videogame field but selectively legitimize it so as to exploit it to generate *surplus cultural value* to convert into their own economic capital, ensuring the field's status quo is maintained even as its frontiers expand. In the second section, I consider the potential for radical interventions within this current arrangement. If the generation of the field's cultural value increasingly, in the intensely in/formal paradigm, relies on autonomous, self-driven creators that are not formally employed by those in the dominant positions, then what alternative conduits of power and value could the broader field foster instead? What could a more egalitarian and collective videogame field look like? Here, I look particularly at the call for videogame makers to unionize that has been building momentum globally to argue that this was only able to catalyze due to the increased autonomy of those at the field's periphery—those least likely to fit within traditional union structures, but also those least able to be punished for advocating for such structure. New sites of exploitation, I argue here, are also potentially new sites of resistance, and movements striving for worker agitation in the videogame field would do well to link to broader movements throughout the gig economy. Ultimately, a videogame industry—or perhaps videogame industries—can't exist without a broader videogame field to which it is not reducible.

Making Videogames Better

In their research on queer gamemakers, Bo Ruberg (2019, 779) details the ways in which the responsibility falls on marginal, precarious, often poor independent gamemakers to make videogames better. "Better" here stands in for a range of social and cultural values: making videogames more diverse, more creative, more accessible, more artistic, more vibrant, more mature, more progressive, cooler. Ruberg shows how the rise in visibility and critical acclaim of creators such as Porpentine, Liz Ryerson, Robert Yang, Natalie Lawhead, Anna Anthropy, and others have provided inspiration and ideas for less marginal videogame makers, and how they are often held up by trade discourses as evidence of the growing creative potential of the videogame medium. By recognizing and legitimizing such gamemakers with awards, talk invites, namedrops, and imitations, the peripheral work of these gamemakers allows those in the dominant positions of the field to make claims to the field's diversity, artistic merit, and cultural significance without having to invest labor or resources toward these accomplishments themselves. As Ruberg (2019, 786) argues, this is effectively an exploitation of queer independent gamemaking labor for the benefit of industrial stakeholders: "Queer indie games are seen as *adding value* to video games—as a medium, an industry, and a culture—by making them more 'diverse.' This, in turn, brings financial rewards to stakeholders other than queer indie game-makers" (emphasis added). The queer independent gamemakers themselves see little financial return for this value they create, continuing to live in highly precarious circumstances reliant on platform visibility, personal networks, and hustling hobbies to scrape out a living.

Ruberg's observations among queer independent gamemakers and the Australian government's showreel I detail above are each emblematic of the ways in which the dominant positions of the videogame field extract social and cultural value from the broader field they simultaneously obscure. We can expand Ruberg's question of who is responsible for making videogames better and who benefits from this betterment to ask, more broadly, who generates the social and cultural value that circulates in the videogame field (constituting its autonomy), and who is most able to accrue and convert these symbolic capitals into economic capital (which then provides material advantages in the field of power).

In trying to answer these questions, some of the limits of Bourdieu's theorizations of field of cultural production come to the fore. As David Hesmondhalgh (2006) notes, Bourdieu builds his theory of cultural fields by focusing almost exclusively on the more autonomous cultural fields of literature, art, and theater while paying only passing attention to more industrialized fields of popular culture such as cinema or journalism. This allows Bourdieu to focus predominately on questions of how social and cultural value are generated and circulated in autonomous cultural fields, but it means we require other lenses to make sense of the currently asymmetric situation facing videogame producers. In Bourdieu's work, the relationship between a field's avant-garde "newcomers" and its "established figures" is primarily formulated as one of direct antagonism where each works to legitimize their own taken position as they (directly or indirectly) disavow all existing position-takings. In such a configuration, a field becomes the struggle between two parties: "those who cannot make their mark without pushing into the past those who have an interest in stopping the clock, eternizing the present stage of things" (Bourdieu 1993, 60). But what we see in the videogame field, and in industrialized cultural fields more broadly, are newcomers making a mark at the field's fringes—winning awards, attracting audiences, appearing in headlines—even as the dominant, most industrialized positions seemingly *do* eternize the present state of things. Despite the rise in legitimacy of more autonomous positions at the videogame field's periphery, heteronomous values that align with larger economic forces persist. The rise of experimental gamemakers using Twine or Bitsy has not dethroned the popularity of first-person shooters or open-world role-playing games. The rise of small independent videogame studios has not weakened the profits of EA,

Activision, or Ubisoft—indeed, a growing independent studio is more likely to be bought by a larger company than they are to dethrone them.

Crucial to transferring symbolic capital into economic capital in industrialized cultural fields, and only passingly considered by Bourdieu (1986, 247), is who owns the means of cultural production and, perhaps more importantly, the means of cultural circulation. Record labels, book publishers, film distributors, and, in the case of videogame production, publishers, platforms, and console manufacturers control access to the field's dominant positions for autonomous and heteronomous creators alike. Fringe videogame makers rely on platforms like Steam and the App Store for circulation (or sacrifice access to audiences by refusing such platforms); they rely on software tools such as Unity and Unreal and GameMaker for production (or sacrifice the ability to make games of a certain scale by refusing such tools). Under the context collapse of intense in/formalization, fringe and dominant videogame makers alike rely on the same discourses, events, and spaces on social media, at conferences and festivals, and in their local communities. They compete for the same government funding programs. We have already seen examples of this throughout this book, such as chapter 3's detailing of how platforms like Steam operate on a model of maximum royalty capture where the more independent developers release their games on the platform, and the more successful they collectively are, the more revenue Steam is able to make. Or, in chapter 6, we saw the anxieties expressed by peripheral gamemakers in terms of the rise of commercial studios working on more "artistic" titles to appeal to government funding programs. We could also consider the "Made with Unity" branding used by Unity where any innovative or experimental videogame created with the Unity game engine can become marketing fodder for Unity to enroll even more producers to its platform ecosystem, further solidifying its position as a central tool in the field (Nicoll and Keogh 2019).[1]

Newcomers to the videogame field today typically depend on means of production and circulation they themselves do not own, and so they are unable to push the established positions into obscurity as they claim their own legitimate positions. Instead, their position-taking further enhances the autonomy of the whole field and generates cultural capital not just for themselves but for the dominant positions who are then most able to exchange that cultural capital for economic capital. The newcomers still innovate by necessity of taking a new position, but the position-takings of the established positions remains undisturbed—indeed they become further entrenched. The newcomers' innovations, their new positions, are by necessity in relation to and reliant on the dominant positions and are thus then exploited by the incumbents of the field for their own capital generation. And so the broader videogame field is tasked with making the videogame industry better while reaping few of the economic rewards themselves. In the videogame field, autonomous producers don't simply produce symbolic capital for themselves but are also exploited for symbolic capital by the dominant in order to sustain the dominants' dominance. Their autonomy remains a circumscribed one.

This situation is similar to how the labor of consumers is exploited by brands to increase their own value. Adam Arvidsson (2005) demonstrates how "the meaning-making activity of consumers [forms] the basis of brand value" (2005, 237). Brands like Coca-Cola, Nintendo, Nike, and Apple are valuable—that is, can generate capital—not just because of the use-values of the commodities they represent but because of the emotions, tastes, aesthetics, and contexts associated with them through the social discourses and activities of consumers. In other words, it is consumers themselves who generate the value of brands. Arvidsson shows how this is a form of surplus-value, the key Marxist concept of how capitalism extracts more value from workers' labor than it pays the worker in return. In Marxist theory, capital is produced, essentially, by paying the worker for less time than the worker spends transferring value from their own embodied labor-power into the commodities that the capitalist then sells on the market. Put differently, the worker's work is split between a period of paid labor (for themselves) and a period of unpaid labor (for the employer) (Marx 2011 [1867], 585). It's this period of unpaid labor that produces the surplus-value that capitalism relies on, and capitalism sustains and grows itself by intensifying and expanding the period of unpaid labor while decreasing the period of paid labor. The unpaid work of consumers in producing "a social relation, a shared meaning, an emotional involvement that was not there before [that] can be understood as the direct basis of [a brand's] economic value" (Arvidsson 2005, 237) thus generates surplus-value for the brand owners—what Arvidsson calls an "ethical surplus" or a "surplus community"—which the brand owners can then translate into economic profit.

For Arvidsson, that the value of brands is produced in part by consumers means that the act of consumption is itself a form of immaterial labor,

Maurizio Lazzarato's (1996, 142) term for how the forms and conditions of communication are continually created and modified, "which in turn acts as the interface that negotiates the relationship between production and consumption":

> the "raw material" of immaterial labor is subjectivity and the "ideological" environment in which this subjectivity lives and reproduces. The production of subjectivity ceases to be only an instrument of social control (for the reproduction of mercantile relationships) and becomes directly productive, because the goal of our postindustrial society is to construct the consumer/communicator—and to construct it as "active." . . . The fact that immaterial labor produces subjectivity and economic value at the same time demonstrates how capitalist production has invaded our lives and has broken down all the oppositions among economy, power, and knowledge. The process of social communication (and its principal content, the production of subjectivity) becomes here directly productive because in a certain way it "produces" production.

The ways in which the unpaid labor of *players* contributes surplus-value to videogame companies has been extensively researched through similar frameworks (Kücklich 2005; Banks and Humphreys 2008; Stanfill 2019). Players that create and distribute mods of popular games (Dyer-Witheford and de Peuter 2009), user-generated content makers for games such as *Dreams* or *Mario Maker* (Brock and Johnson 2021), fan activities such as producing walkthroughs or streaming videos or cosplaying at conventions (Johnson and Woodcock 2019; Chia 2019), angry gamer mobs that attack any dissenting voice critiquing the industry (Polansky 2018) are all examples of consumers producing a surplus of symbolic value for commercial videogame companies through unpaid immaterial labor.

Just as commercial videogame companies and platforms have long intermediated and profited from the immaterial labor of their audiences, translating their informal and productive play activities into economic value, they now similarly exploit the labor of the broader range of videogame makers positioned throughout the field. Just as a *Half-Life* modder adds value to *Valve* by producing a mod, a *Roblox* player adds value to *Roblox* Corporation by producing a new game for other *Roblox* players,[2] or an *Overwatch* fan adds value to Blizzard by cosplaying as their favorite character, independent gamemakers add value to Unity by using the game engine for their next game, to Steam or the App Store by using it as their distribution platform, to the Game Developer Conference (GDC) by presenting a postmortem, to the Independent Games Festival (IGF) awards by being nominated (and perhaps by judging other nominees), to local governments by applying for a funding program, to large conventions by holding satellite parties or events, to other game studios by experimenting with new ideas that prove to be financially viable (or not) and which can then be imitated (or avoided).[3] Throughout this book we've seen concrete examples. In chapters 2 and 3, the Australian field's recovery following the crash in the early 2010s was driven by communities and scenes of noncommercial gamemakers, whose artistic and entrepreneurial work provided a pathway forward for an industry of gamemakers now required to "go indie." In chapter 4, the vast range of reasons students undertake videogame production education are filtered, ultimately, into an enlarged talent pool to be tapped as required by the needs of commercial companies. In chapter 5, embedded gamemakers selectively relied on the creative and artistic reputation of videogames as an autonomous field to pitch their skills for marketing and education firms. In chapter 6, most literally, we saw how the growth of local companies are built on and formalized through the collective skills and knowledge of local communities and scenes.

Importantly, this isn't just causal cases of one subjugated position producing surplus economic value for one dominant position, such as when Steam directly accumulates 30 percent of a gamemaker's every sale through the platform. Rather, more nebulously, gamemakers throughout the field, paid or unpaid, through their gamemaking labor, enhance the value of the brand—the autonomy—of the videogame field as a whole. They ensure particular emotions, tastes, aesthetics, and contexts are associated with videogames generally and with the dominant positions directly (such as Unity, Unreal, Steam, the IGF, the Australian videogame industry). In other words, they increase the total amount of cultural and social value generated by and circulating around the videogame field. As the autonomy of the field is increased by those who have no choice but to strive for autonomy, the fact that they remain tied to the dominant positions through the means of cultural production and circulation means those dominant positions aren't disavowed by this rise in autonomy. Instead they are themselves buoyed and able to exploit the associated cultural capital without having to show a disinterest in economic interests themselves.

Gamemakers in marginal positions produce surplus cultural value for the dominant agents in the field who are then able to turn that cultural value into more cultural value (that is, use it as cultural capital) and then to exchange that cultural capital for their own economic capital. For instance,

Unity strives to make a profit but provides access to its game engine for free. It makes surplus economic value in royalties of successful projects and sales on its asset store, and through the collection and commodification of user data. By also allowing all sorts of gamemakers to use the engine for free, Unity is then able to boast about what Unity is capable of producing, and of its ubiquity in the field broadly, to then enroll even more users and increases its centralization even further. The marginal newcomers change the shape of the field (i.e., what capitals are flowing, where, and how). But this doesn't push the existing positions back in history because they continue to control the means of cultural production and distribution that the new positions are subservient to. The autonomous gamemaking activity of the fringes produces a resource the dominant positions extract to reproduce their dominance of the field in its new shape—to make videogames "better" for themselves.

Organizing the Disorganized

In *Developer's Dilemma* (2014), Casey O'Donnell outlines the aggressive methods of surveillance and control that dominant videogame companies have long used to sustain their own dominance and to police the borders of legitimate videogame production. O'Donnell describes legal, material, and discursive strategies taken by companies since the 1980s to control the means of videogame production, including expansive patents, lock-and-key hardware systems, nondisclosure agreements, geographically distributed teams unsure of who has access to what information, and an enthusiast press functioning first and foremost as a branch of the marketing department—sometimes literally. For O'Donnell, this system of control and the secrecy it enforces creates the titular developer's dilemma that, just like the prisoner's dilemma that it draws influence from, is an atmosphere where individual gamemakers are encouraged to keep their head down and look out for themselves and, consequentially, are less likely to work collectively toward fairer work conditions. It's these same conditions that I've argued contributed to the aggressive formalization of videogame production, and which narrowed how the videogame field has been imagined as a space of possibles to only those positions that are economically productive.

The system of control that O'Donnell maps is the one by which, in a Bourdieusian framing, the dominant positions of the videogame field sustain their dominance by striving to present themselves as the full extent of the field, delegitimizing any position they are unable to directly control or exploit. But the systems of control have transformed in the years since O'Donnell undertook his study. The period of aggressive formalization has given way to a period of intense in/formalization as platform logics of both distribution (Steam, the App Store, the PlayStation Store) and production (Unity, Unreal, Roblox) have restructured videogame production labor. As we saw in chapters 2 and 3, and as is increasingly prevalent throughout a number of gigified sectors, the workers that videogame companies rely on to generate their profit are increasingly not employees. Platform holders, publishers, and toolmakers no longer need to provide the obligations of employment—a minimum wage, paid leave, superannuation, and, in the United States, health insurance—to those whose labor generate their value. Increasingly, they don't even have to provide the resources required to produce the videogames they will eventually publish, with independents increasingly funding themselves until near completion before a publisher shows any attention at all. The largest videogame companies increasingly instead provide the platforms through which gamemakers are expected to be self-driven while the company still takes their cut for providing the opportunity. This enrolls videogame makers as active participants in their own heightened exploitation as they take on the lion's share of the creative and financial risks that were once shouldered by an employer or publisher.

As the previous section detailed, this new arrangement of platform-facilitated entrepreneurism where gamemakers are (seemingly) more autonomous and independent does not necessarily actually liberate gamemakers from the control of those in the dominant positions of the field. Rather, it expands the breadth of positions from which those in the dominant positions are able to extract value to anyone enrolled in the network effects (Srnicek 2017) of particular platforms, participating in particular communities, or involved in particular discourses. Mark Banks (2007, 130) builds off Michael Wayne (2003) to understand this business model, rife throughout the cultural industries, as one of "decentralized accumulation": "whereby large firms may adopt an apparently 'disintegrated' and flexible corporate structure, so creating a space for the 'indies' and localized subcontracting, but still ultimately [ensuring] (through an elaborate system of relationships, partnerships and contractual arrangements) that profits and power remain firmly in their grasp." Such decentralized accumulation underpins the intense in/formalization of videogame production and has "disorganized" (Lazzarato 1996) the labor-power that those who control the means of cultural production and circulation rely on. By opening to new sites of exploitation and capital generation without organizing them, deploying them without employing them, the dominant positions of the videogame field have allowed—have required—the broader videogame field to legitimize, for the field itself to be reshaped and made more autonomous through the consecration of new positions and new tensions. Those the dominant positions previously worked to delegitimize through aggressive formalization now must be legitimized as videogame producers so that their surplus-value can be extracted.

As chapter 3 explored in depth, this provides an alternative, far less optimistic assessment of the seemingly growing ability of videogame makers to obtain autonomy or independence in their work. Decentralized and localized cultural production in the current age remains a "strongly corporate-controlled and conglomerated regime" where "workers are now inveigled into an internationalized division of labor where they can expect to be further exposed to precarious work regimes that suppress wages, disavow unionization and compromise 'local powers'" (Banks 2007, 130–131). Consequentially, however, as gamemakers move beyond formal employment into more ambiguous and informal relationships with the platforms, publishers, and investors of commercial game production, they gain through the modes of entrepreneurship and independence forced upon them a limited and circumscribed autonomy that was previously unavailable. Whereas the developer's dilemma of employment in the aggressively formalized videogame field prevented collaboration and communication, and consecrated commercial videogame production as the only legitimate form of videogame production, the disorganized and in/formalized videogame field depends on such activities. The "industry," the field's dominant positions, rely on the labor of the rest of the field to generate the cultural capital that secures their dominance. As Banks (2007, 166; original emphasis) notes, this comes with new opportunities as "one of the 'unintended consequences' . . . of neo-liberal globalization, with its credo of rationalization, a rolling back of institutions and the promotion of 'choice' is to facilitate conditions under which individuals may actually *choose to reject* those individualizing systems that place them at the capricious mercy of the market." The broader field of gamemaking positions is exploited for their ability to make videogames better, but in their disorganization the potential exists, too, for gamemakers to create a videogame field that looks radically different.

Tentative optimism that the capitalist disorganization of the videogame field could be co-opted into a more equitably structured videogame field is warranted. It's hard to deny that throughout the 2010s, largely thanks to the work and risks taken by its most marginal and precarious positions, the field of videogame production greatly increased in its autonomy, and a broader, more diverse range of dispositions were able to take a legitimate position within the field. The transition from a period of aggressive formalization to one of intense in/formalization allowed a wider range of creators, from a wider range of backgrounds, to produce a wider range of videogames for a wider range of audiences. As the discursive, technological, and legal bottlenecks O'Donnell details became increasingly ineffectual against the growing pervasiveness of high-speed Internet, gamemakers were able to take advantage of digital distribution channels, open-access tools, social media platforms, and alternative media outlets to create alternative spaces of videogame production and circulation to change the space of possibles. The 2010s saw the rise of a range of alternative genres and aesthetics, such as Twine games (Harvey 2014) and walking simulators (Muscat 2018) that directly challenged the field's most hegemonic genres and aesthetics, and led to long overdue debates over what a legitimate or "real" videogame even is (Consalvo and Paul 2019). This decade saw a great increase of feminist and queer game criticism, as well as the violent backlash against it that laid bare videogame culture's misogynistic foundations. We saw the rise of casual and mobile videogame formats, with radically different notions of audience and aesthetics that cared little for the dominant "gamer" aesthetics of the field—formats that are overwhelmingly responsible for the field's dramatic economic growth over the past decade. We have seen, and continue to see, topics of sexuality, gender, race, and ability take an increasingly prevalent position in videogame discourses and research and in videogames themselves.

Most importantly of all, the later years of the 2010s saw for the first time the notorious labor conditions through which the videogame field operates seriously and collectively challenged by gamemakers themselves. Agitation for gameworker unions has persisted since at least 2004 with EA Spouse's public letter decrying conditions at the major publisher. While only 35 percent of game developers were in favor of unionization in 2009 (Legault and Weststar 2015), Johanna Weststar and Marie-Josée Legault (2017, 316) analyze data from IGDA's Developer Satisfaction Survey to estimate that in 2017 "66 percent of [game developers] would vote for a union at their studio." Then, as Weststar and Legault (2019, 851) themselves identify, 2018 became a watershed year for gamework unionization movements. In early 2018, as I was first commencing the interviews for this book, a small group of gamemakers (mostly North American) were coming together on a Discord server to strategize ways to disrupt a panel at the Game Developers Conference (GDC) hosted by the explicitly nonunion International Game Developers Association (IGDA) called "Pros, Cons, and Consequences of Unionization for Game Devs." This grassroots community rapidly become Game Workers Unite (GWU), growing over the following years to become a beacon for gameworker rights across the globe. Responding to GWU's sudden visibility and prominence at the 2018 GDC conference, GDC added an explicit question to their 2019 State of the Industry survey, asking respondents if they thought workers in the videogame industry should unionize (GDC 2019, 7). The results were striking: 47 percent of respondents replying in the affirmative, another 26 percent saying maybe, and only 16 percent saying they shouldn't (11 percent were not sure). In the following years, GWU chapters and similar organizations set up around the world. Typically, they start informally but are increasingly formalizing into legally recognized unions, such as GWU Ireland (a branch of the Financial Services Union), IWGB Game Workers in the UK (a branch of the Independent Workers Union), Vodeo Workers United in the US, or, in Australia in early 2022, Game Workers Australia (a division of Professionals Australia).

The story of GWU's grassroots origins, rapid growth, and occasional failings has been detailed extensively in the journalistic press and, increasingly, by game production scholars (Weststar and Legault 2019; Bulut 2020; Ruffino and Woodcock 2020; Ruffino 2022; Keogh and Abraham 2022). What's worth reiterating, though, is how GWU emerged out of the activities of marginal gamemaker communities and occupations. Two of GWU's founders, Emma Kinema and Liz Ryerson, both held peripheral positions in the videogame field—the former a quality assurance tester, the latter an independent writer and artist. Ryerson had long been an outspoken critic of gendered harassment in the industry (see, for example, Ryerson 2014), and Kinema in 2019 organized a walkout at Riot Games over that studio's response to sexual harassment allegations (Klepek 2019). The current push toward unionization among videogame makers—alongside growing critiques of videogame production labor conditions from journalists and players—not only coincides with but has been instigated by a diversification of just who

Figure 7.1
The cover of the GWU *Game Workers Unite* zine distributed at GDC 2018.

is visible and has the authority to speak as a legitimate gamemaker positioned within the field. While the young middle-class men who have long
dominated videogame production have been extensively critiqued for being
highly apolitical about their work, considering it an individual passion rather
than collective labor (Dyer-Witheford and de Peuter 2009; Peticca-Harris,
Weststar, and McKenna 2015), the growing number of visible feminist and
queer gamemakers, such as those that cofounded GWU, are particularly

outspoken about videogame production working conditions and the need for unionization. Once again, just as was the case when EA Spouse and the subsequent letters from spouses of gameworkers at other studios exposed poor conditions across videogame companies in the mid-2000s, it is those outside the dominant positions of the field, those who are increasingly legitimized by the field's decentralized accumulation, that are most vocally agitating and advocating for alternative approaches to videogame production work. The rise in gameworkers agitating for better conditions and pay at the same time as a broader range of gamemakers are legitimized in the field points to how the shifting business models that strive to exploit those disorganized, unemployed, entrepreneurial, informal videogame makers for the generation of surplus-value (both economic and cultural) also provide those gamemakers, in acknowledging them, a radical potential to influence and alter the shape of the field.

While I never explicitly asked the gamemakers I interviewed for their views on unionization and collective action more broadly, its ubiquity in videogame production discourses at the time of my interviews from 2018 to 2020 means gamemakers regularly brought it up themselves, most often in the context of the daily challenges of gamemaking and future career prospects. Cheese, a 36-year-old solo developer in Launceston, Tasmania, bluntly claimed that "if we could find a way to have some kind of French Revolution where we got rid of those people at the top and then more equally distributed [the resources of videogame production] around, then I think maybe that would be better." In the previous chapter we heard from Ben Kerslake, who worked in a two-person remote team in Melbourne. Kerslake identifies himself as "aggressively anti-crunch" and "very much a proponent of unionization" because of his previous experiences working in both large game and tech companies. Kerslake was skeptical that a "traditional union" for gamemakers would ever be formed in Australia but nonetheless insists that "corporate has a lot of power" and that gamemakers need to be educated "as to their value and their negotiating power." Leena van Deventer, also in Melbourne, when discussing the ways in which videogame production culture is "hostile to women, hostile to mothers, and to carers and parents in general" insisted that "we've got to unionize, collectively organize against this bullshit." Other developers directly lay the blame for the challenges of their current situation at the feet of capitalism. Tania Walker, a contract artist in Hobart, noted that her work is precarious and unpredictable, and that "obviously capitalism is to blame. If we had universal basic income where at least no matter what else was happening I'd know I can pay my rent, I can buy some food this week, that would be a game changer. You could do your passionate work and you know you're not going to starve." Likewise, we can think back to Leigh Harris in chapter 3 referencing Marx when he noted the importance of gamemakers owning the means of production.

There is a paradox here that those disorganized videogame makers who are most exploited by the decentralized accumulation model of platformized videogame production are also those who can most confidently and vocally decry work conditions and power imbalances in the field and be most explicitly pro-unionization. As they are not employees, they have no boss who can punish them for advocating for unionization. However, they are also those for whom formal workplace unionization and traditional shopfloor organizing is least likely to improve conditions. After all, as they are not employees, they have no boss to unionize *against*. Tanya X. Short, in Montreal, articulated this contradiction explicitly. Short is the cofounder and codirector of commercial indie game studio Kitfox. During an extensive discussion on endemic crunch and burnout among gamemakers, Short insisted that "I very strongly think people need to unionize as soon as possible" but also added the caveat that "I can't do that because I'm a business owner." Further into the discussion, Short complicated the situation even further:

> Honestly, unions will never be very effective in the indie space. It's too ragtag. There'll never be a fist of unionists crushing [our studio]. So it's a safe place for me to be like, "Oh, yeah, unions are great." But I feel if you have the privilege to be able to say that . . . because I feel safe saying things that [people who work in triple-A studios] don't feel safe saying, I feel like I have to. I have to be pro-union loudly.

Thus, many "disorganized" independent gamemakers feel it is their responsibility to be vocal about unionization explicitly because they can afford to be. They have no employers threatening to fire them if they discuss collective action or speak out publicly about work conditions. Yet, the same lack of large-scale formal employers means that the traditional union structures independent gamemakers are so vocal about are unlikely to improve their own conditions—indeed, their own mode of entrepreneurial and platform-dependent work has been directly shaped by capitalism as a means of destroying traditional collective power.

Those precarious gamemakers that are the majority of positions in the field and who are most capable of being vocal for unionization have little sense of how their desire for political change can be translated into meaningful collective power. The interviewees and survey respondents who brought up the importance of unionization or collective power more generally struggled to articulate how it could become a reality, especially for those working in small teams or as contractors. Cheese caveated his revolutionary calls by noting that "I don't know what I can do as an independent developer who does freelance contract work. I have no skin in that game, but I'm very happy to cheer from the sidelines." Van Deventer, despite her insistence of the importance of unionization, acknowledges that actually unionizing independent gamemakers is challenging when "there's no one to unionize against, when there's no bosses." On the other hand, Ian MacLarty, a solo developer in Melbourne, despite being "kind of curious to see what happens with the union stuff," was not sure where he would fit in such a union himself as he sometimes hires contractors on his games and is thus, technically, an employer. Likewise, Paolo Ruffino and Jamie Woodcock's (2020; see also Ruffino 2022) research with IWGB Game Workers in the UK details the challenges that union had with a rule that only employees, not employers, could become union members. This failed to account for the realities of intensely in/formal gamework where the same gamemaker may simultaneously be both an employer and a contract employee at the same time. It's hard to unionize when there are no bosses, and it's harder still to unionize when *everyone* might be a boss for a time.

The individualizing and competitive nature of contemporary, platform-dependent videogame work, in its exploitation and disorganization, has dormant within it the possibility of becoming differently organized gamework, but it requires gameworkers to imagine alternative modes of collective action that can complement and enhance the traditional shopfloor organizing of single workplaces. Gamemakers themselves had a few suggestions for how a more equitable videogame field could be achieved for its workers. Most suggestions relied on the idea of grassroots change. For instance, one gamemaker I've decided to keep anonymous lives in regional Australia and works remotely into a large North American triple-A studio. For this gamemaker, the fact that videogame production is a cultural field in which producers are primarily motivated "because they love making games," rather than solely a desire to make money, means it is easier to imagine scenarios where commercially successful gamemakers use their resources to help bring up others:

> I think the best hope is that someone is feeling grateful and generous enough that they incorporate it into their studio and they say, "Well, my studio is going to create open-source software. We're going to have this crib and it's going to form the basis of a game developers union."

Originally, this gamemaker admits, they thought disruptive Silicon Valley start-ups would achieve such a situation, "but Silicon Valley is so capitalist." Yet, they remain optimistic that the noneconomic drivers of autonomous gamemakers may allow such a situation to emerge. Some scholars might cautiously agree. Mark Banks (2007, 124), for instance, argues that while decentralized accumulation accelerates individualization and precarity, for autonomy-desiring cultural workers it "can also lead to enhanced opportunities for reflexive critical judgement, and the development of alternative forms of economizing. When coupled to deep-rooted aesthetic impulses and hard-to-destroy (moral) desires for social re-embedding, this can prove a powerful impetus toward economic diversity and remoralization."

Some commercial independent gamemakers are already making inroads in this area. In late 2021, the workers of Vodeo Workers United became the first certified game developers union in North America with explicit and voluntary support from the studio's founder, Asher Vollmer, himself an independent gamemaker (Kilkenny 2021). Short, in Montreal, details how her studio at the time of our interview paid all workers the same rate, and that while this was likely to change in the near future once they release their next game, begin generating more revenue, and hiring more juniors, Short wanted to introduce "a cap that's like 'nobody can be paid more than five times more than anyone else'. . . . So we're in the process of figuring out how to determine all that." Short's studio Kitfox shares an office space with another independent studio, KO_OP, which true to their name experiments with a cooperative studio structure. As KO_OP co-founder Saleem Dabbous explained to *Games Industry*:

> In our studio, our business decisions are a flat hierarchy. We're fully transparent with all of our decision making; people vote about what we do. But we also have systems and rules in place that prioritize people's experience and reaching consensus. It's not unanimous; it's about consensus. There are rules requiring a quorum in meetings to decide on studio business, rules about what percentage of a quorum needs to agree for motions to be passed, and importantly, rules to ensure meetings don't stretch on endlessly. There are designated project leads and they ultimately get to make the final calls in their discipline. (Quoted in Sinclair 2020)

KO_OP is not the only videogame studio cooperative, and the idea is being experimented with by several small-scale teams, such as the Glory Society in the US, and Motion Twin in France (Grayson 2018; McCarthy 2019). While precarity and exploitation remain as rife at the independent scale of videogame production as at the blockbuster scale, now that those that would have formally been employees are now developing their own teams and businesses, they have the opportunity to build those businesses in more equitable ways.

While such experiments within discrete workspaces are constructive pushbacks to videogame production work's endemic labor issues, they remain too concentrated to demand field-wide change or any sort of meaningful resistance to the dominant positions of the field. Indeed, worker co-operatives have faced criticism for accepting, rather than challenging, the normative logic of the market (Sandoval 2019). Field-wide change would require a more radical and unified approach—one that neither gamemakers, unionists, nor researchers are yet to fully formalize. Ultimately, a collective response that organizes the videogame field's disorganized workers would have to identify and target the field's dominant exploiters, which increasingly are not the individual gamemaker's employer but the digital platforms that hobbyists, indies, employees, and employers alike depend on and produce value for. As argued by MacLarty explicitly, in lieu of formal employers it is the platform holders who control the means of production and circulation of videogame products that collective energy ought to be directed at:

> The platform holders have so much power. It's almost like they're our employers, right? . . . They're the ones that run it [the videogame field] in a sense. But I don't know how you'd get any power over them because they're global. There is no way I can make a living just selling my games on my website. I need a platform that's kind of like a storefront.

In this sense, and as Jamie Woodcock has argued (2021), gamemakers and their allies would do well to look toward alternative, nascent modes of collective action taking place elsewhere in the gig economy, such as among delivery drivers (Cant 2019) and temp workers in the software industries (Brophy 2006), where capital has also successfully disconnected itself from the traditional employment contract.

Ian Thomas MacDonald (2018, 18) goes so far as to argue that "the prevailing model of firm-centered collective bargaining is a dead letter when lead firms which derive most of the profits of production have separated themselves institutionally from the firms that actually oversee the labor process" and insists we need "more ambitious labor strategies." It is too late, MacDonald argues, for unions to simply "put the genie back in the bottle" and "re-create the standard employment relation." Indeed, returning to "how things used to be" under the traditional wage contract should probably not be the goal of precarious workers generally when one remembers that such a contract only ever benefited narrow demographics of workers anyway. This is especially true for videogame workers that, despite the broad range of endemic problems and widespread capitalist exploitation, have also arguably never been as organized as they are now. As Greig de Peuter (2014, 276) argues, precarious labor politics, especially among cultural workers, needs to "go beyond opposing precarity . . . to go a step further to propose and experiment with political-economic infrastructures of cultural creativity that produce an alternative to the dominant social relations of production." This would require not an obliteration of the platform models that underpin contemporary capitalism and which empower a broader range of videogame producers than ever before (so as to better exploit them), but broader social changes such as a universal basic income, accessible health care and education, *and* adequate regulation of platform business models that increase the profit share and protections of those who generate the value.

Of course, addressing the videogame field's power imbalances and inequalities still requires the workers of the largest companies to organize their labor-power through the modes that have traditionally worked for such large workplaces. But unionization of the largest companies alone is insufficient without strategies that address precarity and exploitation across the entire field—and, indeed, had previously failed to emerge *until* the broader field began taking action. Perhaps what is most exciting about the current state of the intensely in/formalized videogame field is that through a growing awareness and articulation of the labor issues and power imbalances of the field, videogame makers are increasingly discussing and beginning to consider alternatives to the dominant models of both exploitation and resistance. While we have yet to see any one strategy emerge to successfully challenge the dominance of the videogame field's major employers and platform capitalists, that videogame makers with legitimized positions in the field feel increasingly empowered to explicitly discuss unionism, capitalism, labor, neoliberalism, exploitation, and Marxism among their peers, in the press, and at the field's most prestigious events justifies a cautious optimism for even the most critical cultural theorists.

Conclusion

The videogame industry as it is popularly imagined—as the discrete, exclusive site where legitimate videogames are produced—cannot exist without the labor of a broader field of disavowed producers and the cultural, symbolic, and economic value they generate. Those companies, platforms, and employers that situate themselves as the entire field of videogame production are but its most dominant, most consecrated positions. Videogames are made *beyond* these positions by artists, by amateurs, by students, by hobbyists, by independents, by contractors. Videogames are made *before* these positions secure their dominance in specific local contexts, commercializing and industrializing years after hobbyists and designers and players first began producing videogames as culturally and socially meaningful artifacts. And, as this final chapter has strived to show, videogames are made *beneath* these positions as the foundations, as the raw materials of skill, taste, and innovation that the dominant positions rely on for their ongoing dominance, extracting economic and cultural value from the risks, innovations, experimentations, and advocacy of the field's multitudes. The dominant positions of the videogame field no longer merely obscure and delegitimize all other positions in the field. Through the rise of platformization and independent modes of production, the multitudes of the field are increasingly recognized and legitimized by the dominant positions of the field—but currently only in a circumscribed manner that reinforces rather than challenges the status quo of the field.

But with this peripheral legitimization and disorganizing of labor that are prerequisites of platform capitalism's distributed accumulation, new, slim opportunities exist for imagining alternative models and more equitable structures of videogame production. While traditional worker solidarity methods have historically been dead in the water among gameworkers, the current moment is as exciting as it is dire. It is no coincidence that a growing push for unionization; the experimentation with alternative modes and hierarchies of gamework; and the more vocal debates of labor, diversity, inclusion, and inequality happening within gamemaking discourses has grown alongside this disorganization. While workplace fragmentation, precarization, and individualization have been extensively critiqued for weakening traditional labor power's ability to unionize and demand better conditions and pay, for gameworkers it has also weakened the ability of managers to stop gameworkers from discussing collective issues and imagining alternative arrangements. While the situation remains grim for most gamemakers, that many are developing a collective political consciousness and beginning to conceptualize potential alternative modes of resisting platform power is worthy of hope and, more importantly, support.

Ultimately, however, effective resistance won't occur in the videogame field alone. Rather, gameworkers and those who research them need to connect and build solidarity with broader movements across society that are working to resist the worst excesses of neoliberalism and precaritization. Broader, more equitable societal changes such as a universal basic income, housing rights, and accessible health care will do more to alleviate the precarious conditions of most gamemakers than any field-specific changes could hope to achieve.

Conclusion: Centering the Field of Videogame Production

The Australian Centre for the Moving Image (ACMI), located in downtown Melbourne's Federation Square, positions itself as Australia's national museum of screen culture. It collects and exhibits a wide range of texts and material related to media art, film, television, and videogames. Since the early 2000s, ACMI has supported Australia's videogame field with residencies, dedicated exhibitions, and a commissioned interactive game installation, *AcmiPark* (2003; see Stuckey 2005). Few, if any, formal cultural institutions in Australia have shown as much interest in or provided as much support for the videogame field as ACMI.

In 2018, I conducted a group interview with ACMI's chief experience officer Seb Chan, producer for public programs Arieh Offman, and director of exhibitions Paul Bowers to learn how videogames fit within ACMI's remit. Despite the institution's ongoing support and enthusiasm, ACMI faces several challenges when it comes to being a national museum of videogames. For instance, at the time of our interview ACMI had no dedicated employee focused on videogames. Instead, as Chan explained, "We have a bunch of us who are in different roles who program and advocate for videogames, who support and design things for these experiences, but we don't have a [programmer], a specific role."[1] Like a similar story at a number of cultural institutions and government agencies, there was a general sense that videogames mattered and should be included in the remit of ACMI. But where videogames actually fit within the institution's organizational structure remained ambiguous (see McMaster 2023 for a similar example).

Further, like all cultural institutions concerned with videogames, ACMI faces struggles in terms of shaping audience expectations for how to confront videogames in the gallery space in ways that are both engaging and educational. Offman explains: "I think the challenging thing is that audiences have over time built up an understanding of how to approach a film within a museum or within a gallery context. How to approach a painting within a gallery context. Whereas . . . there isn't that understanding and that literacy in the audiences [for approaching videogames in a gallery context]." Bowers added, "Also, when I go to an art gallery, an art gallery is where I experience art, you know what I mean? Whereas the place I experience videogames is in my living room. So I'm not in the frame of mind to see it [in the gallery] because that's when I sit on my sofa." When audiences perceive videogames first and foremost as entertainment commodities rather than as cultural works, integrating them into a gallery space in a way that is meaningful to audiences becomes extra challenging.

The trio also noted how both institutional and audience perceptions and expectations of videogames compared to other media forms raised questions about artistic freedoms and cultural significance. As a point of comparison, Bowers draws attention to *Terror Nullius*, a film work by collective Soda_Jerk that mashes together clips of Australian film performances and public figures to provide a scathing (and controversial) commentary of contemporary Australian culture.[2] In part, *Terror Nullius* uses footage from graphic R-rated films such as *Mad Max 2: The Road Warrior*. At the time of our interview, *Terror Nullius* was playing in ACMI's theater, which general members of the public could enter at any time with no barrier or proof-of-ID check. While *Terror Nullius* "is probably unsuitable for a 10-year-old," Bowers notes that ACMI is "okay with that because it is art." However, he reflects, "We're not okay with presenting [videogames such as] *We Happy Few* or *The Last of Us* in that frame, but we probably should be."

Bowers's point here is that while both ACMI as an institution and the general public were able to distinguish the artistic merit of, and thus justify the exhibition of, a film-based artwork not appropriate for children, they would struggle to do the same for a videogame-based work. What struck me, however, were the videogames presented as analogous to *Terror Nullius*: the blockbuster zombie shooter *The Last of Us*—developed by large American studio Naughty Dog and published by Sony—and relatively large-scale commercial independent title *We Happy Few*—developed by 40-person Montreal studio Compulsion Games and published by Gearbox software. I noted that these were both commercial videogames and that the videogame equivalent to *Terror Nullius*—in terms of controversiality, artistic merit, and production context—would perhaps be something more akin to Robert Yang's

Cobra Club (an experimental and explicit game about taking and sending dick pics, exploring themes of data privacy and surveillance culture) or dreamfeel's *Curtain* (a short narrative-driven first-person game about being trapped in an abusive relationship). I pointed this out to my interviewees, noting that ACMI probably wouldn't show a commercial R-rated film such as the *South Park* movie in the same theater as *Terror Nullius* is exhibited in. The production context (where in the field the work and its creators are positioned) surely matters relatively, more so than how appropriate or offensive a given film is in an absolute sense. Bowers justified the comparison thus:

> We're the only place where you're going to be able to see a new Tarkovsky print, for example. That's not going to come to your Hoyts [commercial cinema], and it's something we chose to reflect upon. We wouldn't exclude that to show *Black Panther*. For videogames I don't know if there is yet that obvious distinction between [mainstream and art house] which comes about from a very long canon.

While the distinction is never clear or straightforward, a sense exists among curators and audiences alike that most cultural forms contain both more commercial and more artistic works that require different frames of reference and different modes of evaluation and engagement. Videogames, however, lack any distinction between mainstream and art house. When all videogames are perceived first and foremost as commercial entertainment products, regardless of their production context within the field, institutions such as ACMI become limited in what videogames they can present and how they can present them.

My point with this final anecdote is not to single out or critique ACMI's considerable and ongoing efforts to recognize the cultural significance of videogame production—that they are facing and reflecting on such challenges at all speaks highly of their efforts to overcome them. Rather, the challenges faced by ACMI and other cultural institutions in terms of not just how to collect and exhibit videogames but *which* videogames to collect and exhibit exemplify the challenges exposed throughout this book of how a dominant subset of commercially feasible videogame producers and products has obscured and disavowed a much broader field of cultural production. Processes of aggressive formalization over decades have allowed the positions which are, together, perceived as "the videogame industry" to remain so dominant in the videogame field that they are able to position themselves *as* the videogame field in scholarship, in policy, in curation, in the public imaginary. They are so dominant that any distinction between the subfield of restricted production and the subfield of mass production, any distinction between autonomous and heteronomous principles of hierarchization, any distinction between symbolic and economic values, any distinction between mainstream and art house videogames remains difficult to parse.

Bourdieu (1993, 38) warns that if the heteronomous principle of hierarchization reigns unchallenged, then "losing all autonomy, the [cultural] field [would] disappear as such." Through decades of aggressive formalization, the videogame field did all but disappear as a cultural field. Consequentially, as the field transitioned to what I have called its period of intense in/formalization since the late 2000s, with new positions at the field's frontier advancing the autonomous principles of hierarchization in newly visible ways, it remains difficult for publics, for cultural institutions, for funders, for researchers, and for gamemakers themselves to understand and articulate the cultural contexts, the position-takings, of videogame production as occurring within a cultural field at all. If the videogame field lacks a "long canon" as Bowers puts it, despite videogames having been produced for close to 60 years now, it's because the commercial positions in the field have for too long successfully limited the legitimate positions of the field to their own products and practices. The difficulty faced by cultural institutions, policymakers, researchers, and the public in fully articulating videogames as a cultural form is itself a direct outcome of commercial videogame companies' historic disavowal of the broader field's legitimacy. The dominant positions that we call the videogame industry have instrumentalized an economically redundant notion of cultural significance. This collapses ambiguous but nonetheless useful differentiations such as "mainstream" and "art house" to those of "legitimate videogames" and "not actually videogames at all" so that *The Last of Us* becomes analogous to *Terror Nullius* when one tries to imagine a legitimate R-rated videogame with artistic merit that belongs in a public gallery space.

This is the predicament that this book has strived to address by recontextualizing commercial videogame companies as exiting within, and emerging from, a broader cultural field of videogame production. If videogames are truly art, as the medium's advocates, producers, consumers, and scholars have long insisted, then that means going further than simply accepting or demanding that every videogame is provided some arbitrary recognition of artistic merit or cultural significance. It instead means accounting for the complex ways in which cultural value itself operates and is constituted within and through the field. As Paul Callaghan, a creative producer in Melbourne who has worked with cultural institutions and festivals in both Australia and the UK, put it to me:

> A person making art might not want to start a business . . . people play piano without becoming concert pianists. People engage in creative practice without commercializing it, and it's fine. . . . If games talk about being this cultural force . . . what "cultural" is is someone writing a poem for their wife, like, or making a game for their wife, or learning to play guitar, or learning to dance so they can dance at their wedding. Culture . . . is a thing that someone does in their life day-to-day [and that's] just totally absent from the conversation [of videogames as culture]. If someone made a game for their wife and never showed it to anyone, that's what being cultural is. Someone having the skills to do that. . . . [Games] are important because people care about them. Ultimately that's it.

Videogame companies generate well over $100 billion of revenue every year. This is impressive, important, and demands attention. But it is not why videogames are *culturally* significant. Instead, they're culturally significant because people care about them and because people use them to communicate with each other, to express ideas, and to understand their world.

Research on the economic conditions of global videogame production remains crucial, especially in regard to the consolidation of power over the means of videogame production and circulation by a smaller and smaller number of technology companies and platform holders. But such economic analyses also need to be contextualized within videogame production's broader, contested field as only one aspect of how, and why, people care about and generate value with videogames. The symbolic capitals of the videogame field that accrue, circulate, are sought after, and are inconsistently converted into economic capital must also be accounted for. Starting with the label of "videogame industry" and stretching it across the entire field presupposes an economist, homogenous, commodified set of values that only benefits a few dominant positions. Instead we need to begin from a position that understands how a videogame industry can only exist as an extraction of capital from, a concentration of value beyond, and a disavowal of legitimacy of a broader, contested field of videogame production.

With the rise in visibility and circumscribed legitimacy of a wider range of positions—hobbyists, artists, students, contractors, indies, outsource studios—the videogame field is more autonomous than ever before, and can no longer, if indeed it ever could, be reduced to a singular industry of commercial positions. Such commercial positions never truly existed without the broader, informal, unmeasurable, intrinsically valuable work of a field of positions. Just as a Hollywood blockbuster, an avant-garde art house film, or a TikTok video recorded on a phone can be readily distinguished for where they are positioned within the filmmaking field, so too should a triple-A videogame, a commercial independent project, a student project, a personal project only shown to a few close friends, a contracted advergame, and an experimental art-game be so contextualized within the field of videogame production. The struggles in the videogame field outlined in this book—between creativity and commerce, between professional and amateur, between client dependence and creative independence, between precarity and entrepreneurship, between career and side-hustle, between colocated scenes—point to a cultural bottleneck where the ability for a wider range of gamemakers to create and distribute a wider range of works now clashes with entrenched and limited commercial expectations and imaginations of what videogames can and should be.

My goal with this book, ultimately, has been to address this cultural bottleneck by accounting for different gamemaking positions as all vying to be situated within, and in turn constituting, a field of videogame production. Leena van Deventer, in Melbourne, captured both the need and the urgency of this task with an analogy that has stuck with me throughout this project:

> Look at the market on a Sunday morning, right? You look at all the jewelry stores. Some of the people make everything from scratch themselves, by hand. And then some of them buy it all from overseas and sell it on. They're both making jewelry; they're both in the jewelry making business; they're both in the jewelry selling business; they have the same kind of market that they're pushing towards. . . . And I think people understand very clearly the difference between the handmade bespoke thing and the mass-produced thing. In games we don't really have any way to differentiate the support that is available to each one . . . Like there's room for each. . . . I think if we look at analogies like the jewelry thing, that's a more productive place to have a conversation than bringing values into it, by associating like a profit motivation as being inherently bad. It's not. . . . *It's just a matter of finding a new way to discuss things and having that space.*

Just as one can understand and appreciate both the differences and similarities of the bespoke and mass-produced jewelry sellers, we need ways to understand the different positions and dispositions of videogame makers as all sharing—all constituting—a cultural field of videogame production.

To stress, what I am calling for here is not simply a distinction between "arty" videogames and "commercial" videogames. Such a clear distinction is impossible in today's intensely in/formalized field with the required hustle of forced entrepreneurship and the expanded reach of digital platforms. Instead, I am calling for a more nuanced appreciation of the contexts of videogame production and a dehomogenizing of the measures against which all videogames are evaluated. Just as ACMI can clearly differentiate between *Black Panther* and *Terror Nullius*, cultural institutions, policymakers, educators, researchers, labor organizers, and gamemakers themselves need to be able to differentiate between the varied contexts and positions of videogame production. Looking at and taking seriously the lived experiences of videogame makers within a videogame field across economic, cultural, and social axes provides an opportunity to consider the full range of positions held by videogame makers within a videogame field and to ask what a cultural field of videogame production might look like beyond the extractive and top-heavy paradigms of the videogame industry as it has been traditionally imagined since at least the mid-1980s.

Cultural industries don't come from nowhere. They come from cultural fields. The videogame industry, as the exclusive site of legitimate videogame production, does not exist—at least not in the manner that we are used to imagining it. It is instead entangled with and dependent on the skills, communities, and innovations of a broader field of cultural production. Before there were videogame companies, people made videogames. Beyond the limits of videogame companies, people make videogames. Beneath and holding up the foundations of global videogame production, a vast range of people in a vast range of contexts make videogames. I hope I have shown that this is more than a simple semantic replacement of one word with another. I hope that by looking at the current frontiers of the field such as entrepreneurial and precarious indies, client contractors, students, scenes, and nascent labor movements that I've instead shown the limitations of the videogame industry as a conceptual frame and the need for more expansive framings that capture the full extent of labor, of identity, of experimentation, of exploitation, and of radical potential.

Accounting for the entire field of videogame production means accounting for how social and cultural capital are generated by and circulate within a semiautonomous field in complex, dynamic relationships with economic

capital. This is important for researchers of game production and industrialized cultural production more broadly so that the greater diversity of
production contexts can adequately be accounted for and critiqued without
being reduced to purely economic considerations. But it's also vital for those
policymakers, curators, and educators that wish to support videogame production. At present, most models of public games funding both in Australia
and around the world speak the neoliberal language of jobs growth and innovation, requiring elaborate business strategies, commercial feasibility studies, and a proven ability to make a financial return. This makes sense for
the support models, such as Australia's recent tax offset, targeting the field's
largest companies and employers. But as should be typical for arts funding
more generally, tax offsets for large companies should be complemented
by more modest but less stringent direct funding programs that encourage experimentation, creative expression, and diversity with no commercial
requirements. It's this mode of support that grows the field in such a way
that it is then able to support the growth of a local industry.[3]

Funding that aims to grow an industry without growing the field, exhibitions that legitimize the artistry of videogame companies while ignoring
the work of fringe gamemaker artists, curricula that strive to make students
"industry-ready" without focusing on fostering a student's own craft as
an amateur gamemaker: all reinforce the dominance of the global field's
most dominant positions. Alternatively, developing sustainable local videogame industries requires fostering the full videogame field by supporting
the autonomy of local videogame producers and their ability to generate the
required social and cultural capital to be recognized as legitimate videogame
makers. There can be no videogame industry without a videogame field.
The field must come first.

There's more to be done and this book is far from exhaustive in its
examination of how the videogame field operates. I have largely ignored
the logics and business models of the largest and most lucrative videogame
companies that dominate the field and which others have examined in detail
(Dyer-Witheford and de Peuter 2009; O'Donnell 2014; Kerr 2017; Legault
and Weststar 2017; Bulut 2020; Cote and Harris 2020; Weststar and Dubois
2022). Instead, following Bourdieu's warning, I have focused on describing
the formative tensions of the field's frontiers, where the legitimacy of various
positions is most highly contested. I've also largely ignored the role of what
Bourdieu (1993, 41) calls "cultural intermediaries," who are responsible

for translating the productions and values of an autonomous field to "the logic of the economy." Publishers, curators, critics, journalists, livestreamers, investors, and event organizers all have crucial and complex roles to play in the field that have not been considered here (see Parker, Whitson, and Simon 2017; Vanderhoef 2020; Parker 2021; Nieborg and Foxman 2022). Further, while my primary focus on Australian videogame producers has allowed me to detail the entrepreneurial and self-driven activities of those gamemakers in positions lacking access to the major publishers and studios of North America, western Europe, and East Asia, Australia is nonetheless a Western, developed, English-speaking country with relatively strong (albeit deteriorating) social welfare support. Other case studies of videogame production (not just consumption) in locations such as Africa, the Middle East, Latin America, eastern Europe, and Southeast Asia would reveal drastically different configurations of dispositions, positions, and position-takings within the videogame field. Researchers from these locations are already producing such analyses (Chung 2016; Fung 2018; Ozimek 2018; Fiadotau 2019; Garda and Grabarczyk 2021; Guevara-Villalobos 2021; Anonymous 2022; Daiiani and Keogh 2022). I hope to see more such research in the future, in particular ones that consider local videogame production as a field in its own right, not simply as an appendage of an expanding global industry.

Another area deserving more attention that I've deliberately avoided in this book is the blurring of videogame play and production. In a sense, as the research around mods, user-generated content, and fan communities has made clear for decades, playing and making videogames have always had an ambiguous and overlapping relationship (Kücklich 2005; Banks and Humphreys 2008; Boluk and LeMieux 2017; Chia 2019; Swalwell 2021). In this book, I deliberately distinguished videogame production from videogame consumption to articulate concerns aligned with production and producers specifically. But now, players are increasingly recruited as creators in the platform logics of ecologies such as *Roblox*, using production tools in ways that are almost indistinguishable from play. As this book goes to print, videogame publishers drawn to the carbon-intensive wild west of cryptocurrencies and blockchain are speaking of dystopian "play-to-earn" business models that vividly literalize Arvidsson's (2005) proposition that audiences are immaterial laborers for brands. The intensifying overlap of what I call the videogame field (of production) and what Graeme Kirkpatrick (2015) calls the gaming field (of consumption) requires closer examination. A renewed consideration of playbour within the context of an intensely in/formalized field of videogame production could consider how players themselves are positioned as either legitimized or disavowed creators within the field of videogame production.

What I hope this book has instilled is not a reductive privileging of gamemakers' creative or cultural drivers over economic ones but a more holistic conceptual shift in how to examine videogames and their creators. Gamemakers' commercial ambitions and concerns must be situated within the cultural, social, and aesthetic ambitions and concerns that—individually and collectively—motivate and exploit them in equal measure. As I said in the introduction of this book, we have long understood how videogames operate as an industry but not how they operate as a *cultural* industry, with all the contradictions and juxtapositions that term implies. This book has been an attempt to address this.

Not all videogames are made by companies. Those that are made by companies might be made by a thousand employees, five contractors, or one teenager with a registered business name. The vast majority of videogame makers will never generate an economic profit from their gamemaking activity. Some videogames are made for billions of players, others for the creator alone. The contexts in which videogames are made, the reasons for which they are made, the resources with which they are made, and the audiences for whom they are made are no less diverse than they are for films, paintings, or music. To truly account for videogames as an industrialized cultural form is to account for the full breadth of commercial and noncommercial, formal and informal, professional and amateur ways in which videogames are made across the full field of videogame production. The videogame industry doesn't exist—at least not without an entire cultural field of videogame production to support it.

Notes

Introduction

1. Throughout the book I use the terms *gamemaker* or *videogame maker* to refer to the broadest category of people who make videogames in any context, and I use *videogame production* to refer to the very broad range of activities that contribute to the creation of videogames. The reasons I have chosen these terms instead of the conventionally used "videogame developer" and "videogame development" are examined in detail in chapter 1.

2. The competing debates and objectives of cultural industries and creative industries approaches will be detailed in chapter 5.

3. The unfortunately very limited number of Southeast Asian interviews is due to the advent of the COVID-19 pandemic in 2020 preventing my travel to these locations for more dedicated fieldwork. I'm particularly grateful to these two participants for agreeing to be interviewed remotely via teleconferencing software.

Chapter 1

1. I discuss the tensions of "cultural industries" and "creative industries" approaches in more detail in chapter 5.

2. Indeed, noncommercial videogame production at the time was largely dependent on the dominant positions in the field, as the popularity of mods exemplifies (Kücklich 2005). Often celebrated as exemplary of the endless creativity of players, rather than game developers, the rise of modding culture in the early 2000s also, more critically, points to how modifying existing commercial products was the only feasible means through which amateur videogame makers at the time could access the tools to create the three-dimensional videogames most legitimized at the time.

3. You can access my publicly available videogames at brkeogh.itch.io.

4. In calculating this, I have only included interviewees to whom I directly asked these questions. I did not ask these questions of those I interviewed in their capacity

as government officials or representatives of cultural institutions. For a variety of circumstantial reasons, the questions were also not asked of a small number of gamemakers, and they have been excluded from these calculations.

5. *Production* comes with its own problems as the word is already commonly used to refer to a specific project management role within videogame studios and teams. I have chosen to use the word in its general sense nonetheless due to its common use by both Bourdieu and cultural industries researchers to refer to the broad activity of cultural production. Readers can assume that throughout this book I am always using *production* in this more general sense unless I have explicitly stated otherwise.

Chapter 2

1. See http://www.ourdigitalheritage.org/archive/playitagain/ for the full archive produced by the Play It Again project.

2. Not to be confused with the International Game Developers Association (IGDA), which is a global organization compared to the IGEA's Australian (and increasingly New Zealand) focus. Historically, Australian gamemakers have been represented by the Game Developers Association of Australia (GDAA), which represented individuals, and the IGEA, which represented game production companies' interests in Australia. The distinction between the two organizations became increasingly blurred as the Australian videogame field in/formalized until the GDAA was eventually merged into the IGEA in 2020.

3. At the time of writing, a new federal tax offset for videogame production has been announced for Australia. This is discussed briefly in chapter 7.

4. The second stage of Swalwell et al.'s Play it Again project, focusing on the 1990s, is beginning to rectify this. See https://playitagainproject.com/.

5. $100 here refers to a number of related debates among indie game developers in the early 2010s as both the Independent Games Festival (IGF) and the Steam Greenlight program (initially the only way for independent games to access Valve's Steam platform) each introduced a $100 submission fee as a form of quality control. Indie developers were split on these decisions. Some saw it as necessary to filter out spam and trash, while others saw it as elitist and exclusionary to a broader range of truly independent (and poor) gamemakers (see Hernandez 2012; Klepek 2012; Salgado 2012).

Chapter 3

1. At the time of writing, Valve collects 30 percent of each sale through Steam. Apple also collects 30 percent for App Store sales but only 15 percent for companies that make under $1 million a year. Unity's game engine provides a free license for those whose projects generate less than $100,000 a year, after which one must upgrade to a $400 per seat yearly license. Epic is something of an outlier. Its distribution platform,

the Epic Games Store, takes only 12 percent of each sale through the Epic Games Store, and its development platforms, the Unreal Game Engine, has no upfront cost, and takes 5 percent of revenue on projects that have generated more than $1 million.

2. While here Burdak talks about the imminent "completion" of *Paperbark*, it is worth noting how increasingly the release of a videogame is no longer the point at which its creators stop working on it. The online and live nature of digital storefronts means that videogames are increasingly expected to be revised and updated following release with bug fixes and new content. This has led to the servitization of videogame production and to a shift in tone of the grueling work conditions of gamemakers from crunch to grind (Weststar and Dubois 2022).

3. The survey question asked, "Which of the following types of game developer might you also identify as?" directly following the question "Do you consider yourself a professional game developer?" Respondents were able to tick as many or as few as they wished of the following options: aspirational, student, hobbyist, DIY, indie, independent, artisanal, trash, punk, zinester, and serious. Respondents could also enter their own labels under an "Other" option and provided alternative labels such as "experimental," "arcade," and "consultant."

4. Bitsy is a free, accessible gamemaking tool developed by Adam Le Doux, which, like Twine, has a large community of noncommercial practitioners. See Reed 2020.

Chapter 4

1. Despite my use of *videogame production* throughout the book to refer to the broad group of activities that contribute to videogame making, in this chapter I have decided to use the term *game development* when describing tertiary programs as this is most commonly how they frame themselves.

2. We manually removed six programs from the dataset that mentioned game development as a potential job outcome (and thus technically met the second criteria) but only in a fleeting or secondary manner that suggested no direct focus on game development education within the program.

3. Outrageously, in Australian universities, vice chancellors often earn more in one week than the casualized academics that do the vast bulk of the teaching earn in an entire year (Lyons and Hill 2018).

4. The assumption that game development educators are unqualified or unexperienced is a common yet unfair stereotype among both professional videogame developers and students. As Ashton (2009) notes, the assumptions by both developers and students that game development education exists, first and foremost, to prepare students for a job in industry, means those developers already in industry are seen to have greater authority than the teachers who are themselves constantly questioned and doubted for *not* working in the industry.

5. In Australia, the "sandstone" universities (also known as the Group of Eight) are the more prestigious and older institutions, so named for the prominence of sandstone buildings on their campuses. An American equivalent might be the reputation of Ivy League universities.

6. Of course, and as numerous game studies scholars have shown (Kücklich 2005; Banks 2013; Boluk and LeMieux 2017; Brock and Johnson 2021), gameplaying and gamemaking *are* overlapping practices, and all sorts of complex relationships exist among the identities, skills, and labor of videogame production and those of videogame consumption. This is especially true in the context of a resurgence in popularity of user-generated, content-driven business models such as those of *Dreams, Super Mario Maker,* and *Roblox*. For the consideration of this chapter, it is appropriate to talk of a conflation between, or perhaps a reduction of, these two nevertheless overlapping positions.

7. As other scholars have shown, the same sort of masculinist gamer identity is similarly privileged in how videogame companies talk about their internal culture and advertise for open positions (Bulut 2020; de Peuter and Dyer-Witheford 2005).

8. I provide a much more extensive consideration of videogame production as a craft elsewhere (Keogh 2022).

9. The idea that students would start as indie then move into triple-A speaks to how students continue to see triple-A blockbuster production as more central and legitimate in the field. In cities where large studios actually exist, however, the opposite trajectory is much more common: students are recruited en masse by large studios into graduate positions and then, years later, leave to found their own studios with the skills and contacts obtained while working in triple-A.

10. This is not stated explicitly in the report. Rather, the report states that "84% of the respondents were currently employed" (Higher Education Video Game Alliance 2019, 14) and that "Just over 36% of employed respondents with degrees in game-related programs found work outside the games industry" (19). Thus, I have inferred here that the remaining 64 percent of the employed respondents (that is, 54 percent of the total number of respondents) are those who are currently employed within videogame companies.

Chapter 5

1. My personal stance regarding the claims of serious games and gamification advocates is one of extreme cynicism. I have previously argued that the notion that videogame players are "more active" than the audiences of other media relies on concepts of interactivity and immersion that misrepresent the actual embodied engagements required by all forms of media (Keogh 2018). For valuable critiques of serious games and gamification directly, see Abraham (2022, 27–57); Boluk and LeMieux (2017, 202–224); Ruffino (2018, 26–44); Pedercini (2014); D'Anastasio (2015); and Ruberg (2020a).

2. Chaos Theory, "Our Work," https://www.chaostheorygames.com/work/.

3. Opaque Media, https://www.opaque.media/.

4. GOATi Entertainment, https://www.goatientertainment.com/company.html.

5. Bondi Labs, https://www.bondilabs.com/.

6. Secret Lab, https://secretlab.games/.

7. 2pt, https://2pt.com.au/.

Chapter 6

1. Since completing my fieldwork, the GDAA was absorbed into the Interactive Games and Entertainment Association (IGEA), who then took control of The Arcade. In February 2022, after two years of the COVID-19 pandemic and extensive periods of lockdown, The Arcade's lease on its building was ended with no immediate plans to reopen elsewhere. In August 2022, the IGEA announced that this closure would be indefinite. This has no bearing on the period discussed in the following pages, however.

2. See de Peuter, Cohen, and Saraco (2017) for a more detailed discussion of the phenomenon of coworking spaces.

3. Participants interviewed in other parts of Australia often expressed a frustration that The Arcade, especially due to its close affiliation with the GDAA, also diverted attention and resources away from the field elsewhere in the nation. As one Tasmanian gamemaker put it, "They're meant to be the Game Development Association of Australia, not the Game Development Association of The Arcade!"

4. I am indebted to Adelaide gamemaker Kathy Smart for providing me with extensive details of Adelaide's videogame production community. Any mistakes, however, remain solely my own.

5. On the day of my interview with Reece, the South Australian state government had abruptly announced that it would be ending the state's short-lived game funding program.

6. Thorsland's insistence on aggressive economic growth and job development is challenged by Mighty Kingdom's more recent financial challenges. In September 2022, the studio announced a major cost-saving restructure that involved approximately 25 redundancies—in the vicinity of 20 to 25 percent of the entire studio workforce (Williams 2022).

7. Perhaps unsurprisingly, this was of particular importance to the two Southeast Asian gamemakers I interviewed, who felt that connecting with Western gamemaker communities was crucial for their broader visibility to press and potential audiences.

Chapter 7

1. A similarly interesting trajectory to follow, but one which would require its own dedicated study, is how design and aesthetic experimentations by more marginal videogame makers eventually find their way into blockbuster commercial titles. For instance, in the late 2000s and early 2010s, a number of independent videogame makers were experimenting with videogame experiences that focused less on player empowerment and more on embodied audiovisual participation (see, specifically, Twine games and walking simulators). While creators in these spaces (especially women and queer folk) were often abused and harassed for making "nongames," it would seem that such design considerations have, in more recent years, found their way into blockbuster titles such as *Alien: Isolation* and *Red Dead Redemption 2*. The rapid growth and expansion of the genre of "wholesome" games provides another example (Lupetti 2021). Tracking the actual influences and motivations from the fringes of the field to the designers at the central studios would be a fascinating and valuable project.

2. In 2021, game production platform Roblox, in response to a lawsuit between Apple and Epic, removed all reference from their website that Roblox users created "games" at all, instead stressing that they merely create "experiences" (Robertson 2021).

3. Especially in regard to platformization and games-as-a-service business models, Alexander Bernevega and Alex Gekker (2022; see also Joseph 2021) have convincingly argued that the relationship of videogame publishers and consumers is increasingly one of rentier capitalism where players don't buy a videogame commodity at all but instead purchase temporary access to a videogame service that continues to be owned by and generating value for the videogame publisher. In this section, I am effectively saying that a similar landlord-renter dynamic defines the relationship between the dominant and peripheral positions of the field of videogame production.

Conclusion

1. As of the time of writing, Offman now has the title of videogames curator.

2. The Ian Potter Cultural Trust, which funded *Terror Nullius*, withdrew its support of the artwork on the eve of its debut at ACMI (Di Rosso 2018).

3. As this book goes to press, Screen Australia has announced a direct funding program that looks set to address exactly this gap in Australia. Where the refundable tax offset discussed in the previous chapter will support those videogame companies spending more than $500,000 in Australia, Screen Australia's "Expansion Pack" will provide up to $150,000 to projects spending less than $500,000. That both the Australian federal government and local trade associations like the IGEA seemingly understand the importance of supporting gamemakers at both ends of the field is a highly promising development.

References

Abertay University. 2017. "Grand Theft Auto Creator to Mark 20 Years of Games." Abertay University, November 10. https://www.abertay.ac.uk/news/2017/grand-theft -auto-creator-to-mark-20-years-of-games/.

Abraham, Benjamin. 2022. *Digital Games After Climate Change*. New York: Palgrave Macmillan.

Adamson, Glenn. 2007. *Thinking through Craft*. New York: Bloomsbury.

AIE. 2021. "About AIE." https://seattle.aie.edu/about-us/about-aie/.

Anonymous. 2022. "Reverse Engineering North Korea's Gaming Economy: Intellectual Property, Microtransactions, and Censorship." *Game Studies* 22 (1). http://gamestudies.org/2201/articles/anonymous.

Anthropy, Anna. 2012. *Rise of the Videogame Zinesters*. New York: Seven Stories.

Anthropy, Anna. 2014. *ZZT*. Los Angeles: Boss Fight Books.

Appadurai, Ardun. 1996. *Modernity at Large: Cultural Dimensions of Globalization*. Minneapolis: University of Minnesota Press.

Apperley, Thomas H., and Daniel Golding. 2015. "Australia." In *Video Games Around the World*, edited by Mark J. P. Wolf and Toru Iwatani, 57–69. Cambridge, MA: MIT Press.

Arsenault, Dominic. 2017. *Super Power, Spoony Bards, and Silverware: The Super Nintendo Entertainment System*. Cambridge, MA: MIT Press.

Arvidsson, Adam. 2005. "Brands: A Critical Perspective." *Journal of Consumer Culture* 5 (2): 235–258. https://doi.org/10.1177/1469540505053093.

Arvidsson, Adam, Giannino Malossi, and Serpica Naro. 2010. "Passionate Work? Labour Conditions in the Milan Fashion Industry." *Journal for Cultural Research* 14 (3): 295–309.

Ashton, Daniel. 2009. "Making It Professionally: Student Identity and Industry Professionals in Higher Education." *Journal of Education and Work* 22 (4): 283–300. https://doi.org/10.1080/13639080903290439.

Banks, John. 2013. *Co-Creating Videogames*. New York: Bloomsbury.

Banks, John, and Stuart Cunningham. 2016. "Creative Destruction in the Australian Videogames Industry." *Media International Australia* 160 (1): 127–139.

Banks, John, and Sal Humphreys. 2008. "The Labor of User Co-Creators: Emergent Social Network Markets?" *Convergence* 14 (4): 401–418.

Banks, Mark. 2007. *The Politics of Cultural Work*. New York: Palgrave Macmillan.

Banks, Mark, and Kate Oakley. 2015. "UK Art Workers, Class, and the Myth of Mobility." In *The Routledge Companion to Labor and Media*, edited by Richard Maxwell, 1st ed., 170–179. New York: Routledge.

Banks, Miranda, Bridget Conor, and Vicki Mayer, eds. 2015. "The Crunch Heard 'Round the World: The Global Era of Digital Game Labor." In *Production Studies, the Sequel!*, 216–230. New York: Routledge.

Bartlett, Marigold, and Sam Crisp. 2013. "How to Destroy Everything." *Sam Crisp*, October 1. https://web.archive.org/web/20131005041535/https://samcrisp.tumblr.com/post/62718211352/how-to-destroy-everything-or-why-video-games-do-not.

Bennett, Andy, and Richard A. Peterson, eds. 2004. *Music Scenes: Local, Translocal and Virtual*. Nashville: Vanderbilt University Press.

Bernevega, Alexander, and Alex Gekker. 2022. "The Industry of Landlords: Exploring the Assetization of the Triple-A Game." *Games and Culture* 17 (1): 47–69.

Biggs, Tim. 2021. "Australian Video Games 'Could be Billion-dollar Industry' if Given Support: Peak Body." *Sydney Morning Herald*, February 2. https://www.smh.com.au/technology/video-games/australian-video-games-could-be-billion-dollar-industry-if-given-support-peak-body-20210129-p56xu3.html.

Boluk, Stephanie, and Patrick LeMieux. 2017. *Metagaming*. Minneapolis: University of Minnesota Press.

Bourdieu, Pierre. 1983. "The Field of Cultural Production, or: The Economic World Reversed." *Poetics* 12: 311–356.

Bourdieu, Pierre. 1984. *Distinction: A Social Critique of the Judgement of Taste*. Cambridge, MA: Harvard University Press.

Bourdieu, Pierre. 1986. "The Forms of Capital." In *Handbook of Theory and Research for the Sociology of Education*, edited by John G. Richardson, 241–258. Westport, CT: Greenwood.

Bourdieu, Pierre. 1993. *The Field of Cultural Production: Essays on Art and Literature*. New York: Columbia University Press.

Bridges, David. 1993. "Transferable Skills: A Philosophical Perspective." *Studies in Higher Education* 18 (1): 43–51. https://doi.org/10.1080/03075079312331382448.

Bridgstock, Ruth, and Stuart Cunningham. 2016. "Creative Labor and Graduate Outcomes: Implications for Higher Education and Cultural Policy." *International Journal of Cultural Policy* 22 (1): 10–26. https://doi.org/10.1080/10286632.2015.1101086.

British Academy. 2020. *Qualified for the Future: Quantifying Demand for Arts, Humanities, and Social Science Skills*. https://www.thebritishacademy.ac.uk/documents/1888/Qualified-for-the-Future-Quantifying-demand-for-arts-humanities-social-science-skills.pdf.

Brock, Tom, and Mark R. Johnson. 2021. "Video Gaming as Craft Consumption." *Journal of Consumer Culture*, May 10. https://doi.org/10.1177/14695405211016085.

Brophy, Enda. 2006. "System Error: Labour Precarity and Collective Organizing at Microsoft." *Canadian Journal of Communication* 31 (3): 619–638.

Brown, Fraser. 2019. "Superhot Team Is Now Funding Games but Says It's 'Totally Not a Publisher.'" *PC Gamer*, August 15. https://www.pcgamer.com/superhot-team-is-now-funding-games-but-says-its-totally-not-a-publisher/.

Brown, Phillip, Anthony Hesketh, and Sara Wiliams. 2003. "Employability in a Knowledge-Driven Economy." *Journal of Education and Work* 16 (2): 107–126. https://doi.org/10.1080/1363908032000070648.

Browne, Pierson. 2015. *Jumping the Gap: Indie Labor and the Imagined Indie Community*. Montréal: Concordia University.

Bulut, Ergin. 2020. *A Precarious Game: The Illusion of Dream Jobs in the Video Game Industry*. New York: Cornell University Press.

Burns, Matthew Seiji. 2013. "Our Immiscible Future." Author website, April 27. https://matthewseiji.com/notes/2013/4/27/our-immiscible-future.html.

Cant, Callum. 2019. *Riding for Deliveroo: Resistance in the New Economy*. Cambridge, UK: Polity.

Chess, Shira. 2017. *Ready Player Two: Women Gamers and Designed Identity*. Minneapolis: University of Minnesota Press.

Chia, Aleena. 2019. "The Moral Calculus of Vocational Passion in Digital Gaming." *Television & New Media* 20 (8): 767–777. https://doi.org/10.1177/1527476419851079.

Chia, Aleena. 2022. "The Artist and the Automaton in Digital Game Production." *Convergence: The International Journal of Research into New Media Technologies* 28 (2): 389–412. https://doi.org/10.1177/13548565221076434.

Chia, Aleena, Brendan Keogh, Dale Leorke, and Benjamin Nicoll. 2020. "Platformisation in Game Development." *Internet Policy Review* 9 (4).

Chung, Pei-chi. 2016. "Revisiting Creative Industry Models for Game Industry Development in Southeast Asia." In *Global Game Industries and Cultural Policy*, edited by Anthony Fung, 125–152. Cham, CH: Palgrave Macmillan.

Clarke, M. J., and Cynthia Wang. 2020. *Indie Games in the Digital Age*. New York: Bloomsbury Academic & Professional.

Consalvo, Mia. 2007. *Cheating: Gaining Advantage in Videogames*. Cambridge, MA: MIT Press.

Consalvo, Mia, and Christopher A. Paul. 2019. *Real Games: What's Legitimate and What's Not in Contemporary Videogames*. Playful Thinking. Cambridge, MA: MIT Press.

Cote, Amanda C. 2020. *Gaming Sexism: Gender and Identity in the Era of Casual Video Games*. New York: New York University Press.

Cote, Amanda C., and Brandon C. Harris. 2020. "'Weekends Became Something Other People Did': Understanding and Intervening in the Habitus of Video Game Crunch." *Convergence* 27 (1): 161–176. https://doi.org/10.1177/1354856520913865.

Cunningham, Stuart. 2011. "Developments in Measuring the 'Creative' Workforce." *Cultural Trends* 20 (1): 25–40. https://doi.org/10.1080/09548963.2011.540810.

Cunningham, Stuart. 2013. *Hidden Innovation: Policy, Industry and the Creative Sector*. Creative Economy and Innovation Culture Series. St. Lucia: University of Queensland Press.

Cunningham, Stuart. 2014. "Creative Labor and Its Discontents: A Reappraisal." In *Creative Work Beyond the Creative Industries: Innovation, Employment and Education*, edited by Hearn Greg, Ruth Bridgstock, Ben Goldsmith, and Jess Rodgers, 25–46. Cheltenham, UK: Edward Elgar.

Cunningham, Stuart, and Stuart Flew, eds. 2019. *A Research Agenda for Creative Industries*. Cheltenham, UK: Edward Elgar.

Curtin, Michael, and Kevin Sanson. 2016. *Precarious Creativity: Global Media, Local Labor*. Oakland: University of California Press.

Daiiani, Mahsuum, and Brendan Keogh. 2022. "An Iranian Videogame Industry? Localizing Videogame Production Beyond the 'Global' Videogame Industry." *Media Industries Journal* 9 (1). https://journals.publishing.umich.edu/mij/article/id/89/.

D'Anastasio, Cecilia. 2015. "Why Video Games Can't Teach You Empathy." *Vice*, May 16. https://www.vice.com/en/article/mgbwpv/empathy-games-dont-exist.

Darling-Wolf, Fabienne. 2015. *Imagining the Global: Transnational Media and Popular Culture Beyond East and West*. Ann Arbor: University of Michigan Press.

de Peuter, Greig. 2011. "Creative Economy and Labor Precarity: A Contested Convergence." *Journal of Communication Inquiry* 35 (4): 417–425. https://doi.org/10.1177/0196859911416362.

de Peuter, Greig. 2014. "Beyond the Model Worker: Surveying a Creative Precariat." *Culture Unbound* 6: 263–284.

de Peuter, Greig, Nicole S. Cohen, and Francesca Saraco. 2017. "The Ambivalence of Coworking: On the Politics of an Emerging Work Practice." *European Journal of Cultural Studies* 20 (6): 687–706.

de Peuter, Greig, and Nick Dyer-Witheford. 2005. "A Playful Multitude? Mobilising and Counter-Mobilising Immaterial Game Labor." *Fibreculture* 5.

Deuze, Mark, Chase Bowen Martin, and Christian Allen. 2007. "The Professional Identity of Gameworkers." *Convergence* 13 (4): 335–353. https://doi.org/10.1177 /1354856507081947.

Di Rosso, Jason. 2018. "Terror Nullius Review: Controversial Australian Film Offers a Radical Critique of the Nation." *ABC News*, March 23. https://www.abc.net.au/news /2018-03-23/terror-nullius-review-jason-di-rosso/9576730.

Donovan, Tristan. 2010. *Replay: The History of Video Games*. East Sussex: Yellow Ant.

Dyer-Witheford, Nick, and Greig de Peuter. 2009. *Games of Empire: Global Capitalism and Video Games*. Minneapolis: University of Minnesota Press.

EA Spouse. 2004. "EA: The Human Story." *LiveJournal*, November 10. https://ea-spouse .livejournal.com/274.html.

Fiadotau, Mikhail. 2019. "Dezaemon, RPG Maker, NScripter: Exploring and Classifying Game 'Produsage' in 1990s Japan." *Journal of Gaming & Virtual Worlds* 11 (3): 215–230.

Fiadotau, Mikhail. 2020. "Growing Old on Newgrounds: The Hopes and Quandaries of Flash Game Preservation." *First Monday* 25 (8). http://dx.doi.org/10.5210/fm.v25i8 .10306.

Fisher, Mark. 2009. *Capitalist Realism: Is There No Alternative?* Winchester, UK: Zero Books.

Foxman, Maxwell. 2019. "United We Stand: Platforms, Tools and Innovation with the Unity Game Engine." *Social Media + Society* 5 (4). https://doi.org/10.1177 /2056305119880177.

Frank, Allegra. 2018. "This Is the Group Using GDC to Bolster Game Studio Unionization Efforts." *Polygon*, March 21. https://www.polygon.com/2018/3/21/17145242 /game-workers-unite-video-game-industry-union.

Freedman, Eric. 2018. "Engineering Queerness in the Game Development Pipeline." *Game Studies* 18 (3). http://gamestudies.org/1803/articles/ericfreedman.

Fung, Anthony Y. H. 2018. *Cultural Policy and East Asian Rivalry: The Hong Kong Gaming Industry*. Asian Cultural Studies: Transnational and Dialogic Approaches. London: Rowman & Littlefield International.

Game Developers Conference (GDC). 2019. "State of the Industry 2019."

Game Developers Conference (GDC). 2021. "State of the Industry 2021."

Game On: More than Playing Around. The Future of Australia's Video Game Development Industry. 2016. Canberra: Senate Printing Unit.

Garda, Maria B., and Pawel Grabarczyk. 2021. "'The Last Cassette' and the Local Chronology of 8-Bit Video Games in Poland." In *Game History and the Local*, edited by Melanie Swalwell, 37–56. Palgrave Games in Context. Cham, CH: Palgrave Macmillan.

Gelber, Steven M. 1999. *Hobbies: Leisure and the Culture of Work in America.* New York: Columbia University Press.

Gibson, Mark. 2018. "Independent Games and the Remaking of the 'Fringe.'" *CAMEo Cuts* 7: 1–13.

Gillen, Kieron. 2008. "Exclusive: Warren Spector Interview." *Rock Paper Shotgun*, February 13. https://www.rockpapershotgun.com/rps-exclusive-warren-spector-interview-2.

Gillespie, Tarleton. 2010. "The Politics of 'Platforms.'" *New Media & Society* 12 (3): 347–364.

Golding, Daniel. 2013. "Videogames and Politics: Why Was Escape from Woomera So Divisive?" *ABC Arts*, September 2. https://web.archive.org/web/20140912115852 /http://www.abc.net.au/arts/blog/Daniel-Golding/videogames-politics-Escape-From -Woomera-130901.

Goldsmith, Ben. 2014. "Embedded Digital Creatives." In *Creative Work Beyond the Creative Industries*, edited by Greg Hearn, Ruth Bridgstock, Ben Goldsmith, and Jess Rodgers, 128–144. Cheltenham, UK: Edward Elgar. https://doi.org/10.4337/9781782545705 .00017.

Grayson, Nathan. 2018. "Game Studio with No Bosses Pays Everyone the Same." *Kotaku*, July 25. https://kotaku.com/game-studio-with-no-bosses-pays-everyone-the -same-1827872972.

Greene, Daniel. 2021. *The Promise of Access: Technology, Inequality, and the Political Economy of Hope.* Cambridge, MA: MIT Press.

Grimes, Sara M. 2015. "Little Big Scene: Making and Playing Culture in Media Molecule's *LittleBigPlanet*." *Cultural Studies* 29 (3): 379–400. https://doi.org/10.1080 /09502386.2014.937944.

Guevara-Villalobos, Orlando. 2021. "Playful Peripheries: The Consolidation of Independent Game Production in Latin America." In *Independent Videogames*, edited by Paolo Ruffino, 193–208. New York: Routledge.

Halberstam, Jack. 2011. *The Queer Art of Failure.* Durham, NC: Duke University Press.

Hall, Stuart, and Tony Jefferson, eds. 2006. *Resistance through Rituals: Youth Subcultures in Post-War Britain.* 2nd ed. London: Routledge.

Hardwick, Taylor. 2023. "Safety, Accessibility and Inclusion at Digital Games Events in 2020." PhD diss., Swinburne University.

Harvey, Alison. 2014. "Twine's Revolution: Democratization, Depoliticization, and the Queering of Game Design." *Game* 3: 95–107.

Harvey, Alison. 2019. "Becoming Gamesworkers: Diversity, Higher Education, and the Future of the Game Industry." *Television & New Media* 20 (8): 756–766. https://doi.org/10.1177/1527476419851080.

Harvey, Alison. 2022. "Making the Grade: Feminine Lack, Inclusion, and Coping Strategies in Digital Games Higher Education." *New Media & Society* 24 (9): 1986–2002. https://doi.org/10.1177/1461444820986831.

Hearn, Greg, Ruth Bridgstock, Ben Goldsmith, and Jess Rodgers. 2014. "Creative Work Beyond the Creative Industries: An Introduction." In *Creative Work Beyond the Creative Industries*, edited by Hearn, Bridgstock, Goldsmith, and Rodgers, 1–22. Cheltenham, UK: Edward Elgar. https://doi.org/10.4337/9781782545705.00008.

Helmond, Anne. 2015. "The Platformization of the Web: Making Web Data Platform Ready." *Social Media + Society* 1 (2). https://doi.org/10.1177/2056305115603080.

Hernandez, Patricia. 2012. "You Shouldn't Have to Be Middle Class or Rich to Make Video Games." *Kotaku*, September 8. https://www.kotaku.com.au/2012/09/you-shouldnt-have-to-be-middle-class-or-rich-to-make-video-games/.

Hesmondhalgh, David. 2006. "Bourdieu, the Media and Cultural Production." *Media, Culture & Society* 28 (2): 211–231. https://doi.org/10.1177/0163443706061682.

Hesmondhalgh, David. 2018. *The Cultural Industries*. 4th ed. Thousand Oaks, CA: SAGE.

Higgs, Peter, Stuart Cunningham, and Janet Pagan. 2007. *Australia's Creative Economy: Definitions of the Segments and Sectors*. https://eprints.qut.edu.au/8242/1/8242.pdf.

Higher Education Video Game Alliance (HEVGA). 2019. *2019 Survey of Program Graduates*. https://hevga.org/wp-content/uploads/2020/02/HEVGA_2019_Survey_of_Program_Graduates.pdf.

Holmes, Len. 1998. "One More Time, Transferable Skills Don't Exist (and What We Should Do About It)." *Relational Skill & Learning* (blog), February 27. http://www.re-skill.org.uk/relskill/transkil.htm.

Hopewell, Luke. 2014. "Government Pulls Funding for Aussie Video Games Industry." *Kotaku*, May 13. https://www.kotaku.com.au/2014/05/government-pulls-funding-for-aussie-video-games-industry-in-federal-budget/.

Interactive Games and Entertainment Association (IGEA). 2019 "Australian Video Game Development: An Industry Snapshot." November 28. https://igea.net/2019/11/australian-video-game-development-industry-contributes-to-exports-and-job-opportunities/.

Ito, Kenji. 2005. "Possibilities of Non-Commercial Games: The Case of Amateur Role Playing Games Designers in Japan." In *Proceedings of DiGRA 2005 Conference:*

Changing Views—Worlds in Play. http://www.digra.org/digital-library/publications /possibilities-of-non-commercial-games-the-case-of-amateur-role-playing-games -designers-in-japan/.

Jiang, Qiaolei, and Anthony Y. H. Fung. 2019. "Games with a Continuum: Globalization, Regionalization, and the Nation-State in the Development of China's Online Game Industry." *Games and Culture* 14 (7–8): 801–824. https://doi.org/10 .1177/1555412017737636.

Jin, Dal Yong. 2015. *Digital Platforms, Imperialism and Political Culture.* Routledge New Developments in Communication and Society Research 3. New York: Routledge.

Johnson, Mark R., and Jamie Woodcock. 2019. "The Impacts of Live Streaming and Twitch.tv on the Video Game Industry." *Media, Culture & Society* 41 (5): 670–688. https://doi.org/10.1177/0163443718818363.

Jørgensen, Kristine, Ulf Sandqvist, and Olli Sotamaa. 2017. "From Hobbyists to Entrepreneurs: On the Formation of the Nordic Game Industry." *Convergence* 23 (5): 457–476. https://doi.org/10.1177/1354856515617853.

Joseph, Daniel. 2013. "The Toronto Indies: Some Assemblage Required." *Loading* 7 (11): 92–105.

Joseph, Daniel. 2021. "Battle Pass Capitalism." *Journal of Consumer Culture* 21 (1): 68–83.

Juul, Jesper. 2010. *A Casual Revolution: Reinventing Video Games and Their Players.* Cambridge, MA: MIT Press.

Keogh, Brendan. 2013. "'Just Making Things and Being Alive About It': The Queer Games Scene." *Polygon*, May 24. https://www.polygon.com/features/2013/5/24 /4341042/the-queer-games-scene.

Keogh, Brendan. 2016. "Hackers and Cyborgs: Binary Domain and Two Formative Videogame Technicities." *Transactions of the Digital Games Research Association* 2 (3). https://doi.org/10.26503/todigra.v2i3.58.

Keogh, Brendan. 2018. *A Play of Bodies: How We Perceive Videogames.* Cambridge, MA: MIT Press.

Keogh, Brendan. 2019a. "Are Games Art School? How to Teach Game Development When There Are No Jobs." Author website, June 22. https://brkeogh.com/2019/06/22 /are-games-art-school-how-to-teach-game-development-when-there-are-no-jobs/.

Keogh, Brendan. 2019b. "From Aggressively Formalised to Intensely In/Formalised: Accounting for a Wider Range of Videogame Development Practices." *Creative Industries Journal* 12 (1): 14–33.

Keogh, Brendan. 2022. "Situating the Videogame Maker's Agency through Craft." *Convergence* 28 (2): 374–388. https://doi.org/10.1177/13548565211056123.

Keogh, Brendan, and Benjamin Abraham. 2022. "Challenges and Opportunities for Collective Action and Unionization in Local Games Industries." *Organization*, March 17. https://doi.org/10.1177/13505084221082269.

Kerr, Aphra. 2006. *The Business and Culture of Digital Games*. London: SAGE.

Kerr, Aphra. 2017. *Global Games: Production, Circulation and Policy in the Networked Era*. New York: Routledge.

Kilkenny, Katie. 2021. "Vodeo Games Voluntarily Recognizes Worker Union." *Hollywood Reporter*, December 15. https://www.hollywoodreporter.com/business/business -news/vodeo-games-union-voluntarily-recognized-1235063260/.

Kirkpatrick, Graeme. 2015. *The Formation of Gaming Culture: UK Gaming Magazines, 1981–1995*. London: Palgrave Macmillan.

Klepek, Patrick, 2012. "Developers Mixed on Greenlight's $100 Submission Fee." *Giant Bomb*, September 5. https://www.giantbomb.com/articles/developers-mixed -on-greenlights-100-submission-fee/1100-4351/.

Klepek, Patrick. 2019. "'League of Legends' Studio Faces Employee Walkout, Promises Changes." *Vice*, April 30. https://www.vice.com/en_us/article/gy4qv7/league-of -legends-studio-faces-employee-walkout-promises-changes.

Kline, Stephen, Nick Dyer-Witheford, and Greig de Peuter. 2003. *Digital Play: The Interaction of Technology, Culture, and Marketing*. Montréal: McGill-Queen's University Press.

kopas, merritt. 2015. *Videogames for Humans: Twine Authors in Conversation*. New York: Instar.

Kruse, Holly. 2010. "Local Identity and Independent Music Scenes, Online and Off." *Popular Music and Society* 33 (5): 625–639.

Kücklich, Julian. 2005. "Precarious Playbour: Modders and the Digital Games Industry." *Fibreculture* 5. http://five.fibreculturejournal.org/fcj-025-precarious-playbour-modd ers-and-the-digital-games-industry/.

Lazzarato, Maurizio. 1996. "Immaterial Labor." In *Radical Thought in Italy: A Potential Politics*, edited by Paolo Virno and Michael Hardt, 133–148. Minneapolis: University of Minnesota Press.

Leaver, Tama, and Michele A. Willson, eds. 2016. *Social, Casual and Mobile Games: The Changing Gaming Landscape*. New York: Bloomsbury Academic.

Legault, Marie-Josée, and Johanna Weststar. 2015. "The Capacity for Mobilization in Project-Based Cultural Work: A Case of the Video Game Industry." *Canadian Journal of Communication* 40 (2): 203–221.

Legault, Marie-Josée, and Johanna Weststar. 2017. "Videogame Developers among 'Extreme Workers': Are Death Marches Over?" *E-Journal of International and Comparative Labor Studies* 6 (3): 73–99.

Leone, Matt. 2015. "The Secret Developers of the Video Game Industry." *Polygon*, September 30. https://www.polygon.com/2015/9/30/9394355/the-secret-developers -of-the-video-game-industry.

Lien, Tracey. 2010. "The Rise and Fall of Red Ant." *Kotaku Australia*, June 28. https:// www.kotaku.com.au/2010/06/the-rise-and-fall-of-red-ant/.

Lipkin, Nadav. 2013. "Examining Indie's Independence: The Meaning of 'Indie' Games, the Politics of Production, and Mainstream Co-Optation." *Loading . . .* 7 (11): 8–24.

Lobato, Ramon, and Julian Thomas. 2015. *The Informal Media Economy*. Cambridge: Polity.

Lorusso, Silvio. 2019. *Entreprecariat*. Eindhoven, NL: Onomatopee.

Luckman, Susan. 2015. *Craft and the Creative Economy*. Hampshire, UK: Palgrave Macmillan.

Lupetti, Matteo. 2021. "Against Wholesomeness." *Deep Hell*, August 1. https://deep -hell.com/against-wholesomeness/.

Lyons, Kristen, and Richard Hill. 2018. "Vice-Chancellors' Salaries Are Just a Symptom of What's Wrong with Universities." *The Conversation*, February 5. https:// theconversation.com/vice-chancellors-salaries-are-just-a-symptom-of-whats-wrong -with-universities-90999.

Ma, Eric Kit-wai. 2002. "Translocal Spatiality." *International Journal of Cultural Studies* 5 (2): 131–152. https://doi.org/10.1177/1367877902005002568.

MacDonald, Ian Thomas. 2018. "Rethinking Labor Unionism in Spaces of Precarious Work." In *Global Perspectives on Workers' and Labor Organizations*, edited by Maurizio Atzeni and Immanuel Ness, 3–22. Work, Organization, and Employment. Singapore: Springer Singapore. https://doi.org/10.1007/978-981-10-7883-5_1.

Margolis, Eric, ed. 2001. *The Hidden Curriculum in Higher Education*. New York: Routledge.

Marx, Karl. 2011. *Capital: A Critique of Political Economy*. New York: Dover.

Massey, Doreen. 2008. "A Global Sense of Place." In *The Cultural Geography Reader*, edited by Timothy Oakes and Patricia L. Price, 257–263. New York: Routledge.

Matamoros-Fernández, Ariadna. 2017. "Platformed Racism: The Mediation and Circulation of an Australian Race-Based Controversy on Twitter, Facebook and YouTube." *Information, Communication & Society* 20 (6): 930–946. https://doi.org/10.1080/1369118X .2017.1293130.

Maxwell, Jini. 2021. "How Does the Digital Games Offset Fit into Australia's Screen Incentives?" *ScreenHub*, May 11. https://www.screenhub.com.au/2021/05/11/how -does-the-digital-games-offset-fit-into-australias-screen-incentives-262544/.

McCarthy, Caty. 2019. "Game Developers Behind Dead Cells, Night in the Woods, and More Share Why the Co-Op Studio Model Works." *US Gamer*, March 19. https://www

.usgamer.net/articles/game-developers-behind-dead-cells-night-in-the-woods-and-more -share-why-the-co-op-studio-model-works.

McCrea, Christian. 2013a. "Australian Video Games: The Collapse and Reconstruction of an Industry." In *Gaming Globally*, edited by Nina B. Huntemann and Ben Aslinger, 203–207. New York: Palgrave Macmillan.

McCrea, Christian. 2013b. "Web Zero: The Amateur and the Indie-Game Developer." In *Amateur Media: Social, Cultural and Legal Perspectives*, edited by Dan Hunter, Ramon Lobato, Megan Richardson, and Julian Thomas, 178–184. New York: Routledge.

McMaster, Michael. 2023. "Videogames and the Public Museum: Six Months Behind the Scenes." PhD diss., RMIT University.

McMillen, Andrew. 2011. "Why Did L.A. Noire Take Seven Years to Make?" *IGN*, June 25. https://www.ign.com/articles/2011/06/24/why-did-la-noire-take-seven-years -to-make.

McRobbie, Angela. 2002. "Clubs to Companies: Notes on the Decline of Political Culture in Speeded Up Creative Worlds." *Cultural Studies* 16 (4): 516–531.

McRobbie, Angela. 2016. *Be Creative: Making a Living in the New Culture Industries*. Cambridge: Polity.

Montfort, Nick, and Ian Bogost. 2009. *Racing the Beam: The Atari Video Computer System*. Cambridge, MA: MIT Press.

Mould, Oliver. 2018. *Against Creativity*. London: Verso.

Muscat, Alex. 2018. "Ambiguous Worlds: Understanding the Design of First-Person Walker Games." PhD diss., RMIT University. https://researchrepository.rmit.edu.au /discovery/delivery/61RMIT_INST:RMITU/12248283090001341.

Negus, Keith. 1999. *Music Genres and Corporate Cultures*. New York: Routledge.

Neil, Katharine. 2020. "Conference banner on the wall at the first #freeplay20 in 2004." Twitter, June 10. https://twitter.com/haikus_by_KN/status/1270663901139566598.

Newbigin, John. 2019. "The Creative Economy—Where Did It Come From and Where Is It Going?" In *A Research Agenda for the Creative Industries*, edited by Stuart Cunningham and Terry Flew, 21–26. Cheltenham, UK: Edward Elgar.

NewZoo. 2020. "Top 25 Public Companies by Game Revenues." https://newzoo.com /insights/rankings/top-25-companies-game-revenues/.

Nicoll, Benjamin. 2019. *Minor Platforms in Videogame History*. Amsterdam: Amsterdam University Press.

Nicoll, Benjamin, and Brendan Keogh. 2019. *The Unity Game Engine and the Circuits of Cultural Software*. Cham, CH: Palgrave Macmillan.

Nieborg, David B. 2020. "Apps of Empire: Global Capitalism and the App Economy." *Games and Culture* 16 (3): 305–316. https://doi.org/10.1177/1555412020937826.

Nieborg, David B., and Maxwell Foxman. 2022. "Mainstreaming and Game Journalism." Cambridge, MA: MIT Press.

Nieborg, David B., and Thomas Poell. 2018. "The Platformization of Cultural Production: Theorizing the Contingent Cultural Commodity." *New Media & Society* 20 (11): 4275–4292. https://doi.org/10.1177/1461444818769694.

Nieborg, David B., Chris J. Young, and Daniel Joseph. 2020. "App Imperialism: The Political Economy of the Canadian App Store." *Social Media + Society* 6 (2): 2056305120933329, https://doi.org/10.1177/2056305120933293.

Nooney, Laine. 2020. "The Uncredited: Work, Women, and the Making of the U.S. Computer Game Industry." *Feminist Media Histories* 6 (1): 119–146. https://doi.org/10.1525/fmh.2020.6.1.119.

Oakley, Kate. 2014. "Good Work? Rethinking Cultural Entrepreneurship." In *Handbook of Management and Creativity*, edited by Chris Bilton and Stephen Cummings, 145–159. Cheltenham, UK: Edward Elgar.

Oakley, Kate, and Justin O'Connor. 2015. "The Cultural Industries: An Introduction." In *The Routledge Companion to the Cultural Industries*, edited by Kate Oakley and Justin O'Connor, 1–32. New York: Routledge.

O'Connor, Justin. 2009. "Creative Industries: A New Direction." *International Journal of Cultural Policy* 15 (4): 387–402.

O'Donnell, Casey. 2012. "This Is Not a Software Industry." In *The Video Game Industry: Formation, Present State, and Future*, edited by Peter Zackariasson and Timothy Wilson, 17–33. New York: Taylor and Francis.

O'Donnell, Casey. 2014. *Developer's Dilemma*. Cambridge, MA: MIT Press.

Ozimek, Anna Maria. 2018. *Videogame Work in Poland Investigating Creative Labor in a Post-Socialist Cultural Industry*. PhD diss., University of Leeds.

Parker, Felan. 2013. "An Art World for Artgames." *Loading . . .* 7 (11): 41–60.

Parker, Felan. 2021. "Boutique Indie: Annapurna Interactive and Contemporary Independent Game Development." In *Independent Videogames*, edited by Paolo Ruffino, 129–147. New York: Routledge.

Parker, Felan, and Jennifer Jenson. 2017. "Canadian Indie Games between the Global and Local." *Canadian Journal of Communication* 42 (5): 867–891.

Parker, Felan, Jennifer R. Whitson, and Bart Simon. 2017. "Megabooth: The Cultural Intermediation of Indie Games." *New Media & Society* 20 (5): 1953–1972.

Patel, Karen. 2020. *The Politics of Expertise in Cultural Labor: Arts, Work and Inequalities*. Lanham, MD: Rowman & Littlefield.

Pedercini, Paolo. 2014. "Making Games in a Fucked Up World." *Molleindustria*, April 29. https://www.molleindustria.org/blog/making-games-in-a-fucked-up-world-games-for -change-2014/.

Peticca-Harris, Amanda, Johanna Weststar, and Steve McKenna. 2015. "The Perils of Project-Based Work: Attempting Resistance to Extreme Work Practices in Video Game Development." *Organization* 22 (4): 570–587. https://doi.org/10.1177/13505084 15572509.

Pietsch, Tamson. 2020. "A History of University Income in the United Kingdom and Australia, 1922–2017." *History of Education Review* 49 (2): 229–248. https://doi.org/10 .1108/HER-06-2020-0040.

Plante, Chris. 2013. "The Many Faces of *The Bureau: XCom Declassified*: From 2006 to 2013." *Polygon*, August 19. https://www.polygon.com/features/2013/8/19/4614410 /xcom-the-bureau-development-2006-2013.

Poell, Thomas, David B. Nieborg, and Brooke Erin Duffy. 2022. *Platforms and Cultural Production*. Cambridge: Polity.

Polansky, Lana. 2018. "Worse than Scabs: Gamer Rage as Anti-Union Violence." *Rhizome*, October 30. https://rhizome.org/editorial/2018/oct/30/worse-than-scabs-gamer -rager-as-anti-worker-violence/.

Prescott, Shaun. "Hand of Fate 2 Studio Defiant Is 'Ceasing Development.'" *PC Gamer*, July 24. https://www.pcgamer.com/hand-of-fate-2-studio-defiant-is-ceasing -development/.

Reed, Emilie. 2020. "From Tool to Community to Style: The Influence of Software Tools on Game Development Communities and Aesthetics." In *Indie Games in the Digital Age*, edited by M. J. Clarke and Cynthia Wang, 99–122. London: Bloomsbury Academic.

Robertson, Adi. 2021. "Apple Said Roblox Developers Don't Make Games, and Now Roblox Agrees." *The Verge*, May 14. https://www.theverge.com/2021/5/14/22436014 /apple-roblox-epic-fortnite-trial-what-is-game-name-change.

Robertson, Roland. 1995. "Glocalization: Time-Space and Homogeneity-Heterogeneity." In *Global Modernities*, edited by Mike Featherstone, Scott Lash, and Roland Robertson, 25–44. London: SAGE.

Rocca, Jason Della. 2013. "The Montreal Indie Game Development Scene . . . Before Ubisoft." *Loading* 7 (11): 131–133.

Ruberg, Bonnie. 2019. "The Precarious Labor of Queer Indie Game-Making: Who Benefits from Making Video Games 'Better'?" *Television & New Media* 20 (8): 778– 788. https://doi.org/10.1177/1527476419851090.

Ruberg, Bonnie. 2020a. "Empathy and Its Alternatives: Deconstructing the Rhetoric of 'Empathy' in Video Games." *Communication, Culture and Critique* 13 (1): 54–71. https://doi.org/10.1093/ccc/tcz044.

Ruberg, Bonnie. 2020b. *The Queer Games Avant-Garde: How LBGTQ Game Makers Are Reimagining the Medium of Video Games*. Durham, NC: Duke University Press.

Ruffino, Paolo. 2018. *Future Gaming: Creative Interventions in Video Game Culture*. Goldsmiths Press Future Media Series. London: Goldsmiths.

Ruffino, Paolo. 2021. *Independent Videogames: Cultures, Networks, Techniques and Politics*. New York: Routledge.

Ruffino, Paolo. 2022. "Workers' Visibility and Union Organizing in the UK Video-games Industry." *Critical Studies in Media Communication* 39 (1): 15–28. https://doi.org/10.1080/15295036.2021.1985157.

Ruffino, Paolo, and Jamie Woodcock. 2020. "Game Workers and the Empire: Unionisation in the UK Video Game Industry." *Games and Culture* 16 (3): 317–328. https://doi.org/10.1177/1555412020947096.

Ryerson, Liz. 2014. "Indie Entitlement." \\. . . ..//, June 20. http://ellaguro .blogspot.com/2014/06/indie-entitlement.html.

Salgado, Filipe. 2012. "The Unauthorized and Incomplete Story of the IGF Pirate Kart." *Kill Screen*, February 29. https://killscreen.com/previously/articles/unauthorized-and -incomplete-story-igf-pirate-kart/.

Salter, Anastasia, and John Murray. 2014. *Flash: Building the Interactive Web*. Cambridge, MA: MIT Press.

Sandoval, Marisol. 2020. "Entrepreneurial Activism? Platform Cooperativism between Subversion and Co-Optation." *Critical Sociology* 46 (6): 801–817.

Serrels, Mark. 2012. "The Ski Safari Story: How One Australian Left Rockstar North to Chase His Indie Dreams." *Kotaku Australia*, December 20. https://www.kotaku.com .au/2012/12/the-ski-safari-story-how-one-man-left-rockstar-north-to-chase-his-indie -dreams/.

Serrels, Mark. 2013. "Only 8.7% of Those Employed in Australian Digital Game Development Are Women." *Kotaku Australia*, June 18. https://www.kotaku.com.au/2013/06 /only-8-7-of-those-employed-in-australian-digital-games-development-are-women/.

Serrels, Mark. 2020. "The Secret Avengers Video Game the World Never Got to Play." *CNET*, September 3. https://www.cnet.com/features/the-secret-avengers-video -game-the-world-never-got-to-play/.

Shaw, Adrienne. 2012. "Do You Identify as a Gamer? Gender, Race, Sexuality, and Gamer Identity." *New Media & Society* 14 (1): 28–44.

Shaw, Adrienne. 2014. *Gaming at the Edge: Sexuality and Gender at the Margins of Gamer Culture.* Minneapolis: University of Minnesota Press.

Simon, Bart. 2013. "Indie Eh? Some Kind of Game Studies." *Loading . . .* 7 (11): 1–7.

Sinclair, Brendan. 2020. "KO_OP by name, co-op by nature." *Games Industry*, June 3. https://www.gamesindustry.biz/articles/2020-06-03-ko-op-by-name-co-op-by-nature.

Šisler, Vit. 2013. "Video Game Development in the Middle East: Iran, the Arab World, and Beyond." In *Gaming Globally: Production, Play, and Place*, edited by Nina B. Huntemann and Ben Aslinger, 251–272. New York: Palgrave Macmillan.

Sotamaa, Olli. 2010. "Play, Create, Share? Console Gaming, Player Production and Agency." *Fibreculture* 16. https://sixteen.fibreculturejournal.org/play-create-share-console-gaming-player-production-and-agency/.

Sotamaa, Olli, Kristine Jørgensen, and Ulf Sandqvist. 2019. "Public Game Funding in the Nordic Region." *International Journal of Cultural Policy*, August, 1–16. https://doi.org/10.1080/10286632.2019.1656203.

Sotamaa, Olli, and Jan Švelch, eds. 2021. *Game Production Studies.* Amsterdam: Amsterdam University Press.

Srnicek, Nick. 2017. *Platform Capitalism.* Cambridge: Polity.

Stanfill, Mel. 2019. *Exploiting Fandom: How the Media Industry Seeks to Manipulate Fans.* Iowa City: University of Iowa Press.

Sterne, Jonathan. 2014. "There Is No Music Industry." *Media Industries Journal* 1 (1). https://doi.org/10.3998/mij.15031809.0001.110.

Straw, Will. 1991. "Systems of Articulation, Logics of Change: Communities and Scenes in Popular Music." *Cultural Studies* 5 (3): 368–388.

Straw, Will. 2004. "Cultural Scenes." *Loisir et Société / Society and Leisure* 27 (2): 411–422.

Stuckey, Helen. 2005. "Keep Off the Grass Acmipark—a Case Study of a Virtual Public Place." *First Monday*, October 6–8. https://doi.org/10.5210/fm.v0i0.1561.

Švelch, Jaroslav. 2018. *Gaming the Iron Curtain: How Teenagers and Amateurs in Communist Czechoslovakia Claimed the Medium of Computer Games.* Cambridge, MA: MIT Press.

Swalwell, Melanie. 2007. "Independent Game Development: Two Views from Australia." In *Videogames and Art*, edited by Andy Clarke and Grethe Mitchell, 160–180. Chicago: University of Chicago Press.

Swalwell, Melanie. 2021. *Homebrew Gaming and the Beginnings of Vernacular Digitality.* Cambridge, MA: MIT Press.

Swalwell, Melanie, and Michael Davidson. 2016. "Game History and the Case of 'Malzak': Theorizing the Manufacture of 'Local Product' in 1980s New Zealand." In

Locating Emerging Media, edited by Germaine R. Halegoua and Ben Aslinger, 85–105. New York: Routledge.

Szeman, Imre. 2015. "Entrepreneurship as the New Common Sense." *South Atlantic Quarterly* 114 (3): 471–490. https://doi.org/10.1215/00382876-3130701.

Takahashi, Dean. 2018. "John Riccitiello Q&A: How Unity CEO Views Epic's Fortnite Success." *Venture Beat*, September 15. https://venturebeat.com/2018/09/15/john -riccitiello-interview-how-unity-ceo-views-epics-fortnite-success/.

Tay, Jinna. 2009. "'Pigeon-Eyed Readers': The Adaptation and Formation of a Global Asian Fashion Magazine." *Continuum* 23 (2): 245–256. https://doi.org/10.1080/10304 310802711981.

thecatamites. n.d. "Business Cosplay." *Harmony Zone*. http://harmonyzone.org/text /businesscosplay.html.

Thornton, Sarah. 1995. *Club Cultures: Music, Media and Subcultural Capital*. Hoboken, NJ: Wiley.

Turner, Graeme. 2012. *What's Become of Cultural Studies?* London: SAGE.

Vanderhoef, John. 2020. "Brews, Burgers, and Indie Bombast: The Antiestablishment Neoliberalism of Devolver Digital." In *Indie Games in the Digital Age*, edited by M. J. Clarke and Cynthia Wang, 17–34. New York: Bloomsbury Academic. https://doi.org /10.5040/9781501356421.

VNS Matrix. 1992. *All New Gen*. https://vnsmatrix.net/projects/all-new-gen.

Walker, Alex. 2018. "What Australia Can Learn from the Canadian Games Industry." *Kotaku Australia*, March 9. https://www.kotaku.com.au/2018/03/what-australia -can-learn-from-the-canadian-games-industry/.

Walker, Alex. 2021. "'This Is a Huge Deal': The Industry Reacts to Australia's New Tax Break for Video Games." *Kotaku Australia*, May 11. https://www.kotaku.com.au /2021/05/this-is-a-huge-deal-the-industry-reacts-to-australias-new-tax-break-for-video -games/.

Warner, John. 2018. "It's Time We Stopped Encouraging Indies." *Games Industry*, October 2. https://www.gamesindustry.biz/articles/2018-10-02-its-time-we-stopped -encouraging-indies.

Wayne, Michael. 2003. "Post-Fordism, Monopoly Capitalism, and Hollywood's Media Industrial Complex." *International Journal of Cultural Studies* 6 (1): 82–103.

Weststar, Johanna, and Louis-Étienne Dubois. 2022. "From Crunch to Grind: Adopting Servitization in Project-Based Creative Work." *Work, Employment and Society*, February 12. https://doi.org/10.1177/09500170211061228.

Weststar, Johanna, and Shruti Kumar. 2020. "Developer Satisfaction Survey 2019: Industry Trends and Future Outlook Report." *IGDA*, November 18. https://igda.org /resources-archive/2019-developer-satisfaction-survey-industry-trends-report/.

Weststar, Johanna, and Marie-Josée Legault. 2017. "Why Might a Videogame Developer Join a Union?" *Labor Studies Journal* 42 (4): 295–321. https://doi.org/10.1177 /0160449X17731878.

Weststar, Johanna, and Marie-Josée Legault 2019. "Building Momentum for Collectivity in the Digital Game Community." *Television & New Media* 20 (8): 848–861. https://doi.org/10.1177/1527476419851087.

Whitson, Jennifer R. 2018. "Voodoo Software and Boundary Objects in Game Development: How Developers Collaborate and Conflict with Game Engines and Art Tools." *New Media & Society* 20 (7): 2315–2332.

Whitson, Jennifer R. 2019. "The New Spirit of Capitalism in the Game Industry." *Television & New Media* 20 (8): 789–801. https://doi.org/10.1177/1527476419851086.

Whitson, Jennifer R. 2020. "What Can We Learn from Studio Studies Ethnographies? A 'Messy' Account of Game Development Materiality, Learning, and Expertise." *Games and Culture* 15 (3): 266–288.

Whitson, Jennifer R., Bart Simon, and Felan Parker. 2021. "The Missing Producer: Rethinking Indie Cultural Production in Terms of Entrepreneurship, Relational Labor, and Sustainability." *European Journal of Cultural Studies* 24 (2): 606–627.

Williams, Leah J. 2022. "Former Mighty Kingdom Staff Confirm Redundances at Studio." *Gameshub*, October 5. https://www.gameshub.com/news/news/mighty-king dom-staff-redundancies-30802/.

Wilson, Jason. 2005. "Indie Rocks! Mapping Independent Video Game Design." *Media International Australia* 115 (1): 109–122.

Woo, Benjamin. 2012. "Alpha Nerds: Cultural Intermediaries in a Subcultural Scene." *European Journal of Cultural Studies* 15 (5): 659–676. https://doi.org/10.1177 /1367549412445758.

Woodcock, Jamie. 2021. "Game Workers Unite: Unionization Among Independent Developers." In *Independent Videogames*, edited by Paolo Ruffino, 163–174. New York: Routledge.

Wright, Steven T. 2018. "There Are Too Many Video Games. Now What?" *Polygon*, September 28. https://www.polygon.com/2018/9/28/17911372/there-are-too-many -video-games-what-now-indiepocalypse.

Yang, Robert. 2017. "Lol We're All Poor." *Radiator*, June 26. https://www.blog .radiator.debacle.us/2017/06/lol-were-all-poor.html.

Yang, Robert. 2018. "What Is the Game University For?" *Radiator*, May 4. https://www.blog.radiator.debacle.us/2018/05/what-is-game-university-for.html.

Young, Christopher James. 2018. "Game Changers: Everyday Gamemakers and the Development of the Video Game Industry." Toronto: University of Toronto.

Zagal, José, and Amy Bruckman. 2008. "Novices, Gamers, and Scholars: Exploring the Challenges of Teaching About Games." *Game Studies* 8 (2). http://gamestudies.org/0802/articles/zagal_bruckman.

Index